Marriage
Between Equals

DR. ROBERT SEIDENBERG is a practicing psychiatrist and psychoanalyst in the city of Syracuse, New York, and is also Clinical Professor in psychiatry at the Upstate Medical Center at Syracuse, State University of New York. He is the author of numerous essays on both clinical and applied psychoanalysis and the co-author of *Mind and Destiny: A Social Approach to Psychoanalytic Theory*.

Marriage Between Equals

Studies from Life and Literature

ROBERT SEIDENBERG, M.D.

Anchor Press/Doubleday
Garden City, New York
1973

Marriage Between Equals: Studies from Life and Literature was originally published in hardcover in 1970 by Philosophical Library as *Marriage in Life and Literature*. This edition is published by arrangement with Philosophical Library, Inc.

Anchor Press Edition: 1973

ISBN: 0-385-02085-6
Copyright, 1970, by Philosophical Library, Inc.
All Rights Reserved
Printed in the United States of America

To FAITH

"She was beginning to look up, to belong,
to depend, to cling, to be an inferior in fact,
however the marriage service may gloss it."
—from *Free Fall by William Golding*

FOREWORD

With a little license, a book, if good, is like a successful
marriage, albeit polygamous. There is a union of ideas,
experience, reading, writing, some thinking, and a host of
beautiful people. Of teachers who inspired, may I recall
Dr. Leland E. Hinsie who told me about psychoanalysis.
Dr. Sandor S. Feldman of Rochester, New York, with his
wit and wisdom, is the patron saint to a host of us west of
New Jersey. And, my patients who made it all possible!
There is no question in my mind after twenty years of
practice that patients can eventually cure the doctor.

A friend, Agnes Weis of Syracuse, New York, gave gen-
erously of her time in ideas and tireless editing. I am left
to praise the memory of the late Patricia Bradford George
who did major editing of this work. Her untimely death is
the cloud over this accomplishment. To Marion Cole again
deep gratitude for excellence of stenographic work and
that wonderful patience that could continue to allow cheer-
fulness through interminable "decisions and revisions."

My wife gave no help except, perhaps, the life she lives.

This book is no Athena suddenly springing full-grown
from the head of the author. Material herein has appeared
in psychiatric and psychoanalytic journals. To them I give
thanks for allowing my essays to see the light of day in the
first place and for their permission to use some of it here.
Material in Chapter One is from a piece in *Dynamische
Psychiatrie;* Chapter Two from *The International Journal
of Psychoanalysis;* Chapter Three, *Archives of General
Psychiatry;* Chapter Four, *The International Journal of*

Psychoanalysis; Chapter Five, *The Psychoanalytic Review;* Chapter Seven, *Psychosomatic Medicine, Archives of General Psychiatry;* Chapter Eight, *The Psychoanalytic Review;* Chapter Nine, *The Psychiatric Quarterly, The Psychoanalytic Quarterly;* Chapter Ten, *The Journal of Nervous and Mental Disease.*

I am grateful to Mrs. Caroline Meline of Philadelphia, Pa., for permission to use her letter to *The New York Times Magazine,* (Nov. 12, 1967) in Chapter 15.

I am especially indebted to Mr. Alan Dugan for permission to use his poem, "Speech for Aeneas" in Chapter One. Similarly, to *Saturday Review Inc.* where it appeared Jan. 30, 1965.

Robert Seidenberg, M.D.

Syracuse, N.Y.

CONTENTS

MARRIAGE
BETWEEN EQUALS

PREFACE

This book is about people, not phenomena. As people, they have been acted upon by hidden and overt forces in the past and present which are of great importance in their lives and destinies, but they are in their own right individuals with hopes, convictions, and ideals. Most of all, they are inherently educable with great capacities for growth and change. If they show distortions and incongruities, which we may euphemistically call quirks or neuroses or mental illness, we must never confuse them with their troubles. The phenomenological approach to human beings does a grave disservice to mankind, converting man into a thing of mechanisms, defenses, and symptoms. Modern psychology, in the last few years, is, thanks be, veering away from its previous preoccupation with "cases" and "diseases." This change is seen in the new emphasis on the importance of "identity" as a principal motivation in our lives. It explains much of behavior formerly attributed solely to the capriciousness of internal fluids and "poisons" of past contaminations. In the concept of identity is the acknowledgement that much of what one does, rational or crazy, really has to do with what one strives to be and achieve as an individual in the mass of humanity through and in a complex of inherited and potentially modifiable social institutions. And the new emphasis is on the inheritance of social institutions rather than the inheritance of patterns of behavior.

"Identity" means the acquisition of character, through being, feeling, or achieving, that somehow, to some minimal extent, may distinguish an individual from some three billion others around him. In this hope for personal individuation, there is also the persistence of the qualities of others with whom one shares an existence. So we see that identity is two-faced: one looking inward for a sense of uniqueness, and the other looking toward communality. The task of achieving identity may entail excruciating distortions, but also challenges and accomplishments which have brought men to remarkable heights. Inextricably united with the quest for identity is the promotion of conjugal living with its life and growth promoting force. It is the need for "affinity," to be and do with another, that brings mature fulfillment and ultimately insures the stability of identity.

This book will principally discuss marriage and its partners. This institution has contributed to troubles and neuroses and worse for many, but also probably most that is good and just in humanity. Homo sapiens is the only animal which forms and maintains kinships. Man alone sanctifies kinship, and this has made all the difference. "City and hearth and kinship," said Pindar, "this gives a man something to stay and love." In this era of social experimentation, we hear of attempts to break down family ties and substitute the national image, as in Russia and Red China. Parents there are encouraged and pressured into giving their children over to state boarding schools where they will be raised and tutored by professionals. Here they will be inculcated with correct attitudes and character traits with the emphasis of course on primary loyalty to the state rather than to kin. Siblings are separated and parents are permitted to visit only at certain times. In this way, an attempt is made to correct or do away with all of those neurotic traits and undesirable neuroses that stem from family living.

To the student of humanity, this social engineering appears patently absurd, for while it must be freely admitted that family living has produced a goodly share of monsters and could improve itself, the substitution of hordes which the Communist favor for the refinement of instinct, inherent in the relationship of kin, is a retrogression for which any adopting society will pay dearly. Fortunately, these experiments usually are abraded under the pressure of better sense and the returning recognition that in throwing out the siblings and parents in the dirty water, you eliminate the infant's chance for the exchanges of warmth, for the taming of instincts, for the development of basic trust, and most of all, for the building of pride in personal heritage which in turn is inextricably bound to gaining an identity.

The collectivistic societies jeopardize all of these in their quest for "cooperative" man. Instead of the family, they offer loyalty, trust, warmth in relationship to all citizens, called the State. Such a conversion is doomed to failure because "citizenry" or "comrades" or "the state" are too abstract for human needs; they are "things" which are at best substitutes for human object relations. How warm is the milk from the state's breast? The organs of the state don't have the necessary contents as well as concavities and convexities to offer comfort and stimulation for human emotional growth. The state, by taking over the family role, may acierate its populace but the accretion will be rust.

The apotheosis of the state and the downgrading of kinship are clearly found in the ballad of Communist China reported in the October 25, 1964 magazine section of the *New York Times:*

> "To sing a ballad for the party,
> I compare the party to my mother,
> My mother gave me only my body.
> But the party's brilliance lights up my heart."

Here is a life-and-death struggle between Oedipus and Mao.

If the family and kinship are as important as I have indicated above, then marriage—that social, legal, sexual, and religious bond—is their foundation and cantilever. Again, marriages are often as varied, strange, and spooky as are the people who make them. Also, certain religious and political forces may distort them into compacts beyond human capacity or endurance. The Clown in *As You Like It* is quite cagey in this matter and would have only civil bonds, resisting the religious aspect: "I am not in the mind, but I were better to be married of him than of another, for he is not like to marry me well: and not being well married, it will be a good excuse for me hereafter, to leave my wife." We hear about the agonies of people existing in enforced unions, to everyone's detriment. Similarly, we are astounded by the purported mounting divorce rates, which make us wonder if an institution seemingly so vulnerable or so little respected is being abandoned by humanity.

Others feel that human beings are as yet not developmentally up to the renunciations and responsibilities which the marriage union asks. And, there are a few who have postulated that marriage is an archaic social form which has outlived its usefulness and should be replaced by something more consonant with the modern scene. They see a basic hypocrisy between love and marriage and, although some do not disclaim the need for marriage, they would caution against "unrealistic" expectations. The French politician Leon Blum once wrote: "Yes, girls ought to be told and the young men ought to have it dinned into them too, that marriage will not satisfy their craving for love, or rather for passion. They ought to be told that marriage is contrary to it by definition since marriage is organized monogamy, while passion in the first phase of love-life corresponds to a polygamous instinct. We must emphasize, we must keep on emphasizing, that marriage is a necessary and beneficial institution but only on the strict condition that resort is not made to it until the time comes when the instinct has exhausted its strength."

Denis de Rougemont similarly saw an inevitable conflict between passion and marriage in the West. He saw it as a disease having its origin in the 12th-century myth of Tristan and Iseult. With Blum he advocates that we purge ourselves of the expectation of passion in marriage or suffer the disillusionment that must inevitably ensue. Both of these writers have oversimplified the human situation. The passion between two human beings cannot, and should not, be separated from over-all passions of living. It is true that if the marital union is expected to embrace and fulfill inordinate needs it must fail. On the other hand the passion of marital love is likely to endure if it marches hand in hand with other great affective concerns. In other words, the marital circuit can be overloaded and burnt out. In sex, after all, there is a communion, an act of friendship. Its vicissitudes correlate very closely with the feelings of compassion and struggle between its partners. There are no sexual problems; there are problems of the sexes.

To these critics one can reply that the conjugal condition should never be a categorical imperative. It never has been, as evidenced by ecclesiastical and other abstentions. For, for the mainstream of civilization, this union characterized by varying degrees of loyalty, trust, cooperation, sexual and social gratification, financial and emotional security, incentive for growth and personal development, transmission of cultural heritage, and providing for the needs of children, is not likely to disappear. The marriages of "love" or passion are apt to be and remain quiet, and thus forgotten. It takes an account like Laurence Whistler's *The Initials in the Heart* to remind us of the enduring love that can exist between two married people.

Of all the theories mentioned above, the one that may prevail is that man has yet to gain the maturity to live more happily and effectively in the marital state. Lest a reader emit a sudden groan of impatience, I add that marriage as an institution changes as society itself evolves; that roles of husband and wife change as new situations and opportunities arise. The wife of the 19th century, whose place was almost exclusively in the home, has been replaced by her granddaughter, who finds a new role for herself as an active person in the community or on a job as well as tending to her home duties. This was made possible in part by her education and in part by the changes in concepts of what is feminine and what is masculine. This new role has wrought a change in marriage, perhaps for the better. Attitudes and relationships too have changed as children are no longer needed to contribute to the financial support or work on the farm and are thus liberated to pursue their own goals. So the roles change and relationships are modified within the framework of the basic man-woman union.

It is not herein proposed or suggested that the correction of social evils, real or fancied, will bring happiness to men and women or bring correction to all of the sinister maladies of mating we see. It is indeed a vast oversimplification, the work of dreamers, to conceptualize man as an innocent victim of the social institutions around him. A tension between the public and private world has been and will always be intrinsic to the human condition. And man will, as he always has in the past, confuse the sources of his anxieties, at one time attributing them all to the outside, at another to the enemy within. His history has been a movement from the paranoid to the depressive position and back again with almost monotonous predictability. When all the injustices are righted, when there is no longer oppression or submission, no masters or slaves, no exploitation of body and soul, no more myths or follies, what will be left for him to do? Either he must then rail against justice, equality, science, and brotherhood, or go mad with boredom. Man is indeed a giddy animal.

It is with this caveat against militancy for perfectibility or windmill hunting that some of the social issues and forces of mating and human affinities will be presented. Some of the ambiguities, myths, injustices, and follies of society are presented. Their exposure or correction will not produce everlasting happiness, or even promote better relationships than are already achieved. Instead, they are presented in the spirit of science, in an attempt to call a spade a spade, for whatever that exercise and result is worth. Finally, it should be said that discontent, displeasure, and pain are, have to be, and should be, "organic" to man's nature. Without them he would be quickly destroyed before he could even get started or, once started, he would never achieve the second rung. Those who see these as malignant products of a hostile environment need some of Freud's tragic vision.

This said, the following chapters have been written by one who envies the novelist's skill. Clinical studies as well as allusions to belles-lettres will be presented to demonstrate not just the things that can go wrong with marriage, or the burdens that unresolved or latent problems of individuals place on it, but also the magnificence of the obsession.

This is not a primer on marriage or a "how to do it" book. My role is that of a neutral observer who tries to keep moral judgment to a minimum with the personal disclaimer that my own marriage prevents me from being a completely "objective" scientist.

Rosalind in *As You Like It* knew that no one could be an objective scientist in these matters, saying: "Love is merely a madness, and I tell you, deserves as well a dark house, and a whip, as madmen do: and the reason why they are not so punish'd and cur'd, is that the lunacy is so ordinary, the whippers are in love too; yet I profess curing it by counsel."

Robert Seidenberg, M.D.

CHAPTER I

MARRIAGE, MOTIVES, AND MIXTURES

Two people who know they do not understand each
    other,
Breeding children whom they do not understand
And who will never understand them.

T. S. Eliot, The Cocktail Party

We are all familiar with the common slip of the pen which
makes it come out "martial." Some capricious god of vocabulary made marital and martial easy to confuse. This
same god made it easy to write "marred life" for married
life. But this is understandable, since Zeus himself, with all
his thunderbolts, could not evade the nagging and retribu-
tions of a jealous, possessive wife, and was always on the
make. The spirit of Mount Olympus was no favorable
paradigm for marital bliss. Was there hope then that mortals could behave better?

It seems that the Judeo-Christian tradition either thought
the marital situation hopeless or cleverly avoided the issue.
Our deities not only shunned conjugal love but made
celibacy one of the highest virtues. Western man, in this
tradition, thereby inherited a built-in ambivalence. Although his religion and morality promote the sanctity of
this union, he is faced with the knowledge that his Gods
did not partake of it, and his high priests transcend it in
their own lives to this very day.

Jehovah was to take Israel as His bride but there has been an obvious breach of promise. His feelings for Israel were expressed to Hosea as follows:

"Therefore, behold, I will allure her, and bring her into the wilderness and speak tenderly to her. . . . And there she shall answer as in the days of her youth, as at the time when she came out of the land of Egypt. 'And in that day,' says the Lord, 'you will call me, "My husband," and no longer will you call me, "My Baal." For I will remove the names of the Baals from her mouth . . . And I will betroth you to me for ever. . . .' "[10a]

We face the paradox that Western man's religion promotes an inherent antimarriage force. Such concepts (elevated to fact) as the Immaculate Conception and the Virgin Birth are extramarital, and thereby compound the testimony against marriage. The effect and power of these paradigms should never be underestimated. In my own years as observer and psychoanalyst, I have yet to come across a woman who, in some part of her fabric, has not at least a fragmentary identification with the Virgin Mary. Similarly, every Western male, Christian and Jew, feels himself, or would like to be, Christ-like. Before the reader offers a personal disclaimer, let him spend some time reviewing his life and thoughts. Judaism, with its monastic childless God, and Christianity, with its celibate, unnaturally born Deity, create inexorable doubts about both sexuality and the ultimate "nobility" of the marital state. You and I, as well as our children, ask and are under the influence of the question, "Why isn't God married?"

Although we do not practice or believe them today, who can say that we are uninfluenced by medieval moralities? As described by Rattray: "In the eyes of the Church, for a priest to marry was a worse crime than to keep a mistress, and a mistress was worse than to engage in random fornication—a judgment . . . completely reverses secular conception of morality, which attaches importance to the quality and durability of personal relationships. When accused of being married, it was always a good defence to reply that one was simply engaged in indiscriminate seduction, for this carried only a light penalty, while the former might involve total suspension."[17]

A twenty-eight-year-old wife of an Anglican priest fully agreed with the ancient church fathers, if for different reasons. She stated that she was tired of playing second fiddle to her husband's congregation and offered advice to today's young women: "Never marry a cleric." Said she: "It is almost like being a favored mistress of a married man." She agreed that celibacy might, after all, be the best state for a clergyman.[12]

We must therefore not be led to believe, just because there are income tax advantages and other inducements for marriage, that our culture has done everything it can to encourage the marital state. To go from the sublime to the vulgar, it is to be noted that we raise our children on movies and television programs in which the heroes are mainly unmarried. Heroism and marriage apparently do not mix well. It is almost inconceivable to us that the Ranger could be anything but "Lone." Our cowboys and marshals roam their Western hills of Galilee righting injustices and evangelizing. A good many of their problems are the result of the difficulties the married settlers get themselves into. On the other hand, television serials about married life are invariably comedies in which the children are the innocent victims of their parents' fumbling and ineptness.

A man's devotion to his work or his cause may appear as a deterrant to married life. Although work and marriage would generally appear quite compatible in everyday living, the zealot may feel that marriage would be incompatible with his major goals. Many bachelor politicians have explained that politics was their whole life, that they never had time for anything else.

The competiton between love and ambition is no new discovery. Alan Dugan expressed it in the following poem entitled "Speech for Aeneas":

"Dido cried at the innocent fact
that I had to leave and not come back,
but a public official must be brave,
and dare the women and dare the waves
because he is bound to do his duty
to be the king and burn the booty,
so, 'Peace,' I said. 'Your Majesty,
pity the hard-hearted part of me:
a roll in the hay is good for you
but a man of gods has work to do,'
so we sailed on the earliest possible tide
and she went and committed suicide:
a great queen, and a swell dish,
and I'm sorry it had to end like this,
but an ecumenical society
is more important than matrimony."[3]

Mr. Dugan is true to his heritage and calling, for poets through the ages have done little for the marital state. When they have written of love, it has been outside of marriage; novelists and playwrights write either comically or morbidly about it. Kierkegaard writes: "Poetry follows the ancient custom in taking love as its domain, leaving marriage to get along as best it can. But in modern poetry (the drama and the novel) things have even reached the point where it is common to use adultery as a refined background for a new love affair. The innocent poesy explains nothing about marriage; the guilty poesy explains it as adultery."[9a]

Aside from these singularly motivated persons, we are also confronted with what has euphemistically been called the male-dominant society. This dominance has been of such long duration in history that we come to think of it as "natural"—the way things are or have to be. Whether it is natural, or the result of the natural use or abuse of power, is a question beyond the scope of this essay. The dominance of the male has shown itself in the virtual monopoly of the professions, politics, business, and, of course, in the military and church establishments. This exclusiveness leads to the thesis that men like to be with one another both in serious matters and at play.

Freud commented on two of these social institutions, the military and the church, as exclusive male societies where women have no place. In the idiom of psychoanalysis, he indicated that the binding force in these two instances is homosexual love. Freud wrote: "In the great artificial groups, the church and the army, there is no room for women as a sexual object. The love relation between men and women remains outside these organizations."[4] In limiting his observations of the love between men to these two institutions, Freud perhaps missed the overall implications of the exclusion of women and the concomitant union of men in practically every major social, political, economic, and recreational endeavor which our civilization fosters. Perhaps former Prime Minister Harold Macmillan intuitively knew of the masculine affinity, for, on first being told of the (John) Profumo case, he is reported to have remarked: "Thank God it's a woman."[9] We cannot escape the conclusion that men's major energies are directed and spent with one another, rather than in heterosexual or mating pursuits. The argument that the having and holding of the woman underlies all of the above pursuits may have validity, but one gets suspicious of the exclusion of the woman as a necessary prerequisite for the acquisition of them. In the words of wise Rosalind: "Men have died and worms have eaten them, but not for love."[19]

We must recognize that our society is overwhelmingly dominated by male "homosexuality" in religion, politics, higher education, law, big business, the armed forces, and practically all the other important institutions.[24] I use "homosexuality" not in the vulgar sense of the orificial few, but in the reality that men in general prefer to spend most of their time in each other's company, compete, make contracts, plan and make decisions together, and in their leisure time, play together. Very little time is spent with women; their opinions are generally held in low esteem;

they are never present in the higher echelons of decision-making, and are not brought into games of leisure. They are sexual partners, but this takes but a few minutes a week, just enough time to establish that the male is heterosexual, which he obviously is not, based on his apparent preferences as found in time-spent studies. Goethe knew this in the remarks of the Tutor: "A man needs another man; he would even create a second man for himself if no other existed. But a woman could go on living for ever and ever without even dreaming of creating a being like herself."[8] For most men, women are good to sleep with—not to stay awake with. The marriage condition must be understood in the light of these circumstances, drawing away that curtain of mythology which has obscured basic anti-marriage orientations.

It may be that current writers, Genet, Burroughs, Selby, and Baldwin, with their emphasis on homosexuality, have really caught up with a long-hidden hypocrisy. Of course, in so doing they have offended conventional minds, and have gotten themselves labeled as, at the very least, misanthropic. What they write of homosexuality has been shocking, as the "return of the repressed" often is, and they have made of Fanny Hill and Lady Chatterley, by contrast, welcome parlor guests. But in the license of their profession, in the dramatic forms that are designed to make an impression, they are perhaps at last bringing home the message, not of the depravities of a few, but of the overriding homosexual feelings which dominate our institutions, feelings best recognized and faced.

These feelings are not to be interpreted as bad. On the contrary, they are good, in the sense that they promote good feeling, cooperation, get things done, and may lead to world peace. They are bad only when they are ignored or denied, for then unnecessary defensive attitudes and actions result. These take the form of massive protests of "maleness," with a concomitant thwarting of all feelings of tenderness, justice, and civility. And, in the absence of these, war and hell break loose. It may be the paradox of our civilization that the disdained Genet or Selby, those provokers of vomit, by lifting a societal repression, may truly be the saints of our age, as Sartre has already suggested. This is not to imply that the solution of all misery is now at hand.

The honest recognition of the affinity of men for each other, not just in the church and army, is long overdue; likewise, the organized exclusion and persecution of their "loved ones"—women, under specious slogans of "equal but separate," or "natural" or "God-given roles," must at last be faced for what they are. If one is born into a situation, or if it has gone on for a long time, or if it has been happening to a large number of people, it takes on a naturalness and justice that is hard to shake. The remarks of a former Governor of Florida, LeRoy Collins, are pertinent. "What seems just at one time in a man's life may come to seem unjust at other times. I grew up in a segregated society. It never occurred to me that this was unjust."[13]

Once married and safely ensconced in her suburban home, the average woman rarely has the opportunity even to talk to a male, much less take any serious role in important matters of the day. With the end of her schooling, her contacts with important and stimulating personages are apt to be fleeting at best, and usually nonexistent. For the male's is a closed society and what is left to the woman is the clothed society. Her chances in marriage for intellectual survival are meager in comparison to that of her husband, who is apt to have the stimulation that is so vitally necessary for continued growth. She, then, cut off from the mainstream of worldly activity, becomes Homo Stagnans, causing a further exaggeration of the differences between the sexes. This leads to a sexual imbalance, which for some may augur well for a contented relationship, mainly of the dominant-submissive variety, but for others may spell unending, unfathomable struggles, often lowering both members into a morass of pettiness.

Yet we have overcome to some degree both past and

current, spiritual and temporal, forces of antimarriage, and to some degree find happiness and contentment in it. The best evidence for this is our own ability to be witty about it. No institution of our civilization has been as much a subject of humor and jokes as has marriage. They seem to have universal appeal and rarely give offense to anyone. Indeed they invariably have hostile content. But this is, in part at least, evidence of contentment and security. The dangerous and the inimical can rarely be joked about.

By contrast we find bitter misogamy in the existential words of Hamlet in his advice to Ophelia: "Get thee to a nunnery. Why wouldst thou be a breeder of sinners? I am myself indifferent honest, but yet I could accuse me of such things, it were better my mother had not borne me. I am proud, revengeful, ambitious, with more offences at my beck, than I have thoughts to put them in, imagination to give them shape, or time to act them in. What should such fellows as I do, crawling between Heaven and earth. We are arrant knaves all, believe none of us. Go thy ways to a nunnery. Where is your father?" In his next speech, Hamlet adds: "If thou dost marry, I'll give thee this plague for thy dowry. Be thou as chaste as ice, as pure as snow, thou shalt not escape calumny. Get thee to a nunnery. Go, farewell. Or, if thou wilt marry, marry a fool: for wise men know well enough what monsters you make of them. To a nunnery go, and quickly too. Farewell."[21]

Hamlet calls for an end to civilization, for he finds compounded evil and corruption in everyone. Man deceives woman and woman undoes her mate. This is Hamlet, the existential philosopher, absorbed in abstractions. But these are thoughts that most of us have when we are depressed, caused not so much by the banefulness of the world as by our own impotence and ambivalence in dealing with or solving problems. Hamlet had plenty of that. We all become existentialists when we are losing our personal fight. Winners are rarely philosophers; they are so busy with their harvesting that they have neither time nor inclination to worry about the issue of whether the race should continue or not.

Perhaps the perceptive Rosalind knew of what she spoke in regard to the male's mating reluctance when she said: "No, faith, die by attorney: the poor world is almost six thousand years old, and in all that time there was not any man died in his own person (videlicet) in a love-cause."[20]

A boy generally marries the girl next door, whether she lives right there or not. Even though in America we espouse the romantic concept of free choice of mate as opposed to the prearranged mating of nonliterate societies, there are forces which in fact prearrange marriages far beyond what we, as self-respecting individuals, would care to admit. We marry because we fall in love. But with repetitive monotony, well known to the sociologist, we "just happen" to fall in love with those in the same social class, educational level, financial bracket, religion, color, political beliefs, nationality, size, mannerisms, intelligence, and looks as ourselves. Not exactly alike, but within a range which does not disprove the rule. Indeed, the sex must be the opposite but even here there are some who lament, "Why can't a woman be more like a man?" There are many exceptions in those who can either accept differences or are attracted to differences. These, however, are not typical; for the majority a social segregation, as pointed out by Glazer and Moynihan, keeps the pot "unmelted" and grossly determines whom the youth will marry.[7] There is a sociological mating machine working night and day—one that was operating for centuries before the advent of IBM and the families of computers. We know whom you will marry as surely as we know that Jack will fall and Jill will be tumbling after.

A sociologist, John Finley Scott, makes provocative observations of the mating machinery as it applies to middle-class girls and sororities at our American colleges. He sees American parents as fearful of leaving the serious business of marriage to the caprices of love.[25] He indicates that the sorority system of our colleges is a device to control the dating and marriage possibilities of their daughters. He likens them to the fatting houses and convents of the primitives. Noting that many ethnic groups in America are endogamous in their marital desires for their children, he indicates that there is also a strong element of hypergamy, the ambition to marry the daughter to a man of higher status. Scott states: "The American middle class has a particular place where it sends its daughters so they will be easily accessible to the boys—the college campus. Even for the families who worry about the bad habits a nice girl can pick up at college, it has become so much a symbol of middle-class status that the risk must be taken, the girl must be sent. American middle-class society has created an institution on the campus that, like the fatting house, makes the girls more attractive; like the Canary Island convent, teaches skills that middle-class wives need to know; like the shtetl, provides matchmakers; and without going so far as to buy husbands of high rank, manages to dissuade the girls from making alliances with lower-class boys. That institution is the college sorority."

Apparently the big danger of sending a girl off to college is the random factor of love which seemingly has no regard for class boundaries. Scott observes: "There seems to be no good way of preventing young girls from falling in love. The only practical way to control love is to control the type of man the girl is likely to encounter; she cannot fall dangerously in love with a man she has never met." The three functions of sororities, according to Mr. Scott, are: "It can ward off the wrong kind of men." "It can 'facilitate' moving-up for middle status girls." "It can solve the 'Brahmin problem,' the difficulty of proper marriage that afflicts high-status girls."[18]

It is after these sociological, economic, and cultural givens that we exercise a personal choice. Within this segregated community, we then fall in love with the girl of our dreams who, as we all know, is really our mother or sister!

The perceptive Gloria Steinem tells us that "falling in love" for women is not as crazy as it seems. Because

women as a group generally have no worldly power of
their own in our society (or when they do it is poorly tolerated), they gain it through marriage. Marrying a man of
importance, wealth, or potential, will enhance her own
prestige and importance in a socially accepted way. She
gains either by identification with her husband or basks in
his reflected glory, thereby overcoming to some degree
deprivations she inevitably suffers in a basically misogynous
society. And, for the male, marrying a woman who might
enhance his career or ambitions with her charm, social
standing, family wealth, etc., falling in love similarly is no
act of insanity. Therefore, "choice of object," we can reasonably deduce, is not totally (sic) derived from the
Oedipus Complex. Yet, these social and worldly motives,
generally unconscious to the participants, are legitimate ingredients of *love*.[22a]

The anti-mating forces in us were detected by the keen
national observer, Joseph Wood Krutch. He is rightly suspicious of all the pornography and titillation rampant on
the American scene. Why the need for all of this stimulation? Is sexual desire always in danger of dying out? He
writes:

"Anthropologists tell us that in primitive societies fertility cults involve erotic dances and the exhibition of
realistic or symbolic representations of the sex organs.
But some of them, at least, add that this means, not that
primitive people are obsessively attracted by sexual activity, but that they are not. The purpose of the rites is to
work up an interest in something they tend to forget all
about.
"I am about to ask a question rather than make a statement. But I cannot help wondering if the dutiful wolf
whistle and the mammary fetichism do not suggest a
similar state of affairs. If we are really so randy as we
pretend to be, would we need all of this stimulation?
Certainly the names of and the publicity for the more
expensive perfumes suggest that women are compelled
to use desperate means to provoke even the most liber-

tine of proposals. After all, the night clubs, the musical shows, the 'continental' movies are only Barmecide feasts. Do most of the spectators proceed from them to their private games or (depending on age) do they either resume their longing for a sports car or their perusal of the *Wall Street Journal?"* [10]

Benedick in Shakespeare's *Much Ado About Nothing* was a bachelor, but one who relinquished his misanthropic tendencies in favor of carrying on the human race. With his passion for Beatrice, he states: "This can be no trick. The conference was sadly borne. They have the truth of this from Hero. They seem to pity the Lady: it seems her affections have their full bent: love me? why it must be requited: I hear how I am censur'd, they say I will bear myself proudly, if I perceive the love come from her: they say too, that she will rather die than give any sign of affection: I did never think to marry. I must not seem proud. Happy are they that hear their detractions, and can put them to mending: they say the Lady is fair, 'tis a truth, I can bear them witness: and virtuous, 'tis so, I cannot reprove it, and wise, but for loving me, by my troth it is no addition to her wit, nor no great argument of her folly, for I will be horribly in love with her. I may chance have some odd quirks and remnants of wit broken on me, because I have railed so long against marriage: but doth not the appetite alter? a man loves the meat in his youth, that he cannot endure in his age. Small quips and sentences, and these paper bullets of the brain awe a man from the career of his humour? No, the world must be peopled. When I said I would die a bachelor, I did not think I should live till I were married, here comes Beatrice: by this day, she's a fair Lady. I do spy some marks of love in her." [22]

The social scientists would tell us that Benedick has little chance of succeeding in his early resolution to remain a bachelor. He could not readily resist the claims of society and his social class as well as the force of romantic love. It had to be Beatrice, of course.

What makes for this certainty and predictability in mating? It is that quality of mankind that likes the familiar and hates the alien. Social customs and religious edicts, prohibitions against marrying outside of one's religion, racial and color taboos, act to delineate and narrow down choices. Of course, there are parental pressures and guidance, keeping to one's own social sphere, the merging of fortunes and proxies, matters of prestige and, of course, the not-to-be-forgotten element of opportunity. Opportunity is dependent on all the above elements plus the state of autonomy or dependence the individual is in at the time. Some young adults have degrees of autonomy in their twenties or thirties wherein they are able to resist some of the familial pressures to which most succumb. Such a person then might marry, with somewhat greater latitude, someone special, outside of his religion or class or economic bracket. These persons are more adventuresome and willing to take certain risks of alienation from their group for the benefits of extraordinary mates. It is likely that they have, to a measure, overcome their group's xenophobia and find something valuable on the outside to admix with their own talents and resources.

There is another who strays from the fold, not so much out of reasonable choice, but out of revolt against parents and relatives. His xenophobia is no less than theirs, and in most instances considerably more, but he must make a display of his bravado by flouting tradition and marrying an outsider not because of her value as a person, but her value in disturbing his family. Unlike the generally autonomous person who makes a choice of a marriage partner after being liberated from the taboos of his family, this one has no interest in his choice other than her role as a chip on his shoulder.

Both the autonomous individual and the harassed one appear to go against our sociological rule, but their number is not sufficient to threaten the validity of the statement.

The vast majority of us conform dutifully, submit to, and support those forces around and in us unknowingly. "Unknowingly" because who of us would admit, or has the sociological imagination to understand, that in the last analysis we have not only communal minds but indeed predestined hearts as well? Though we go on saying that we lose *our* minds or *our* hearts, all along we were but sharecroppers.

As if this sociological predestination and determinism were not enough, the natural selection in which we may pride ourselves suffers further assaults when we apply the psychological high-powered magnification to our specimen, love. Freud long ago told us that, even within the narrow range of our endogamy, there are internal unconscious motivations which cause us to pick a certain person.[5] Or, if we don't pick a certain type, we try to convert them to it. We marry persons who are attractive to us, but what is the attraction? The man on the street knows something of this, especially when it concerns his neighbors. He says, "Likes attract," or "Water seeks its own level." In more sophisticated circles we hear, "They get along fine; he's a sadist and she's a masochist." We also hear of women who love to marry alcoholics in order to suffer and the wives of wifebeaters who unconsciously are seeking punishment and getting it. We have learned of the Pygmalion complex in men who want nothing more in life than to convert prostitutes into their fair ladies.

Is marriage for growth as well as for security? Should it be a state of comfort or challenge? The traditional advice seems to be that one should, as much as possible, marry someone with similar tastes, attitudes, interests, religion, race, etc. This is based on the homily that life and marriage are tough enough, why complicate either by taking a mate who is "unlike" you. Match up, they say, with someone who is like yourself. And, after all, who could be better than that! Are we to assume that the best that marriage can be is a projected narcissism? The traditional view seems to hold that it is enough that the sexes are different, leave it at that. For the majority in the foreseeable future the fetish for the familiar will prevail. It is safe. It also shows domination of the repetition compulsion to which the masses are heir. For the adventuresome few, however, there will be the excitement and challenge of mating with "foreigners" who may bring to the marital situation a newness and freshness of thought absent from the conventional household. Here Camus' wisdom is relevant: "The pain of not having everything in common and the misfortune of having everything in common."[1] Pain is better than misfortune.

Obviously, diversity in itself is no guarantee of a fulfilling marriage. If a formula might be proposed, it would be intimacy without exploitation. And intimacy must involve both the pleasures and comforts derived from compassion and sharing but also a firm understanding and acceptance of a struggle between the sexes which is as old as civilization itself. It is this struggle that sharpens and quickens its acknowledged and accepted presence, making the difference between an exciting and challenging relationship or a hateful one. Among the most hateful of all are the tranquil relationships which never end in the divorce courts but result in the destructive submission or defeat of one partner and the disillusionment of the other. Hopefully, marriage need not be based on a dominance-submission axis in which one member must always serve the vanity of the other. Too often one hears such remarks as: "My wife must never earn more than I." It would seem that one could attain or earn one's esteem in ways other than in such numbers games. The truly autonomous person does not need to show his superiority at the expense of another's suppression. Artificially derived advantages should be anathemas to the self-respecting.

In this overwhelming vanity the male is the chief offender and in spite of all the calamities allegedly wrought by the so-called castrating female, the burden and onus of oppression is on the male, just as it is on the white man in regard to the Negro. This inequality has been institutionalized and solidified to the extent that it is considered "perfectly natural." The concept of "natural" roles in this regard is the accompanying and encumbering mythology which blinds both the oppressed and oppressors. Women are, as Eric Fromm calls them, the defeated sex. Society hypocritically has gone to great lengths to turn women's chronic deprivations into noble virtues. Psychology has helped in this by calling masochism quite "normal" for women. To wit, if women appear to be a suffering, shortchanged minority, it is basic to their nature to receive such treatment! They must really enjoy it since they never do much about their own plight. How else to explain acceptance of such chronic and unending subjugation. Most marriage "contracts" take this subjugation as "understood." The female, with few exceptions, is foredoomed to her fate; to protest at the altar is to be labeled misanthropic. It would behoove a fair-minded male then out of enlightened self-interest for the present and the future, never to allow such an unearned advantage to accrue to himself. If it is humiliating to be a slave, it is an insult to one's integrity and dignity to be a master. He therefore in good faith and conscience should not expect or demand renunciations and deprivations of another that he is unwilling to suffer himself.

In using the phrase "enlightened self-interest," it is to the male's long-term advantage to demand of his spouse full engagement in the world according to her capabilities, unrestricted by male vanities and societal "roles." For if he does not, he will most likely find twenty years later a weeping "change of life" mess on his hands. For the "natural" role of motherhood, like fatherhood, has no future and if that is all one knows or has going, fate will be most unkind.

"Exogamous" unions may cause many difficulties, but they are never involved in the sin of boredom. Each partner may bring a new enrichment to the other. Why spend one's life looking into a mirror, having one's beliefs and attitudes constantly confirmed? The conventional wisdom of our times militates against differences, even attaches the abel of "deviant" to those who would marry outside of their milieu. Psychoanalysts and psychiatrists have looked upon interracial marriages as the doings of the "sick," and clergymen are very strong against any straying from the flock. In this respect religions act like political parties trying to hold and increase their voting strength. The tradition of Biblical Ezra is still very strong. Dismayed to learn that Jews had been intermarrying with neighboring peoples, his exhortations and threats led them to divorce their "strange wives." (10:10:11:12:14:15:16:17) Governments tend to discourage "fraternization" with other peoples, and the specter of miscegenation is not the exclusive mentation of Southern white racists. It may be easier to stick to your own kind, but it may also be stultifying.

An example of the conventional attitude of the helping professions is the report of a psychiatrist on interracial marriages. From his studies he found "deep-seated psychological sicknesses of various sorts underlie the 'vast majority' of marriages between white persons and Negroes. . . ."[16] He said that problems in such marriage reflect "the vicissitudes of the Negro-white relations" and he indicated that such marriages are based on "acting out" aggressions towards their parents or society at large. "The couple's mutual discontent, hatreds, hostilities and desires for revenge —not love and compassion—brought them together." Admitting that some Negro-white marriages were good and healthy, he had the expectation that these might increase eventually.

Statements such as these may be the result of deep study and perception. However, it is unlikely that this psychiatrist could really know about the "vast majority" of such marriages since they now total some 50,000 and up to 600,000 where the Negro member has "passed" for white. And it would certainly seem both unfair and unscientific to make such sweeping judgmental statements on the basis of those who came for psychiatric help. Judging by what a psychiatrist sees in his office, he could easily say that marriage "between the sexes" has been a dismal failure, and it appears that the vast majority of people come together for horribly "sick" xenophobic motives such as sticking to one's own race, religion, social class, neighborhood, country club, etc.

The mainstream of orthodox psychoanalysis sees nothing but pathology in exogamous marriages. Granting that there may be some of the variety that "succeed," most are doomed. In a recent psychoanalytic study of thirty patients who were partners in racial intermarriage, the following most remarkable statement is found: "Just as endogamous marriages contracted as a result of neurotic needs may succeed through the agency of treatment or benevolent fate, so may exogamous marriages succeed (sic)." The fact that ex-Governor George Wallace of Alabama would heartily concur cannot fairly be used to invalidate this antinomian proclamation of "science." This article concludes with a host of psychopathological findings in the cases studied ranging from "unresolved Oedipus complex and incest taboo problems" to "counterphobic and fetishistic attitudes and choices which defend against castration anxiety." In all there was not one word that would indicate that the author had ever entertained the notion that these young people were attempting to transcend the prejudice and hate of their parents and society.[11]

Sociological studies appear to contradict the pessimism of the psychiatrists. Under the rubric "Mixed Marriages Found 'Doing Fine,'" the *New York Times* reports a study in Seattle of 210 mixed marriages in which the couples "were generally doing fine and meeting few problems based solely on marriage across the color line." And, as would be anticipated, "A white mother sought to defer her daughter's marriage to a Negro by sending her to three psychiatrists, but love prevailed."[15]

"Deep-seated psychological sicknesses" are frightening words which psychiatry teaches its students. Most often these "sicknesses" turn out to be states of being wherein children free themselves of the prejudices and mythologies of their parents. To purge oneself of institutionalized ha tred, to really embrace the Christian ethic of the brotherhood of man, is too often interpreted by psychiatry as "acting out" hostility and revenge. For centuries we heard the demagogues use pseudo-science to tell us of "races" which in fact do not exist, of biological deterioration that miscegenation would cause, of mongrelization. To some extent, these scientisms have been put to rest. It is dismaying that psychiatry, with its casual, impressionistic consultation room data, may become the new replacement. Psychiatry and psychoanalysis show no restraint in reducing complex social phenomena to pet complexes.

Ottenheimer states that the choice of a mate is not accidental or random "but is deeply influenced by unconscious factors."* In her explication of the psychodynamics of choice, all is oedipal or pre-oedipal. It is close to the truth perhaps that choice of a mate is "not accidental or random" but the determinants, though "unconscious" are overwhelmingly social, economic, cultural and even demographic. Oedipus, though necessary, has been overworked. The vital and important contribution that psychoanalysis has and can make to understanding of these matters is vitiated by attempting to explain so much with so little. It was Freud himself who taught us the principle of over-determination—namely the multiplicity of factors behind attitudes and behavior.

Today, however, taking nothing from psychoanalysis, sociology can tell us a great deal about mating and "unconscious" factors in object-choice.

Loyalty to a group builds the character of a people, and may promote certain skills and favorable manners, but the danger of moral hemophilia exists. The desire to marry one's own kind undoubtedly promotes the feeling of collec-

* The Marriage Relationship, Psychoanalytic Perspectives, Edited by Salo Rosenbaum and Ian Alger, Basic Books, New York, 1968.
   Lilly Ottenheimer, "Psychodynamics of the Choice of a Mate," Chapter 5, pp. 59-69.

tive immortality. Since one's own end must ultimately be faced, there is hope through one's family, one's business, one's religion and ethnic ties that there can be a perpetuation of personal values and desires. When a son or daughter marries outside of the given class, religion, or ethnic group, there is the dismay that all that one has built up will fall into the hands of an outsider. For some who love to control from the grave, this is both death and defeat. Or, as Wedekind put it: ". . . his mind is tottering like a rickety fencepost because he wants so much to be immortal."[23] However, endogamy tends to perpetuate demons, for they can only be exorcized by outsiders. And if outsiders are never allowed inside the door, the demons never are exterminated.

Society seems too preoccupied with the question of whether a marriage will "succeed" or not; the concept of marriage as an implement of mutual growth is sorely neglected. Marriage is too often viewed as a safe haven, duly protected by law and Heaven, where one can rest on one's oars. Its value to personal growth can be inestimable if there is a drawing together and admixture of "talents." This would necessitate a large element of diversity which could lead to mutual enrichment. But diversity is actively discouraged by almost all our social institutions today. They say diversity of the mates creates problems. But all of living in a great sense is the challenge of problems. When a man or woman goes to work, he is begging to be confronted with problems to test his mettle, to stretch his muscles, to stimulate his cerebrum. The problem of living with and learning from a far different person can be the greatest stimulus for personal development. Such a person can help in attaining true mastery of the irrationalities within. Can an executive survive in business surrounded by "yes men"? Yet to find and marry a "yes partner" seems to have been made a great virtue. Marriage as an endpoint is a self-deceiver; rather, it should be looked upon as a developmental stage in the humanizing process.

We often hear that people should marry only when they

have maturity. This is fine, but people in their early twenties are never mature, and marriage should provide them stimuli which will hasten the humanizing process: those opportunities for accommodation, for individuation, for the exchange of ideals and values, for the delineation of boundaries, for the testing of moralities and the mastery of errant instincts. All of these are apt to be purely theoretical until one is confronted with the realities of the everyday give-and-take which the intimacy of marriage provides. Here, then, can be an opportunity for getting to know what and who one really is, instead of retaining theoretical images that one has lived by up till then. One can then find out how generous, how tolerant, how unselfish, how brilliant one really is. This testing of ideals is apt to be a painful one, but there can be no substitute for it except a dream world. In marriage lies the opportunity of eliminating self-myths. If a person considers himself adaptable, marriage will tell him; if he seeks to know how tolerant of another he is, he will learn in the conjugal relationship; if he asks himself how he is at sharing, he will know; and, how strong are his defenses against disappointments, frustrations, loss, and capricious blows of fate—this too he will discover. He cannot be truly mature until he has been confronted with, and deals with, and hopefully masters, painful exigencies of living to which the marital state alone is heir. Marriage is one of the great levelers of life; it is a societal headshrinker which, for some, ends illusions about self-importance, courage, honesty, integrity, and generosity. And they are the better for it. For others who start out with low self-esteem, marriage may prove they possess greater moral fiber than they had ever dreamt. Far from a good cure, marriage for still others may be a test of such overwhelming severity as to jeopardize their sanity.

Balzac's words are indeed pertinent: "Two beings on the eve of joining always deceive each other; but the deception is innocent and involuntary. Each, of course, stands in the best light; they are rivals as to which makes the most promising show, and at that time form a favorable idea of themselves which they cannot afterward come up to. Real life, like a changeable day, consists more often of the gray, dull hours when Nature is overcast than of the brilliant intervals when the sun gives glory and joy to the fields. Young people . . . ascribe the inevitable troubles of life to matrimony, for there is in man a tendency to seek the cause of his griefs in things and persons immediately at hand."[1a]

If mastery of the instincts, and by this we mean self-mastery, is a respectable goal of life, then marriage offers an opportunity for this achievement. The exercise of moral muscles is provided in the sense that the conjugal situation will provide all the circumstances for proving virtues and revealing shortcomings. For here is the testing ground par excellence for convictions about democracy, justice, and fair play—all high-sounding and safe until put to the test. It is well and good for a woman to demand the liberation of Rhodesia, but has this wife enslaved her husband and children? Or can she subject them to all types of humiliation and degradation as long as she says she loves them?

Marriage can provide a new suzerainty or it can become an opportunity for the practice of democratic and humanistic "instincts." Since practice makes perfect (we will happily settle for a little less), marriage gives the major opportunity for personal and mutual growth that life provides. Didactic courses on human growth and development generally stop at the end of adolescence and pay all too little attention to the accretions which can occur only during the years of conjugal union. As indicated above, all is theoretical and abstract until put to the test of intimacy which only marriage is likely to provide. Genuine growth comes only with satisfaction and frustrations, in which learning and doing are inextricably involved.

These growth processes might be gotten elsewhere. However, only in marriage is one likely to experience the day-in-day-out *confrontation* with oneself through another, and it is this unavoidable confrontation that makes all the difference. In all of this, not only one's integrative capacity but one's sanity is constantly tested in trying to determine what is fair or not. Generally, in determining who is doing what to whom, one has to make judgments of one's own and the other's rationality. "Am I indeed the tyrant she says I am?" The first instinct to such a pronouncement is to holler "foul," but the accusation has been made. Someone that you love has called you tyrannical. You must now make the judgment of her opinion of you. Once heard, it is part of your learning experience, but now you somehow must test the validity of her statement. You, who had always espoused liberal causes and spoken eloquently on these matters at cocktail parties, are now being called a tyrant in your own home. Perhaps it should be put down as completely ridiculous. She may have said it simply because she was angry. Then you go on to other possible causes—perhaps the children had been getting on her nerves, the cleaning woman had not arrived, or the perennial standby, perhaps her lunch disagreed with her. What to *do* about it is the next issue. Two alternatives come forth immediately: because you are a generous soul, you will forgive her temporary lapse; or you may want to set her right by demonstrating how a real tyrant behaves. There may be a myriad of other alternatives, but none can allow this husband to evade a judgment about his beloved's accusation. Among the possible appraisals, he can discover that he may be exactly what she says and that she has in fact understated the case, or he may have to face the reality that he had chosen as his wife an unfair shrew. Chances are the truth will be found between these extremes, but he must be prepared to face all of the above. Chances are that no one else has ever openly called him a tyrant, so that he has had no prior exercise for his new inquiry. Only his loved one has cared so much or so little for him as to confront him with this. She alone has afforded him the opportunity of proving his judgmental mettle. From this he may grow, and she may too, although unkindness is not here recommended as the only or prime way to heaven. There is truth and there is meanness, but they often come forth as one. The seasoned spouse gets to know that all that is mean is not truth.

Lest the reader mistakenly interpret from the above that growth comes from confrontation with disagreeable events, it should be affirmed that there are the salutary effects of building a family, of living up to contracts and commitments, of giving and taking constructive criticism, of loyalty and fidelity, of teaching and learning, of extending and receiving respect, of consolation in time of tragedy, of striving for mutual enrichment, and of patience. Here we speak of true patience, to be distinguished from indulgence on the one hand and indifference on the other. Sooner or later, we all fall on our faces in public or at home, and there must be someone standing by waiting for the recovery and possibly extending a helping hand.

The pattern of existence will inevitably include those instances when fate will deal a painfully low blow, or one may fall through one's own clumsiness or ineptness. It is part of being human to be heir to these circumstances, and it is part of being human to expect and receive at such times compassion for another. Patience, then, indicates understanding of the universal predicament of intermingled success and failure—in the jargon of psychoanalysis, those periods of progression and regression that characterize the human spirit. Existence has not proved to be an unencumbered, uninterrupted spiraling to heaven, no matter who the person or what the course.

In marriage, there must be patience as each partner seeks his own salvation hopefully and "with diligence." Salvation cannot be found solely in the other, no matter how much love there is or how good the intentions are. The mate must wait patiently until the other has arrived at some personal solution. At such times, "love" is nothing but interference and intrusion. For certain problems in life, there is no substitute for solitude.

Since it would be unrealistic to expect that each mate could develop and grow at the same rate or at the same time, there will be periods when one will have to wait for the other. It goes without saying that each has different integrative capacities which will bear heavily on how, and how facilely, one deals with the problems of living. The acknowledgments of these differences are inextricably involved in the attitude of patience. Sometimes one waits a lifetime.

But patience should be considered for what it is—a compassion that has limitations. It is not an unending subservience to another in which one is subject to inordinate punishment and deprivation, nor is it a substitute for making reappraisals of one's current and ongoing condition of living. There can be too much patience with another or with oneself, leading to an indifference that helps deny a painful reality. No homily or prescription can ever be a substitute for personal, and hopefully wise, judgment.

Marriage is the open formalized bond which hopefully will pre-empt all others. But the hidden bonds which may hold a person to his mother or his father may make this formalized one to a stranger impossible. For instance, linkages to a person of one's own sex and secret marriages which allow for no heterosexual "unfaithfulness." It was understandable then for an analysand with such a problem who thought he was pursuing women who were like his mother, to unwittingly say: "It's like the song: I Want a Girl, Just Like Dear Old Dad!" He corrected himself, but not without embarrassment and dawning understanding.

Children think and play marriage all the time. But their play marriages are completely endogamous without question. Until a certain age when shame enters the picture, the little girl knows and says that she will marry her father. Why not? Who else is there she knows half as well? What boy or man will ever have her interests as much at heart? Every child born to a conventional milieu knows about marriage and its vicissitudes: the child is witness to the married state of his parents and secretly and not so covertly at times feels married himself. He has known and experienced every intimacy with his parents, with the one exception of phallic intercourse itself. He has seen the full gamut of physical sensations, jealousies, lovers' quarrels, abandonments, competition, reconciliations, betrayals, infidelities, reunions, punishments, rewards, estrangements, loyalties, feelings, renunciations, ambitious strivings, social climbing, power-seeking, submission, etc. Marriage to an outsider is a different experience, with the new dimension of the stranger added, but marriage itself is nothing new. Marriage is indeed old hat by the time one finds oneself at the altar. But until that time one has lived in a double marriage to both father and mother, with all the entanglements and ambivalences and competitions, double jeopardy and double protectiveness that such a triangle results in. At times the monogamy that conventional adult marriages provides is a distinct relief.[26]

The growing youth lives in a bisexual polygamy, albeit quite unspoken, and must renounce this when he is expected to choose one object of the opposite sex. He replaces one woman for another but must give up or sublimate or otherwise transfer the "libidinal" ties formerly held with his father. At this point, to the chagrin of some wives, he becomes "married to his work." We are led to the understanding, then, that marriage for the young adult is not a new or alien experience, any more than love itself is. For the person who does not "marry" in adult life, we might conclude that, barring the vagaries of opportunity, availability, etc., he has either already had his fill of human intimacies, and desires freedom, or possibly he is fully contented with his polygamous family linkages of varying intensities between the sexes and simply refuses, or finds no good reason, to relinquish them for the uncertainties of the unknown and untested. He stays "married" in his double bond.

Obviously most people make the change, whether under pressure from some deep social conscience or as a part of an unfolding developmental process. They do it, as our presence gives testimony. Consequently, most of our social institutions cater to "adult" marriages and family life; the "single" person is part of a minority group which is penalized in everything from discriminatory income tax rates to exclusion from a great part of business, social, and political life.

But science tells us a small part of the phenomenon of affinity. There is love, which in spite of our fine statistics and sociological data is *the* overriding consideration in our mating considerations. And love is not the same as sex, although they are very much alike in that neither makes much sense. Love is a human religion in which another person is believed in. It has all the illusions of religion, including the self-effacement, adoration of the other, and above all the ecstasy of certainty. About the latter, more is to be said. With all the ambiguities, ambivalences, and incongruities of living known from childhood and thereafter, there is an intrinsic hope of the individual to be under the spell of certainty. Knowledge and science never can provide this. But love, yes! The lover is certain that he has found the perfect one; he is certain there can be no other for him; he is certain that this will make him happy and, of course, will last forever. In a world that is largely made up of doubt, he is treated for once to the absolute and the infallible. This is religiosity at its zenith. Here human beings worship one another; and, as is well known, lovers in their trance don't think about God very much. Yet it is not accident that the ceremonial act of marriage itself most often has a church setting. This serves to add religion to religion. The mutual feelings of lovers on such an occasion transcend biology, chemistry, economics, and good sense; all become either second runners or casualties of sensation and sentiment. All may be sacrificed for the illusion of certainty.

We know that the idea of romantic love between the sexes had its origin among French noblemen in the 13th and 14th centuries. Before that, mating was a purely business matter, as it still is in many parts of the world today. In ancient Greece, as in China, romantic love and passion was found only between members of the same sex. Relations between the sexes were institutionalized and rarely, if

ever, sung about or glorified by poets. Like many other
European conventions, romantic love gained a foothold,
flourished, and has become the primary mating mode in
America. Whether romantic love and democracy and humanistic traditions go hand in hand are problems for the
social and political historians. However, one cannot help
but be intrigued with the speculation that the belief in a
fellow human being—the flowering of a *human* religion,
now with adoration of one's own rather than an other-
worldly one—was a step toward true brotherly love, a sense
of democracy, and humanistic ideals. And it is true that a
person in love generally has a warm feeling toward the
world. In romantic love, in spite of the "unconscious"
societal structure and boundaries already alluded to above,
the sense of choice is felt to be there—perhaps more so for
the male than the female, but at least the feeling of the
prearranged, of the inevitable, of the unalterable, is largely
absent. The right to choose a mate has become an un-
written inalienable civil right, even though to this day individual states in America have promulgated prohibitions,
mainly along racial lines.

The unlimited right to choose a mate has given great
anxieties to parents, communities and religious leaders.
They see a breakdown of tradition and group solidarity.
But we cannot have it both ways. It is inconsistent to
preach civil rights one day and parochialism the next. And
in some circles, there appears to be a developing polarity
and antagonism between the love of man and the love of
God! I have heard it said from pulpits that a person should
not marry out of his religion; that in a conflict of interests,
one should forsake the person one "purportedly" loves for
his religious fealty, for his love of his religion and his
God.[27] No new conflict, it appears that there will be in-
tensification of it as humanistic values gain ascendancy.
This seems to be the case, in America at least. And if romantic love makes man-worshippers of us all, do we become inordinately vulnerable to the vagaries of fate that
always show that man is destructible, uncertain, fallible,

and capricious? Not so, of course, with God. Belief in man in many respects requires greater blindness, greater faith, and greater powers of illusion than belief in God, for He never reveals "bad" qualities, and He never leaves. For belief, we can concur with Pascal that He is by far the better bet. Relationships flounder because of the difficulty in maintaining the religious fervor which characterized their onset; as in "falling out of love." Hopefully, belief can somehow transcend the assault of disillusionment which reality and everyday living bring with it. It may be that *belief* and *reason*, those notorious "immiscibles," can be admixed in proportions which can overcome the caprices of belief and the heaviness of reason, to give sustaining power and endurance to relationships.

Even the British aristocracy appear to be succumbing to the democracy of romantic love. The Duke of Bedford talking about marriages between aristocrats and commoners is quoted as saying: "Not many years ago the aristocrats would not dream of marrying into 'trade.' Now there's nothing nicer than to marry into a nice chain of supermarkets."[14]

To seek happiness in marriage is consonant with the humanistic tradition. It is a noble goal reflecting the ideal of very personal needs and desires of the individual as apart from the needs of the family, state, or church.

The idea of personal happiness is relatively new in our history—only a century or so old—and not at all permanently entrenched. The French Revolution spawned it and totalitarian regimes would like to extinguish it. At the time of his ascension to power, Hitler was quoted as saying: "The era of personal happiness is closed."[2] The pursuit of happiness has been strong in America, so much so as to be incorporated in its basic political documents. However, even in America there are periodic rumblings against it. Some felt that there was a hint of this in John F. Kennedy's famous 1961 inaugural appeal: "Ask not what your country can do for you; ask what you can do for your country."

It is an orientation to this world rather than another or the next. Robert Frost voiced this modern hopeful attitude when he said: "Earth's the right place for love, I don't know where it's likely to go better."[6]

The difficulty with happiness and its pursuit in marriage, as in many other things, is the *principle* under which it operates. One woman can be made happy by the circumstance of another devoting himself totally to her needs. She can find happiness if carried about as an infant might be, anything short of that being considered neglect. One could envision a state of happiness when indulgence is total and responsibility nil. Similarly, happiness for some can be achieved only by the total subjugation and humiliation of another. This is akin to the "happy warrior" type in the military where one is made happy because a city has been successfully bombed. During the Spanish Civil War one of Mussolini's sons, on a bombing mission, was enthralled by the beauty of an exploding bomb on the target below. In the hands of many, the pursuit of happiness can become less than a thing of beauty for the rest of humanity.

The elucidation of the operative principles of mentation was one of Freud's major contributions. He described the *pleasure principle* under which the neonate is said to operate. Here the outstanding and only consideration is the immediate gratification of a need. It is with maturation that the individual discovers that if he is to survive, and if he is to become "human," he must renounce this reflex behavior in favor of the reality principle which, while never renouncing the pursuit and attainment of pleasure, brings to bear on the subject overall and remote needs and circumstances, and takes into account the identities and importance of other people. It is happiness governed by the reality principle that one can achieve in marriage.

All too often the happiness that many achieve for themselves is directly at the expense of others over whom they have gained power and authority. This is happiness on the basis of forced indulgence which imitates the parent-child or master-slave model. "If you do as I say, it will make me very happy." Hopefully, authentic happiness can be achieved on the basis of reason and justice. This is more difficult, for it means renunciations and compromises instead of demands for subservience or surrender. If more difficult, it is ultimately more rewarding and lasting since, as we learn from politics, deliberately cultivated inequities spawn revolutions.

NOTES

1. Camus, Albert, *Notebooks 1935-1942* (New York: A Modern Library Book, 1965), p. 84.

1a. de Balzac, Honoré, *A Marriage Settlement* (New York: Jefferson Press, 1836), p. 24.

2. de Sales, Raoul de Roussy, "The Idea of Happiness, 1942," *The Saturday Review Treasury* (New York: Simon and Schuster, 1957), p. 206.

3. Dugan, Alan, "Speech for Aeneas," *Saturday Review* (Jan. 30, 1965), p. 6.

4. Freud, Sigmund, *Group Psychology and the Analysis of the Ego*, trans. James Strachey (New York: Liveright Publishing Corp., 1949), p. 122.

5. Freud, Sigmund, "Some Character-Types Not in Psychoanalytic Work," *Collected Papers*, IV (1915).

6. Frost, Robert, "The Death of the Hired Man," *Selected Poems of Robert Frost* (New York: Holt, Rinehart, and Winston, 1962), p. 25.

7. Glazer, Nathan and Daniel P. Moynihan, *Beyond the Melting Pot* (Cambridge, Mass.: M.I.T. Press and Harvard University Press, 1963), pp. 173-287.

8. Goethe, J. W., *Elective Affinities*, trans. Elizabeth Mayer and Louise Bogan (Chicago: Henry Regnery Co., 1963).

9. *Herald Tribune*, Sept. 27, 1965, p. 22.

9a. Kierkegaard, Soren, *Concluding Unscientific Postscript to the "Philosophical Fragments,"* trans. David F. Swensen and Walter Lowrie. (Princeton University Press for the American-Scandinavian Foundation, 1941), p. 237.

10. Krutch, Joseph Wood, "Challenge to an Unknown Writer," *Saturday Review*, LXV (March 10, 1962), p. 12.

10a. Hosea, 2.19.

11. Lehrman, Samuel R., "Psychopathology in Mixed Marriages," *Psychoanalytic Quarterly*, Vol. XXXVI, No. 1 (1967).

12. *New York Times*, Jan. 4, 1965.

13. *New York Times,* Oct. 21, 1964, p. 20.

14. *New York Times,* Jan. 31, 1965, p. 69.

15. *New York Times,* April 30, 1967.

16. Osmundsen, John A., "Doctor Discusses 'Mixed' Marriage," *New York Times,* Nov. 7, 1965, p. 73.

17. Rattray, Taylor G., *Sex in History* (New York: Vanguard Press, 1954), p. 69.

18. Scott, John Finley, "Are Sororities Today's 'Olags' and Fatting Houses?", *The National Observer* (Oct. 4, 1965), p. 13.

19. Shakespeare, "As You Like It," *The Complete Works of William Shakespeare* (Cleveland, Ohio: The World Publishing Co., n.d.), p. 226.

20. *Ibid.,* p. 226.

21. Shakespeare, William, "Hamlet," *The Complete Works of William Shakespeare* (Cleveland, Ohio: The World Publishing Co., n.d.), p. 961.

22. Shakespeare, William, *Much Ado About Nothing,* ed. G. B. Harrison (New York: The Shakespeare Recording Society, Inc., 1963), pp. 35-6.

22a. Gloria Steinem, *Women and Power,* in *Reflections,* vol. 4, No. 3, 1969, p. 15 (reprinted from the *New York Magazine*).

23. Wedekind, Frank, "The Marquis of Keith," *Masters of Modern Drama,* ed. Haskell Block and Robert Shedd (New York: Random House, 1962), p. 279.

24. Tiger, L., *Men in Groups,* New York, Random House, 1969.

25. The *Irigwe* of Nigeria have a matrimonial system which accedes both to parental preferences and to personal romantic choices. The individuals have two successive marriages. The first union is arranged by the parents prior to the adolescence of the participants. Several years later the mates may initiate a separation and then espouse someone of their choice. This arrangement is called *primary* and *secondary* marriage. (This is from material presented by Prof. Walter H. Sangree of the University of Rochester to the Western New York Psychoanalytic Society, Nov. 29, 1969. His paper on this research is to be published in the *American Anthropologist* in 1969 or 1970.)

26. Obviously an oversimplification, one dimension of marriage is, as Sarwer-Foner maintains, an adult expression of infantile patterns of asking for and responding to gratifications and frustrations at the hands of the original love objects and their successors. See Sarwer-Foner, G.J., *Patterns of Marital Relationship,* in *American Journal of Psychotherapy,* vol. 17:31: Jan., 1963.

27. Sklare, M., *Intermarriage and the Jewish Future,* in Commentary, vol. 37:46: April, 1964.

CHAPTER II

CATCHER GONE AWRY

Although his fortune was large and his character sensible, he seemed to feel strangely flattered to become the privileged husband of a woman whom the whole world must find lovely.

Goethe, *Elective Affinities*

There is a therapist in every one of us. Jesus saves, and we wish to identify with Him. Few of us can save lives, but we all at some time or another try to save souls. We all have fancied ourselves as catchers in the tall grass rescuing others who play their games near the brink. For some the highest mission of life is rescue, and they are attracted to the problems of others. And in every rescuer there is invariably found the need to be rescued.

Marriage lends itself to such missionary zeal. If you love someone, it is quite natural that you would want to help him. But one often sees that a person is loved *because* he or she needs help. The distraught person then becomes a challenge, to be helped, to be rehabilitated when everyone else and everything else has failed. "I will straighten her out." "I am what she needs." "I will make her a good life." These are expressions of love and empathy, but they can be derived from a malignant megalomania often leading to severe disillusionment and worse. A person must be enthralled with his own importance to feel that his good intentions, or the examples he sets, or the love he gives, can undo the torment and pain of another, usually wrought by a myriad of destructive and threatening imprints of many decades of living. When a man marries a woman to cure her, he at once identifies himself as a superman. The rescue fantasy is the intellectual counterpart, or perhaps derivative, of having phallic super-potency to gratify when everyone else has failed. His goal does not stop at just being the "right guy" for someone but involves being both the "right" and the "great" guy.

The motive of the rescuer is a selfish one. He unconsciously uses his beloved as a means of glorifying himself. If she does not respond to his magical love potion, he turns on her in a most sanctimonious way and then discards her, accusing her of betrayal and infidelity. She has not been cooperative! At the same time that the rescuer hopes to achieve a miraculous transformation in his mate, he feels very mature and well integrated in contrast to the quivering wretch before him. She makes him look good by contrast, just as the Negro makes the White racist feel good.

We witness an example of this rescue operation in Arthur Miller's *After the Fall*,[1] which is about a "sick" girl, Maggie, and a man who wanted to cure her. She and her mother were abandoned by her father when she was eighteen months of age. Starting at an early age, she readily gave her favors to men. She slept in the park and wandered in strange places, innocently unaware of danger. She became a celebrity as a singer and as a sex symbol. Throughout all of this, she acted foolishly in her business dealings, trusted the wrong people, mainly believed the cunning praise of those who wanted to exploit her, and generally appeared almost biologically incapable of self-preservation. Quentin, the brilliant lawyer, unhappily married to a self-sufficient wife who continually proclaimed autonomy, became fascinated and was drawn to marry the ex-telephone operator, even though she made no demands for marriage. To him, in spite of all her sexual promiscuity, she represented innocence that had to be defended and protected. In all that she did and was done to her, she rarely felt exploited or felt that anyone was acting other than in her interest. This was an innocence that contrasted sharply with the world of sophistication which Quentin knew, where deep, dark destructive and self-seeking motives were always suspected and found. In his circle, there were no acts of generosity or trust. (Who ever signs a paper without a lawyer? Maggie did, because people said it was all right.) This innocence had to be defended, protected, and, of course, stamped out. Quentin could not tolerate the way she would casually play near the edge. As she played brinksmanship on the street, in the park, with agents, she also courted death with drink and sleeping pills. Here indeed was work for some catcher in the rye with a child of nature who either was fatally attracted to the edge of the cliff or never really believed it was there. Quentin was there to rescue and to catch until the ambulances and the emergency rooms, stomach pumps and *gavages* became altogether unnerving. The contrast to his first wife's full self-sufficiency was quite attractive when it came to breaking the gentle falls, but when they turned to threats and dives into the abyss, it was more than he had bargained for. His vigil at the brink tired him and caused the complete disillusionment, which in turn led to hatred of this creature who not only failed to respond to his benevolence, but became worse and worse, as if each successive rescue seemed to intensify her desire to destroy herself. If he hated her because she acted that way, or hated her because she would not learn from him, he hated her most because she threatened to expose his complete naiveté! But he was saved from this exposure by a typical self-deception. Quentin seemed to have explained it all by saying that he was, after all, too good for her.

Maggie was American white trash and Quentin was what former Governor Paul Johnson of Mississippi would call a first-generation alien. Quentin's father was an immigrant who did well in business although he was illiterate.

The parents' marriage had been arranged. The well-to-do businessman was considered a good match for the girl who up to then had been courted by Strauss, a poor boy who read poetry to her. This boy later became a doctor. Quentin laments his mother's fate in being forced into an opportunistic marriage to a boor, his father, instead of with a more cultured individual. Quentin could not rescue his mother, but probably he would have liked to. He himself was intended to work for his father, but he was rescued from that by his older brother, Dan, who took his place, liberating Quentin for more scholarly pursuits, the law, writing, perhaps poetry. Unlike Maggie, who had no one, Quentin knew the family net was always there for him.

There is the inevitable identification with Christ. Quentin is seen on stage standing against the wall with arms outstretched in crucifixion as if he is trying to love everybody. Later, when his megalomania is punctured by defeat, as he sees that both endless love and truth are weak reeds for the task at hand, he espouses humility. He wants to be a human being again.

Quentin's involvement blinds him to the destructive aspect of too much love. He figures that Maggie's rehabilitation has failed not because of the wrong mode of treatment but because of inadequate dosage. In his desperation to love and to save, to give and to find salvation, he finds both object and subject in mortal jeopardy. Is Quentin's motivation solely for power in order to change, to affect another? And is her negativism his chief frustration? Perhaps. We, however, suspect that she made him look good by contrast. She let in darkness so that he could shine more brightly. When there are grave doubts about one's own balance, there is some reassurance in being near the disintegrated. When Quentin says suicide is designed to kill two, he is mouthing a clinical banality. For the death of one can renew life in the other. Christ died for us all. Christians experienced a rebirth in His death. Quentin himself, a most depressive character, may have been saved from suicide by Maggie's death. He did envisage himself as crucified. He saw the concentration camps, the congressional committee betrayal of friends, the estrangement of his wife, the alienation of his own child, etc. His friend Lou did kill himself as he was to be betrayed by a "friend" and past associate in leftist organizations. Quentin himself, in his sanctimonious manner, was about to implicate his friends before the committee. Maggie was a whore but, as everyone knows, the worst whoring never gets done in bed. But she had the name and the game; next to her, at her side, anyone could look respectable.

Underlying the impulse to save, to rescue, and to catch another, is the feeling of imminent loss within oneself of the ability to cope. It appears that Quentin, failing in communication with his wife, suffering from the alienation of his child and from the suicide of a close friend in connection with the congressional investigation in which he himself was involved and was about to name names, was close to personal dissolution and, possibly, suicide. Although he was reassured that he could always count on his own family for help, such help for a "big boy" was impossible to accept. There was too much involved in asking to be rescued, and the only psychological alternative was to save Maggie. Marriage was not her idea.

Thus, Maggie's death may have served to allay Quentin's own existential agonies. As it is said in Christianity, He died for us; it may also be said in interpersonal relations that one may do the dying for another. In witnessing and attending to Maggie's degradation and brinksmanship, her indifference to reputation, her lack of self-preservative instinct, her aimlessness, her rootlessness, her utter simplicity, and her repeated dalliance with life itself, Quentin may have found the motivation to reaffirm and to mobilize his own life-forces. Strange? Not at all when one considers that relationships often have the characteristics of a seesaw; one is up *because* the other is down. Again, the tragedies of others, like ancient myths and anxiety dreams, give a feeling that one is not so badly off after all. Probably this is a macabre reason for the popularity of funerals, lynchings, visits to insane asylums, concentration camps, etc.—and marriage?

Maggie did not want marriage; such "respectability" was outside her spectrum of living. She had never known it as a child and perhaps she had some prescience that it was not for her. She was doing "good" in her own way by being generous with what she understood, trusted, and had mastered—her body. She was a student and teacher and purveyor of biology—never capable of understanding the nuances of love, of loyalty, and of other abstractions quite alien to her. Quentin never wanted to understand this, prescribed love as the alyssum.

Quentin's confidence that the truth saves was revealed early in the play when he insisted on telling his father, critically ill with a heart attack, that this wife, Quentin's mother, had suddenly dropped dead after her visit to him at the hospital. This bit of intellection, in the secret service of hostility, was the prototype of things to come with Maggie. The father was not at all saved nor was there evidence that he was appreciative of, or in condition for, such honesty.

Quentin's tragic defeat was in his inability to gauge properly the receptivity of the other person. For the ill prepared, the power of the intellect may be a weak and disappointing reed. In dealing with Maggie, the power of the intellect became the tyranny of the intellect because it hoped that superficial application would suffice. Then good intentions raged against the forces which did not respond.

It is quite apparent that the conflict between intellect and instinct is an intrapsychic one for Quentin, played out, as it generally is, between antagonists. Did intellect fail because of its inherent weaknesses, or was instinct too strong? Or was the difficulty an apotheosis of the intellect at the expense of common sense? For what was lacking in Quentin's intellection was the good sense to know the limitations of virtue. Coupled with this was his disdain and disgust for the emotions. The physical warmth which Maggie understood and sought was anathema to him. Her requests for the "physical" repelled him; her beauty was a sterile commodity—a sensuous but not a sensual experience for him. This type of reception was entirely alien to her reality and could be viewed by her only as abandonment.

The catcher's game is by no means the exclusive play of prominent people or celebrities. In all walks of life individuals are attracted to those seemingly less fortunate than themselves. Apparently the concept of being helpful has become a virtue of such high moral standing that it has become a facile rationalization for relationships which otherwise would be difficult to explain or understand. Although helpfulness and conscience should not be disparaged, they must have their proper places in the total spectrum of what goes on between people. It is no compliment to be desired *only* because one is crippled or inept or disintegrated. Ideally, people should be attractive for their strengths, with a concomitant acceptance of their inevitable weaknesses.

In international affairs, it is difficult for major powers such as the United States or Russia to understand why small nations remain hostile and antagonistic in spite of huge aid programs and repeated professions of friendliness and sincerity by the former. This, of course, is a complex issue encompassing historical as well as contemporary political and economic exigencies, but an underlying "resistance" to good feeling is the barrier wrought of differences of size and importance. The weak nations may suspect that they are "loved" not because they are nations but because they are *weak*. Whether this is an illusion on the part of ungrateful recipients or has actual substance is difficult to say. There is some evidence that this is not pure illusion, for in the case of France, the United States dearly loved her after World War II when she was down and out. Now, with the present display of authority and autonomy since General De Gaulle, the love affair has, to say the least, simmered down.

Similarly, in race relations in this country, the "darkies" were loved and protected as long as they acknowledged, in word and deed, their inferiority and dependence. As the Negro began to assert his equality, love flew out the window. Why these disenchantments? Quentin agonized over a similar question. He wondered if it were not some basic need to have and maintain power over others. As Lord Acton said, power does things to its possessors. Its most malignant consequence is that corruption which prevents self-examination. That person not only becomes convinced that he is using power in the best possible manner, but he inevitably comes to the conclusion, like sovereigns of old, that God gave it to him. This combination of self-justification and concept of divine appointment leads to blindness and tyranny.

The attraction of weakness is unfortunately an all too usual expectation as far as the woman is concerned. She has been "designed" as the weaker sex and often expresses her overriding ambition as finding some man "who will take care of me." Self-sufficient, assertive women are often shunned by men and condemned by other women.

Although women are normally supposed to be weak and consequently have to be protected, society lifts its eyebrow when a woman is attracted to a male's moral weaknesses and wants to spend her life taking care of him. Women are known to fall in love with obsessive gamblers, alcoholics, dope addicts, and others showing grave moral deficiencies characterized by lack of control. It is known that, like Quentin, they have great hopes of rehabilitating their mates, and this proves to be a chief motivation for marriage. The man who has monolithic intentions, determination, control, and goal-directedness, along with the inherent advantages that life and society give him as a male, may have little appeal and indeed be very threatening to certain women. To these women of competitive bent (and there is competition in all relationships) such a mate would present insuperable odds for her in any contest. In such a marriage, a woman's destiny would be to gain glory in his achievements and/or wither away in his great shadow.

Women may prefer less illustrious mates, so their own

roles and identities in marriage will not be completely eclipsed. This preference suggests a paradox, for one supposedly would want the best of mates for oneself. But, with a little reflection, it becomes apparent that there can be a conflict in the desires to "get the best" and also to "be the better." It therefore is no great surprise to find, clinically and in everyday life, instances of women who are attracted to and marry problem men when they could have done better. In these instances there is no lack of opportunity for better choices, which is sometimes given as a reason for such a match.

An attractive woman of twenty-eight found herself severely criticized by her friends for the attachment she had made. She was a highly intelligent person, had done graduate work at a leading university, and was now holding a responsible job in government. She had "gone steady" with several men, had even been engaged to a young lawyer, but she seemed to recoil from relationships which would seem consonant with a successful marriage. She now had formed an intimate relationship and wanted to marry a man of thirty-five, previously married, and recently discharged from a mental hospital. He had shown marked instability in most of his social relations and had worked at a menial job, far beneath his educational level. Even at this job, his fear of accepting any responsibility made his hold extremely tenuous. They met at a summer hotel and their relationship quickly developed into an intense intimacy. He was seeing a psychiatrist and would discuss his therapy sessions with her. He told her of his past and present weaknesses and anxieties; she became enthralled by the mysteries of the psyche and gratified that a man would divulge to her his many and grave shortcomings. He told her that his mother had abandoned him and his sister when he was three years old. Thereafter, he was raised by an aunt who made the children conscious of the great act of mercy that she was performing. He grew up to be timid and shy, lacking trust in any personal capacity to cope with problems or to sustain relationships in his own work. His first marriage ended when his wife left him for another; she was unable to put up with his lack of initiative and ambition. His grief over this landed him in a mental hospital. His course during hospitalization was a stormy one; he had made a suicide attempt and was beset with many obsessive, destructive thoughts as well as numerous psychosomatic ailments.

Her developmental history contrasted sharply with his. She came from a conventional middle-class background. Her parents appeared devoted to each other, were hard-working, moderate in social and political views, and concentrated chiefly on the education and development of their two children. Her growth pattern and early relationships were normal with the exception of an eating difficulty dating from the birth of a brother when she was five. Since then, she had been a finicky eater and was prone to vomiting, especially when excited or upset. As a result, she remained quite thin; her refusal to respond to her mother's good cooking and other indulgences remained the sore point in the household. Otherwise she was quite obedient, never falling below her parents' expectations, both morally and in school performance.

Later they were concerned that she appeared reluctant to marry, although they were otherwise quite pleased with her outstanding professional achievements. She, on the other hand, was cordial but aloof from the demands of her parents, although she maintained close associations with her brother. She was worried because his school performance and general ability were below average, in contrast to her own. It appeared that there was little likelihood of his being accepted to college; his outlook for achievement seemed bleak. She felt extremely guilty about this, wondering if she in some way had done injury to his motivation since he had had to develop in her shadow. Even though she was proud of her own success at school and thereafter, she hoped it was not achieved at the expense of her younger brother. Regardless of modern views about the equality of the sexes, it was still, she knew, more important for the male to be educated and prepared for worldly activities. Her feelings that she might have directly or inadvertently damaged him were not based on anything that she recalled doing. She had been kind to him. Outside of family squabbles and pettiness, she was generally helpful to him in his school work and social situations. It approached an ideal sister-brother relationship. Her only crime might have been her scholastic success that could have engendered a feeling of hopelessness within him, for it would be difficult for him to match her achievements. But it would have been dishonorable, she reflected, to hold back in order to help him. If she had sinned, it was the sin of developing her talents. She continued to do what she could for him in the way of offering encouragement and advice, and she promised to aid him financially in school or in any business venture he might propose.

Although, while growing up, she was innocent of any active rivalry with her brother, she had apparently been extremely threatened and dismayed by his birth, phantasizing that she might be abandoned by her parents who would "naturally" favor the new male arrival. Her lifelong neurotic symptoms, dysphagia, nausea, and vomiting, beginning at that time, bore evidence of her continuing difficulty in coping with a sibling. We know that phantasies besetting children faced with outer threats of loss of love are destructive ones toward the intruder, perhaps of getting rid of him, of devouring him. To counteract such feelings, one develops the reaction formations of overprotectiveness and concern. This is how she had handled her family feelings, and the situation had left her with a deep ambivalence toward the opposite sex. Because the most acceptable role for her was a helping one, she saw no future in marrying a man who was already self-sufficient. On a deeper level, the presence of a weak and inept male also represented a personal triumph in the struggle to show her parents and her own conflictual psyche that a girl can be more valuable than the exalted male.

Another aspect of her attraction to her new paramour

was the feeling that hers could only be a helping or re-
habilitative role, for he was already ill. Before her was a
"damaged" person; the wounds were already and unmis-
takably inflicted by others—a mother who abandoned her
child, an aunt who made exorbitant demands, and a wife
who knew no compassion. She then could never be accused
of *causing* injury here, as might have been the case with
her brother. The man she now loved had already been
done in by a trio of malefactresses; if things did not go
well with him, she could not be blamed, as she might in a
relationship of greater equality. She thereby protected herself from the anxiety incumbent on "hurting a male"
which haunted her most of her life. This is one prominent
attraction of the already damaged product.

The effects of this union were less than salutary. The
male in this case, finding a seemingly welcome contrast to
his first wife, was temporarily hopeful of finding a woman
who could supply those things which were missing within
himself. But his demands grew greater than even her tolerance could bear, and they parted with mutual willingness,
without recourse to Maggie's solution of suicide. Rocked
and disillusioned by this attempt at mating, she learned
that her correction had to be an internal one first.

The opposite number to the "catcher" is the indifferent
one. Imbued with the philosophy that each person should
be completely autonomous and totally responsible for himself, he develops or assumes a contrived indifference toward
his mate. He shies from giving any criticism, any positive
suggestions, and is fearful of giving a helping hand lest he
be accused of intruding. His paradigm would be the story
of one Englishman extending condolences to the other:
"Sorry, old man. I heard you buried your wife last week."
The reply of the autonomy-loving one was: "Had to. Died,
you know!" One is then left to wonder whether she died
because at the moment of her anginal attack, her nitroglyc-
erine tablets were just out of reach, and her husband did
not want to interfere in her personal struggles. Many husbands and wives try to convert marriage into a psycho-

analytic situation and attempt to imitate the neutrality of the analyst. They would not ever want to be accused of trying to run the life of the other. This behavior is often carried to a compulsive fault and reaps the same destructive results as the love of the militant rescuer.

The responsibility of the husband and father for his family is a given which has been the principal justification for his dominance. He must provide and protect, or give the appearance of doing so. In exchange for his "burden," he is given stature and advantage commensurate with his responsibility. He also has the image of "working hard" in the world for his family. This "work" is generally considered an act of personal sacrifice and deprivation entitling him to special privileges. Although there may be an attritional result from unchallenging and boring work, work generally adds to self-esteem, promotes personal worthiness, and stimulates the vitality of brain cells. It may provide the series of successes that men live by. The term "hard work" should be reserved for those banal activities which do not challenge or tax the mind and where achievement is absent. For instance, having to study for a Ph.D. can, by no stretch of the imagination, be considered hard work; having to read and write needs no added rewards. To demand rewards or special credit is to deceive and hoodwink.

This type of self-serving mythology was part of the life-structure of Jim and Nancy. It led inevitably to an imbalance of values and concerns resulting in a case of sub-criminal negligence. If Maggie suffered the results of ill-advised indulgence, Nancy suffered the effects of a weak, self-preservative "instinct" and of a "catcher" who was not really there.

They had met at a mid-western university where they were involved in graduate studies in the history department. They were both bright, attractive young people of great vitality and worldly idealism. Their familial traditions were similar in religion and class. Both had parents in academic life. These two young people were the envy of their friends; they were well-mated, conveniently congenial, and above all optimistic about the future.

Jim's father was head of a department at a leading university. Nancy's mother was dean of women at an eastern college. Her father was in the diplomatic service and was away from home for long periods of time. Nancy had suffered from loneliness and made resolutions that her married life would be different. She, a latch-key child, was determined that she would be a mother who was home when her children came home from school. Yet she was very bright, excelled academically, and was socially popular. However, her scholarly nature worried her, for she was harassed by occasional slurs from relatives about the necessity of being "feminine." There were times of depression, especially during arid "dating" periods.

In college, although she maintained a serious interest in her academic work, she became increasingly apprehensive about her social life. In her freshman year she dated frequently, but the fellow whom she especially liked dropped her for another girl. Her friends seemed to have better luck in going steady than she did. She began wondering whether there was something wrong with her that she seemed incapable of "holding" the boys. Was she not feminine enough, she thought? On weekends when there were no dates, she suffered severe loneliness and self-doubt. She began having weekend headaches and feelings of despondency. She sought medical help and was reassured that there was nothing wrong. Her academic successes as well as her interest in social issues and politics could not dispel the self-doubts about her worthiness. Her senior year came and went and she was neither married nor engaged as were many of her friends. She decided to go on with her work in graduate school where she had no difficulty in being accepted into the advanced degree program. It was here that she met Jim who was one year ahead of her in course work. In contrast to her previous boyfriends, Jim wanted to stick and within six months they were engaged. They were both happy with each other; Nancy especially so since she would be able to dispel her doubts about her femininity and worthiness. Scholastically, she was the brighter of the two but tried to obfuscate this difference as much as she could.

She became a patient listener and consciously played a passive role in the relationship. She spent long periods of her time researching for Jim's work and typed his papers in addition to her own work, which now began to suffer. She had mild regrets about this neglect of her own productivity but in her gestalt, this was a small price to pay.

Jim was known as an ideologue. His interest was in contemporary world problems. He was a campus activist and also took part in national and international youth organizations. He was immensely pleased with his association with Nancy and saw her as a wonderful helpmate and companion in the achievement of many of his goals. He intended to make a career of academic life, to use the campus as a base from which he could carry on his activism.

They were married after they both earned Master's degrees. Jim was awarded a fellowship at another university leading to his Ph.D. Because of a university rule, husband and wife were not permitted to study in the same graduate program. Nancy was somewhat dismayed by this, and Jim had reservations about this move which would in effect be a deprivation for Nancy. She would hear none of it, however, and insisted that they make the move. She reasoned that she had had enough of studying and was content in her marriage; furthermore she wanted to have a baby as soon as she could. With financial help from the family, they made the move. Nancy became pregnant and continued to help Jim in his work. She welcomed the change, finding her new role quite exciting. The progress of her husband and the advent of motherhood were compensations enough for the renunciation of her own intellectual development.

Jim earned his Ph.D. Thereafter there was an appointment as an instructor as well as travel to remote areas of the world. They had two children in quick succession. Returning to an advanced position at a leading university, Jim's career was well on its way toward success. He now had a book in preparation, he was heralded by his confreres, and his lectures were eagerly attended. Socially Jim and Nancy were the stars of the community. Their company was sought out and they were labeled the ideal couple. Roles seemed clearly and appropriately defined. Jim was the active and worldly one; Nancy was the helpmate, passive and retiring. Jim was a good provider, feeling secure that he was doing his job and content in the knowledge that Nancy was pleased and well-adjusted in her role. He was defined by others as hard-working, selfless, and devoted in both his public and private life. Speaking engagements came which took him away from home at regular intervals. Offers from other colleges were frequent but Nancy began to balk at too many moves and the disruption it caused in trying to establish a social life and maintain friendships.

By the eighth year of their marriage, much of the bloom was disappearing as far as Nancy was concerned, but not to Jim, even though Nancy's headaches were returning and an irritability on her part was becoming evident. She became reluctant to accompany him to certain obligatory campus banquets; she no longer cared to edit his essays for publication. Feelings of loneliness and despair began to overtake her; her children and household duties did not seem to engage her interest as they had done earlier. Though gratified by her husband's successes, it appeared that she could no longer find contentment in his achievements alone. These thoughts were never expressed or communicated. Jim was frankly bewildered by Nancy's disenchantment but felt quite helpless to ameliorate the situation. He suggested more help in the house and that Nancy take up skiing or horseback riding as salutary exercises. Nancy turned a deaf ear to his suggestions; her former helpful passivity had now turned to negativism.

Nancy's behavior then took a new unexpected turn.

Never having shown any but a polite interest in men other than Jim, she became romantically attracted to Jim's best friend, Tom, a bachelor poet-in-residence at the university. The three had been brought together at many university functions and Tom became a frequent visitor at their home. At first Jim brought Tom home to dinner; after the passage of a few months, Nancy would ask Jim to invite Tom at more frequent intervals. Devoid of any suspicion or jealousy, Jim's attitude was of pleasure that Nancy was becoming less irritable and withdrawn.

Tom had never been married and showed a marked reserve in his "object relations." He shied away from intimacies and seemed content with friendships of his colleagues on campus and student gatherings. He was startled and yet excited when Nancy began to make romantic overtures to him. He had not "known" women before and Nancy appeared to offer opportunity for a belated experience. His loyalty to his friend weighed heavily on him but did not prove, at first, to be an inexorable obstacle.

Nancy made overt advances to him and overcame his earlier reluctance. The trysts continued for ten months until Nancy, now convinced that she no longer cared for Jim, became quite possessive of Tom and suggested that they run away together. Apparently contented with an affair, Tom had not entertained the prospect of marriage and could not allow himself to be that disruptive to his friend's household. He had viewed the affair as quite innocent—a thing of play rather than an intimate and far-reaching social matter. He thereupon balked at going further. He told Nancy that he would have to withdraw from the relationship if she had become involved to that degree. He would do this with great reluctance since she had meant a great deal to him.

Nancy was visibly shaken by this response and realized that much of what she had felt and anticipated were hopes and desires of her own rather than anything that Tom had promised. He was a tyro both at the beginning and the end. Yet Nancy felt a sense of betrayal as well as deep humiliation. Her hopes for rescue were similarly shattered. There was no return to Jim at this juncture. Nancy was found comatose one day after there was no answer at the door. The children were at school. She had taken an overdose of sleeping pills and tranquilizers but was saved by prompt medical attention. In a day she was fully recovered but in that time Tom, distraught with guilt, had made a full confession to Jim, who took his cuckolding with complete surprise but in a typically civilized manner. The important thing, both men agreed, was to help Nancy back to emotional stability. The two of them felt that Nancy should seek immediate help. Modern Ophelias are told, "Get thee to an analyst!"

For Jim and for Nancy, what became of their marriage was a transmogrification, totally unforeseen. Was there a sinner here, and if so, who was it and what the sin? The Biblical prophets advise: "Thou shalt not stand idly by!" This apothegm was probably responsible for more intrusive meddling than help that was to be derived. Yet there is a principle of the helping hand, the plant to be watered. What is one's responsibility when there are no requests or appeals? Must one then be an expert in occult sign language?

By ordinary standards of responsibility, Jim's behavior was impeccable. He did all the correct things; he developed his talents, had worldly concerns, and was conventionally responsive to his wife. He did not actually coerce her nor did he set up prohibitions against fulfillment of her needs. On the surface, at least, he treated her as an autonomous person. The main difficulty here is that the institution of marriage itself sets up an imbalance; it contains a built-in coerciveness against the woman who has an ego and yet must deny it because of the bedevilment of femininity. For Jim, being married or becoming a father entailed no renunciation of goals of worldly achievement; for Nancy, however, the price of being a wife and mother proved to be greater than she could pay even though marriage was her "free" choice. However for the woman, there is no success in life if there is no marriage. But for the literate woman, marriage by itself often cannot provide the demiurge of satisfactory fulfillment.

In analysis, Nancy presented the picture of a thoroughly defeated person. Her problems proved to be more existential than genetic. Her frenetic rush into romance with its disastrous results added the crushing addition to her list of defeats. She had been sincere in her love and devotion to Jim. She had resolutely fused her destiny with his but found that she had instincts of her own which could not be denied. His successes accentuated the differences in their status and destinies. She could no longer sublimate her own brightness into duty and devotion. Plagued during her adolescence by the image of femininity as fostered by friends, relatives, and society, she sought an identity in marriage, which had to pre-empt everything else. Yet to be feminine as conventionally defined required renunciations beyond reasonable dimensions for her, as for many other intelligent women.

Psychoanalysis seemed to bring some understanding of her problems. She remained in her marriage without love; Tom left the scene. In the years remaining to her she made abortive attempts to seek her salvation in *"good works."* She died at the age of forty of a heart attack. Jim was no villain; neither was Quentin. They were both caught in an existential web. Nancy never verbalized her needs because she wanted to play courageously the role that she herself sought. But did Jim falter in failing to identify with Nancy as a fellow human with feelings and aspirations that might not be too different from his own? Was he ingenuous in taking her at her word? There are those who have said of this tragic situation that he had no right to let his own ambitions eclipse hers. However, he *had* urged her to go on with her own development. Yet this is easier said than done. Superficially he was an ideal husband for an ordinary wife. Here another dimension of empathy was required that he lacked; he can be faulted on the score of *proper* behavior in an *improper* situation. He was a catcher in the rye but not in blue grass.

NOTES

1. Arthur Miller, *After the Fall* (New York: The Viking Press, 1964).

CHAPTER III

UNDERMINING CONFIDENCE

How easy is it for the proper false
In women's waxen hearts to set their forms!
Alas! our frailty is the cause, not we!

                                        Viola, *Twelfth Night*

Fire is stirred by fire
The same tiny flame will kill two wheat heads together.

                        Federica Garcia Lorca, *Blood Wedding*

In the last chapter, we saw instances of compassion without wisdom. Wisdom, or what stands for it, can be an equally potent instrument of malpractice between human beings. That the strong overpower the weak is no great or new insight. But there are designing individuals among us who work their trade with a subtlety and malice that make Iago ingenuous. Their principal method is to ferment self-doubt in those who can ill afford further attrition to their internal esteem system. And, like Quentin's compassion, it is done "innocently," always under the banner of helpfulness. Freud tried to teach the lesson of the force of authority in the early formative years of development. Harry Stack Sullivan revealed the tyrannies of interpersonal relations of later periods. Some people escape neither, having the misfortune of being hit from below and above.

Although the capacity to test reality is variable in any person, it appears to be critically diminished in those who are labeled "borderline" or "psychotic." The classical scientific literature examines this process mainly as an intrapsychic phenomenon. Freud wrote that in both neurosis and psychosis there is a withdrawal of the ego from reality. He said: "Neurosis does not deny the existence of reality, it merely tries to ignore it; psychosis denies it and tries to substitute something else for it." Freud called the normal or healthy reaction a combination of these two. "It denies reality as little as neurosis, but then, like a psychosis, is concerned with effecting a change in it. This expedient normal attitude leads naturally to some active achievement in the outer world and is not content, like psychosis, with establishing the alteration within itself."[1] The break with reality results "less because of the temptations it holds."[2] Others have made pertinent contributions concerning the topography and dynamics of this problem.[3, 4]

Although generally attributable to or a concomitant of unconscious intrapsychic conflicts involving a narcissistic withdrawal, it is felt that more is to be said on the subject of reality-testing capacity in terms of preconscious forces derived from interpersonal relationships. It is suggested here, as novelists and playwrights have already done, that the capacity for reality-testing of a person can be critically affected by the activities, attitudes, and behavior of a persistently designing person with whom he is inextricably bound, as in marriage, certain friendships, psychiatric treatment, or even at work. Simply stated, it is the phenomenon of being "driven crazy." In a series of cases Meerloo has demonstrated the destructive effects to ego, self-esteem, and life itself of certain types of mental coercion.[5] This appears equally applicable to interpersonal relations and to groups of people and nations (brainwashing, thought control, political campaigning).

There is a tendency for many to hand over reality-testing function to others, to let others decide what is real or not, what is possible or probable, what is authentic or spurious;

what is on the inside or outside. Let the experts decide, we say all too frequently. Yet in certain areas we cannot abrogate this function lest we lose our pride, our identity, and our minds. We must trust others, yet we must not use his trust to encourage laziness and the atrophy of our own capacity.

On the other hand, many have a need to impose their will to make forcibly all decisions of what is right and what is real, and what is fact and what is fancy. Marriage is the relationship where a timid person is particularly vulnerable to such an imposition. Romantic love, of course, encourages this trust and submission. Sometimes it is the authority of maleness, or of being a physician, or a clergyman, which gives this mate a corner on what is or what should be. The mates of such persons, insecure to begin with, may witness the little confidence they have in themselves slowly whittled away, and they may be left like Ophelia, a victim of the struggling giants around her.

They write tragic dramas when the oppression occurs to a man, e.g., Coriolanus, to be discussed in the next chapter. It is the woman, however, who is more often vulnerable to this attrition because she is expected to be docile and cooperative, submitting to her husband's better judgment, or at least the needs of the family as defined by her husband. Freud once said something to the effect that a woman leans on the superego of her husband (something he has been taken to task for by militant feminists). It has been taken to mean that she has little moral conscience and must turn to the male for information concerning the deeper aspects of ethics, convictions, as well as social and political beliefs. Contemporary life may be disproving this statement, but the basic fact, at least in middle-class conjugal living, is that the economic and social status of the family largely hinges on the position, decisions, and convictions of the male. Although it may be true in the abstract that behind every successful man there is a woman, no one as yet says the opposite, even though this is needfully the case. It is probably a greater necessity to have a cooperative and enlightened husband to allow a woman worldly success than the other way around. A husband's success is good for everyone; everyone in the family benefits. A woman's success may bring disharmony, and social condemnation, especially if she outshines her husband. It is for the woman to "know her place," rarely for the man. Males are not generally expected to inhibit themselves because they might stimulate the resentment of jealousy of mates—except, of course, Coriolanus, who gave up Rome for his mother and wife and ended up disastrously. A woman, conversely, would suffer ostracism of the worst kind if she sought and attained worldly success at the expense of her husband.

If father knows best, as the television soap opera says, there is an implicit acknowledgment that he knows best even when he is wrong. It is best for members of the family to go along with him. His pride is at stake and it is best for the family that his pride be maintained at a safe level. The question here is whether this pride is to be maintained at any price, even at the expense of the very sanity of the others. Often, fathers and husbands expect, as part of loyalty, that wives submit to psychological indignities that transcend their own reason and self-respect. A conflict then arises for the woman of knowing her place as a loyal spouse and at the same time holding on to her own truths. It is the time-worn issue of what loyalty demands. We know it is entirely necessary for harmony in a family, and yet it should not be the type associated with suzerainty. It is only within recent history in the West that "ownership" of one's wife is frowned upon. Yet the tradition of owning someone does not die easily; although there are today many legal and moral safeguards, the division of labor and related circumstances tie the woman down to "her lord and master." In order to survive this inequity, women have learned certain survival techniques which are often disparagingly called "the feminine mind." They are known to lie, to play dumb, to act hysterically, to be appropriately scatterbrained, to be sexually unresponsive, and to be hypochondriacal. If there is such an entity as a feminine mind, it may have its origins, partially at least, in the feeling of being "owned" and powerless. Many men surely treat their wives as chattels or as toys, or, as is revealed in psychoanalysis, as parts of their own bodies, to be handled and fondled as such.

As an owned object, the woman is never really respected or taken seriously except when she acts up, threatening to disrupt the peace of the household. Her husband may then mobilize his efforts to quell the riot. Her riot is generally labeled hysteria, which before Freud had been considered an exclusively feminine disease. It is during these occurrences that a husband will even risk his homosexual repression with the lament: "Why can't a woman be more like a man!" He is at his wit's end with his "unfair" lady.

The sickness that can be fostered by domination is seen in the data in many cases. A twenty-six-year-old married woman, teacher by profession, was referred from an adjoining community by her family doctor as an "emergency consultation." She came with her husband who, in his desire to be completely helpful, wished to "sit in" on the interview and was chagrined when told that this would not be necessary. The patient was an attractive young woman whose facial features were distorted by an expression of abject fear. She had a wide-eyed stare that had given physicians the impression of exophthalmos of glandular origin. Thorough examinations had eliminated this explanation.

In the last six months she had become anxious and depressed. She feared that she was losing her mind and would be committed to a large mental hospital in the vicinity of their home. She knew of no problems other than the possessive demands of her mother, but this was nothing new. She was well satisfied with her marriage of five years; she described her husband as loving and devoted, and completely distressed by her present unhappiness. He would spare no time or money to "get her over this thing."

Her husband had been married once before for a brief period, but had extracted a promise from her that neither of them would ever refer to that. This naturally aroused her curiosity, but since he was so kind and devoted she abided by the promise.

She then turned to her early life, which she believed to be the cause of her present difficulties. She had a brother three years older, but she was given most of the family's attention because she had been born with a club foot. Successive operations corrected this malformity so that today there is no sign of it. This meant financial hardship for the family, but it also meant that she was separated from them for long periods between the ages of five and eleven. These hospitalizations were very difficult for her, and she was bitterly hostile and antagonistic to her mother for leaving her; only years later, when she understood the benefits of the operations, did her hostility change to gratitude.

She described her father as a successful businessman who in his fifties had to retire because of severe depressive episodes with hypochondriasis. Her mother's attitude she remembered as completely unsympathetic to his plight, while she herself had strong positive feelings for him. However, her mother had fears of her own. For example, whenever there was a thunderstorm or lightning at night, she would wake her children from a sound sleep, take them downstairs, and huddle with them in the basement. Neither the patient nor her brother had any such fears; however, in late adolescence the patient developed a fear of such phenomena of nature as thunder and lightning.

Later the patient told more of her relationship with her mother. She had written her mother every day while at college, and had followed her wishes about dating. Yet she was aware of being much more comfortable when she was a considerable distance away from her. No such distance was possible after her marriage, since her husband felt that they should take up residence in the same community as her mother. This was near the farm of his own parents. He fully understood her problems with her mother, he told her, and would help her all he could.

He built a home away from the village on a tract on his own parents' farm. Through his attentiveness to her he gained the reputation of a model husband. Because of her fear of the dark and of thunder and lightning, he gave up successive jobs that might keep him away from her overnight. He had large floodlights installed to discourage prowlers, and bought a German shepherd dog as further protection.

On one occasion he turned down a promotion to a large district in another state, because he did not want her to have to leave her job, at which she was happy. This puzzled her, since as a teacher she could have been employed anywhere. The company discharged him, but this only increased his feelings of nobility. Religion became a matter of such intensity to him that he built an altar in their bedroom where they might pray together; he confided to her that his mainstay in living was prayer.

She had complete confidence in her husband's judgment, since so many things he predicted came true. However, instead of responding with a feeling of well-being to her husband's solicitude, she became increasingly depressed and fearful. Her physician treated her principally with sedatives and tranquilizers. This gave some relief but actually lowered her confidence. Only in her job was she sure of her capabilities and judgment. Her husband, friends, and physician suggested that she might be working too hard and should take a leave of absence, but she resisted this idea.

Physical symptoms appeared, such as pain around the heart and numbness in arms and legs. Reassurance that there was nothing organically wrong made her more fearful, since she felt she could not trust her own senses and was imagining things. Sexual relations, which had been pleasant before the move to the family homestead, now seemed revolting. This made her ashamed—to react in this way to such a kind husband. He, however, only became more solicitous. Now he would never leave her alone at home. He would stay by her side. He also suggested that she must confide in him about her fear of losing her mind; he said that he would understand no matter what she told him. This puzzled her, since she did not know what she could tell him and what he wanted to hear.

She agreed to psychotherapy, and this proved most successful after two years of weekly sessions. Early in treatment her husband sent, through her, a barrage of questions: Should she continue to work? Could she drive alone? Should he leave her alone overnight? Should she tell her mother she was seeing a psychiatrist? All were answered with the traditional neutral answer of the therapist, that such questions should be answered by the patient herself, not by the therapist, or her husband, or her mother.

Could she have a prescription for medication in case she became nervous or weak? She was told that in such a situation she would call upon her own resources, just as she had in other stress situations, such as her operations and the death of her father. Loud complaints came from the husband, who would not stand by and see his wife suffer. He would take her to the finest clinics in the country. However, the patient herself resisted this, although she was at first distrustful of what seemed to be a lack of concern on the part of the therapist. Therapy continued. "Panic" or "emergency" appointments were denied, and telephone calls for reassurance were discouraged.

This woman had to learn a basic verity, that in her daily affairs only she had the necessary information to make decisions and to act upon them. The therapist, husband, mother, physician, all others acted in poor faith if they attempted to take over this function, even if she asked or demanded that they do so.

Eventually she was able to abandon her preoccupation with the past and to examine her present predicament. She saw that she had been expected to play a role of helplessness far beyond actual need. Her feelings of gratitude toward her husband were replaced by a more realistic appraisal of what was transpiring. Finally, she allowed herself to understand her husband's emotional difficulties and how they were affecting her. She could then see that her husband also had a fear of the dark, of being away from home, and most of all a need to be near his own parents. Ashamed of these, he projected his own immaturities onto her. He hid his own need for parental protection by taking every opportunity of pointing up her helplessness, real or fancied. She became angered that his principal words of endearment had been, "You're my little girl."

Now, without pills in her purse, she actively managed her own affairs. She remained at home without a "baby sitter." She no longer feared "going insane" or ending up in a mental hospital. A beneficial estrangement took place in the marriage, during which a reappraisal of roles and direction occurred. The husband sought therapy for himself because of the new stresses placed on him by this realignment.

The referring physician was very shaken by his experience with this patient, and later realized that he had been an unwitting accomplice to her husband's machinations. Probably because he was very fearful of her condition, he violated the principle of privacy to which he would have adhered in treating an ordinary physical disease. On many occasions he had private conversations with her husband about her, and the husband was allowed to call him frequently to find out whether this or that activity might be upsetting to her. This had the effect of augmenting her doubts about her ability to get along.

The effect of giving tranquilizers to patients of this kind is to indicate to the patient that the physician is convinced of her helplessness. Although the referring physician had prescribed tranquilizers for this patient in good faith, and although some immediate relief was obtained by their use, her condition worsened. To her, an authoritative figure, the physician, had indicated that her perceptions and activities could not be trusted unless chemically affected. Szász has emphasized some pertinent social implications of the use of tranquilizers, and asks: Whom do we treat, the patient or those around him?[6]

Another illustration of the manipulation of the weak by the strong deals with the particular hazard of being a physician's wife. The 44-year-old wife of an obstetrician came to treatment because of feelings of despondency and fear that she was "losing her mind." She was in a constant state of tearfulness and appeared to have lost her ability to control her emotions. She lacked any confidence in running her household or dealing with her children. She had begun to drink quite heavily from an amply stocked liquor cabinet.

She was the next to the eldest of four children of a country doctor. They were in difficult financial circumstances. For the last fifteen years of his life her father had been unable to practice because of illness. She described him as kind and just, but "we all knew it when father was in the house." She described her mother as passive and placid, with little formal education, devoted to keeping the house orderly so that the father would not be offended. She rarely left the house, feeling that she should always be around when her husband needed her. She kept up contact with the outside world by letter-writing. She seemed happy, with no apparent need for personal distinction or outside social relationships.

The patient's life was overtly conventional; after several years of college she worked at a professional job and gained some distinction in her field. At twenty-eight she married the obstetrician, already successful in his community. He had been married before. For the first few years, before the advent of children, now four in number, she had been happy. Now, however, she was becoming increasingly depressed at the loneliness of what she called "the life of a lady in waiting," the fate of an obstetrician's wife. As the children made increasing demands on her time and energy, she felt more and more discontented with her role.

Her husband could not understand any reason for discontent. Did he not provide all she wanted? He was critical of her because, with all her spare time, she did not care for the house and the children more effectively. He bitterly resented any public activities she might enter into, except those associated with his own, such as medical auxiliaries and so on. He could not understand that she did not derive gratification from *his* many successes both as a physician and community leader.

He was very self-righteous and looked upon his success as proof of his inner strength. One of his chief interests was mental health, and in their many altercations he told her that anyone who could not be happy in the situation he provided had something radically wrong with her. He made an appointment for her for a thorough checkup by a confrere of his to rule out any physical cause for her terrible disposition and unreasonableness. She was reluctant to go, but did not want to cause him embarrassment. She was in perfect health, and the internist assured her he would give her husband a complete report. When she asked her husband about his report, he was ambiguous.

The situation between them continued to deteriorate at a faster rate, and the husband sought out a new psychiatrist in the community, one over whom he had much political control. She saw him a dozen times, but this turned out a fiasco because of the frequent inquiries made by the husband, and responded to by the psychiatrist, who was apparently too involved to maintain confidentiality.

The patient became hopeless, and showed increasing difficulty in dealing with her children. She thought of sending the older two away from home. Her husband then asked an analyst for an appointment for his wife, but was told that the analyst's policy was to refuse any request for consultation except from the patient himself. He could not understand this, but said that he would try to get his wife to call. A few weeks later she did, and psychotherapy was agreed upon.

Even though the arrangements were made privately with the patient, she felt the analyst was an agent of her husband, in spite of reassurances to the contrary. On several occasions, directly and indirectly, he attempted to get information. When he could not control the psychotherapeutic situation, he became enraged and demanded that she quit, since the case obviously was being mishandled with such "secrecy." He told his wife, "Until you can do things the way I want them done, I can't consider you a normal person." However, she continued therapy, and it proved successful for her. She stopped drinking, regained her role in the household, and her tearfulness ended.

Husband and wife were gradually able to argue differences of opinion without mention of "abnormality." There was no happiness here for either of them, but considerably more dignity.

The woman's story demonstrates a very special type of power a physician has and can wield on his family. This is probably even truer in the home of a psychiatrist or psychologist. Judging behavior and giving opinions as to what is nomal or abnormal, by a person with authority and specialized knowledge, can have far-reaching and devastating effects. It can lead to tyranny which holds forth the threat that "if you do not agree with me, you must be abnormal and/or crazy." The specter of the mental hospital is also present. In this the physician can use the power of his relationship with confreres who may be beholden to him in both professional and political ways. The feeling of conspiracy the mate might have would not in any sense be delusional.

In a recent study entitled "Psychiatric Ills of Physicians' Wives" a psychiatrist at a private mental hospital noted the records of fifty wives of physicians who were admitted for psychiatric care. These women were in their early 30s with disorders characterized by depression, drug addiction and bizarre physical complaints. He noted that these women came from middle-class families and seemed socially, intellectually, and culturally well adjusted. However, after marriage they felt increasingly excluded as their husbands became more involved in their practice. Very often drug addiction was initiated by husbands who resorted to their professional roles and gave drugs to their wives. The psychiatrist reports this study indicated that these women needed help in establishing a separate and meaningful role for themselves.[7]

Although the above illustrations highlight the tyrannies of which human beings are capable, it should not be assumed that individuals come into marriage "innocently." There are those without basic trust and autonomy in their development which leaves them poorly equipped for the relatedness that marriage demands. A person with memories from childhood of betrayal, exploitation, and alienation is not likely to have the trust necessary to look beyond temporary grievances, oppressions, and disappointments which must inevitably arise. Instead of being driven crazy by their mates, they continue with the marriage partner the same unresolved struggles that they had known before, the same play with a new leading man. Their internalized, distorted pictures of the world make them misinterpret kindness as hostility, helpfulness as destruction, closeness as oppression, independence as neglect, and autonomy as desertion. They have already been so damaged by disappointments and frustrations at the hands of their intimates as to make further intimacies of a sustained nature difficult or untenable.

Very often the fears and anxieties and hates buried within the self are projected onto the other. Instead of the feeling of being oppressed by inner unresolved problems involving prior objects, relief of sorts is obtained by thrusting these onto the mate. Now one *knows* who is the enemy, who is the real cause of all misery, past and present; it is indeed the person one has married. All one's inadequacies, infirmities, lack of opportunity, failure of achievement, personal illness, the sum total of one's unhappiness and discontent is then due not to oneself but to this witch or Hitler whom one has innocently married. All one's misery is condensed and displaced to the person on the other side of the breakfast table. The underlying fallacy of this state resides in the unreality of ever giving or allowing another to have sole or overwhelming responsibility for one's happiness or contentment or welfare or misery.

Marriage can provide a neat excuse for all sorts of abrogations of personal responsibility or self-examination. Most of all one can easily shift the blame or credit to the person to whom one is linked. Marriage in this sense may obfuscate personal reality-testing and prevent the proper understanding of oneself, one's identity, one's own boundaries—where the "I" leaves off and the "thou" begins. Grave difficulties arise when the merger, which marriage ideally should be, becomes or is promoted as a fusion. Then one is apt to become an appendage rather than a partner—an appendage of varying degrees of value or annoyance. In this fusion, one may gain certain securities, such as being taken care of, of having decisions made, of having opportunities provided, of having work laid out for one, and of being carried along. These may be gained, however, at the risk of losing one's identity, one's integrity, one's pride, and one's mind. There is in many a primitive longing for such a fusion, based on a mother-infant symbiosis, which must be resisted if a person is to "become" or "evolve."

Paradoxically, often this hidden desire to be taken over, and to be fused with a protecting person, causes great hostility toward the protector. Instead of facing the shameful desire to be submerged and taken over, it is simpler to blame the partner for being there, i.e., to be angry at the hand that you want to be fed from. Extreme dependent feelings appear to call forth defensive measures of hating or repelling the person by whom one would secretly like to be taken over. It is an exaggerated show of independence, aided by the distortions of denial and reaction formation, of keeping one's pride and self-respect. This person is apt to appear extremely belligerent and at the same time very demanding. These distortions become soul-deep, and are corrected, if at all, only by the most thorough and often painful introspective efforts.

This chapter has uncovered some aspects of actual and fancied oppressions in interpersonal relations. Both lead to marital divisiveness as well as personality corrosion.

Neither is ever found in pure culture, but in varying combinations and constellations. The complexities of human mentation and interactions are indeed humbling. There are no simple constructions of the conflicts, no easy pointing of the finger of blame, and no facile solutions. The diagnosis that begins: "The sole trouble here is . . ." is destined to make a fool of the diagnostician.

NOTES

1. Sigmund Freud, "The Loss of Reality in Neurosis and Psychosis," *Collected Papers,* II (London: Hogarth Press, 1949), p. 277.
2. Otto Fenichel, *The Psychoanalytic Theory of Neurosis* (New York: Norton & Co., 1945), p. 440.
3. R. LaForgue, "The Ego and the Conception of Reality," *Int. J. Psa.,* XX (1939), pp. 403-07.
4. Hans W. Loewald, "The Problem of Defence and the Neurotic Interpretation of Reality," *Int. J. Psa.,* XXXIII (1952), pp. 444-49.
5. J. A. M. Meerloo, "Suicide, Menticide, and Psychic Homicide," *A. M. A. Arch. Neur. and Psychiat.,* LXXXI (March 1959), pp. 360-62.
6. T. S. Szász, "Some Observations on the Use of Tranquilizing Drugs," *A. M. A. Arch. Neur. and Psychiat.,* LXXVII (Jan. 1957), pp. 86-92.
7. James L. Evans, "Psychiatric Ills of Physicians' Wives," *Amer. J. Psychiat.,* CXXII (1965), pp. 159-63.

CHAPTER IV

FOR THIS WOMAN'S SAKE

My mood, which just before was strong and rigid,
No dipped sword more so, now has lost its edge.
My speech is womanish for this woman's sake.

Sophocles, *Ajax*

This chapter deals with a character type vulnerable to a certain feminine influence which to casual observation might appear favorable and constructive. It is generally a taming and domesticating influence. The woman, responding in her traditional role, exerts pressure for the preservation of home, family, and country. To the susceptible male, however, this influence may be disintegrative. As Freud put it, "If a man, for example, has become overkind as a result of a violent suppression of a constitutional inclination to harshness and cruelty, he often loses so much energy in doing this that he fails to carry out all that his compensatory impulses require, and he may, after all, do less good on the whole than he would have done without the suppression."

In Chapters II and III women appeared to be the chief victims of the marital state. They are more apt to be, just as people or nations with lesser power generally are. However, male functioning has its special vulnerabilities and vicissitudes. If the male has more power and lives by superior rules, he also has the obligation of measuring himself against others' as well as against his own past achievements. Measuring up is the *sine qua non* of maleness. Later in life, if the male feels or finds that he has not measured up, that his identity is incomplete or has suffered erosion, he is apt to view himself and the world in most unkind ways. Obviously, his affinities play major roles in his development and achievements. Recognition of the jealousy and competition of females and their detrimental effects, has led to the derogatory designation of "castrating female."[1, 2]

The character type to be examined here is one very familiar to the analyst. It is the male who operates in life as though the identifying qualities of masculinity are belligerence, arrogance, vainglory, ruthlessness, and sexual insatiability. This image of what is maleness is prevalent among adolescents of both sexes, and also among the socially disadvantaged. The term masculine protest defense was first applied to the woman who would not give up her "tomboyishness" and presented a masculine image in adult life, usually a caricature, as a reaction against fearful instinctual and ego demands. It can also appropriately be applied to the male who projects an image of maleness, held over from adolescent phantasies. We will, therefore, refer to this attitude and behavior as "masculine protest reaction" in the male. Although this defense can be shown to deal with complex lifelong conflicts, it is seen to be a reaction formation against an underlying feminine identification. Alexander described this type of behavior in the male as over-compensation, i.e., overcoming the shame resulting from a failure to live up to one's ego ideal of manliness.[3, 4] A vicious cycle is established. For the overaggressive behavior soon leads to fear of punishment from the superego. This aggressive behavior then succumbs to passivity, inhibition of drives, and turning against oneself.[5]

The motives for this hyperaggressivity, however, are overdetermined. Another source is the oedipal conflict itself. The boy, never able to show aggression towards his own father, displaces these feelings in full measure towards objects of the external world. Meek and docile in the family setting, his boldness knows no bounds outside the home. Herein is seen the classical splitting of objects. The paradigm of this splitting was Freud's case of Little Hans. The white horse on the street and not the father was the fearful enemy towards which he could more safely express his fear and antipathy. At the same time, this behavior unquestionably provides an outlet for homosexual as well as for aggressive cathexis. Fighting, quarreling, and competing with other men are central in their lives. Here, contacts are actively sought out and are well tolerated as long as the tender component is repressed and contact with orifices avoided. The discussion, of course, does not exclude or denigrate the importance of the meaning of maleness and masculine behavior in different social classes.

Illustrations of this type can be seen in analyses of two men whose "taming" led to severe neurotic disturbances, and also in similar character types drawn by Shakespeare in *Coriolanus* and by Sophocles in *Ajax*.

A thirty-six-year-old lawyer came to treatment because of depression, anxiety, and hypochondriacal symptoms. He had a fear of cancer of the bowels, of which his father had died five years earlier. He became depressed on anniversaries, especially those of the deaths of his parents. He had been an only child of immigrants, and had grown up in a slum neighborhood. As a child he witnessed murders and suicides; he saw those who anesthetized themselves with alcohol and narcotics. His relatives' main pride was in their successes in exploiting those even less fortunate than themselves. His father, a peddler, made barely enough for subsistence. His mother bemoaned her fate in having become entangled with a ne'er-do-well, so that she rested all her hopes on her son. The family resources were wholly channeled to the son's education, which was now their only hope for social elevation. When the boy showed some deviant or truant behavior, which might cause him to veer off this course, his mother would demand that he be punished by his father, who usually complied with spankings, but without zeal. Father seemed fearful of both his wife and his son, but he often played with him; his term of endearment for him was an anal obscenity. The mother clearly indicated that "maleness" had been wasted on her husband. Given the equipment, she would have put it to proper use.

The boy was closely guarded as to playmates and games. He was known as a "sissie," but was reassured by his parents that it was because he was superior. At the age of eleven, he became alarmed by recurrent nocturnal emissions, and privately consulted a doctor, who treated the condition with medication, which, the patient recalled, did little good. He subsequently went through college and law school; his success in law practice was early and substantial. But he was aggressive in his dealings, at times ruthless, and hovered on the outer margins of legality and ethical conduct. He had a flair for court work and preferred the toughest cases. Socially, he was brusque, outspoken, and belligerent, often spoiling the welcome given by his confreres and other social contacts. He was a master of sarcasm, and his associates became his victims.

At the age of twenty-eight he married. His wife, very attractive and well-educated, was a timid, fearful person. She was appalled by his boorishness, but attracted by the security he could offer. Thinking herself ostracized from social life as a result of her husband's behavior, she set out on a vast program to rehabilitate him. She incessantly corrected his speech and manners. There were classes in social dancing, golf lessons, etc., to civilize him. She became very critical of his clientele, since he frequently dealt with criminals and had a large income from them. She was appalled when they telephoned him at home, and feared newspaper publicity. The specter of disbarment was constantly with her. By cajoling and threats, she was able to "reform" him in these ways. She held over him the threat of divorce, with concomitant exposure and expenses, which would be destructive to him. She turned him, under threat, into a well-mannered individual, reforming also his professional life.

He later rationalized this obedience and submission by telling himself that it was all for the good, that he was better off, well liked, less notorious, etc. However, as indicated above, he developed agonizing physical symptoms and obsessive thoughts, which made him an anxiously subdued person. His preoccupation was mainly anal in character. He watched his stools, frequently handling them and examining them for blood, and would manipulate and rub his anus until it bled. He would then become terrified, running to his physician or proctologist for reassurance that he did not have cancer. There were concomitant menstruation and childbirth phantasies as the anal bleeding recurred. He, too, now had a receptive organ which bled regularly. There were problems of periodic impotence and self-castrative phantasies. He had the feeling that his razor might slip while shaving and cut off his penis. When staying in hotels, he would barricade the window lest he fall from it in a moment of forgetfulness.

Here we see strong preconscious forces in the pleas and threats of the wife and her need to fit him into a pattern desirable for her which resonated with unconscious conflicts and their attempted solutions. The resonance in this instance served to break down some of his defenses, converting a character neurosis into a psychoneurosis. His feminine identification broke through under the impact of the wife's threats and fears. A flight into sickness ensued. Instead of being a belligerent, boastful person, he was now weak and preoccupied with his body. He became "womanish" as defined by his unconscious. He also became the antithesis of everything he had known in childhood.

As might be expected, the course of treatment was beset by several intrinsic technical problems. First of all, he came with the feeling that he was being sent by his wife for further modification, i.e., to meet her image of the ideal husband. To please the therapist, he became even more passive, making a favorable social adjustment. Yet

his symptoms increased in intensity and frequency. He
retained an internist, and a proctologist, as added protection. It was difficult for him to overcome the feeling that
the analyst was one more agent of his wife, out to civilize
him.

The second but related problem was the intensity of the
submissive dependency resulting from the return of repressed feminine identification. No longer belligerent and
brusque, he "settled down" on the couch, displaying the
cooperativeness and docility which are death to genuine
learning. Much of his time was spent in licking his wounds.
The working-through process was long and difficult, with
several interruptions, some technical, and others the result
of acting out. After five years of treatment, however, the
outcome was favorable. His social adjustment was to his
liking, and he did not lack self-respect. The hypochondriasis had diminished; the preoccupation with his anus
and feces had largely disappeared, although he still takes
more than a cursory look at his feces before flushing. He
appeared, too, no longer to need to be submissive to a
father surrogate.

A twenty-eight-year-old man came for help because of
marital difficulties, anxiety, somatic complaints, and fear of
disease. He had been married for three years, and had one
child. The circumstances of the marriage were unfavorable
and led to a great deal of disharmony. He had frequently
dated his wife-to-be, but with no serious intentions; but
she became pregnant and confronted him with this situation. He had ambitions to be a writer, and had no desire
to settle down until he had experienced a full measure of
freedom. The girl, however, threatened suicide, and great
pressure was brought to bear by both sets of parents. He
relented, gave up his personal plans for the future, and
entered into the marriage. Instead of pursuing his creative
career, he got a job in a factory where his father had been
employed.

The couple fought incessantly; there was never enough
money; each felt victimized by the other. They had dif-

ficulties in their sexual life, the patient suffering at times from premature ejaculation and impotence. One night, on returning from work, he found that his wife had left him and returned to her parents with the infant. At first he looked on this as a good riddance, but as the days passed he became increasingly apprehensive. He had several acute attacks of anxiety and became fearful at being alone in the apartment. He was disturbed by the recurrent thought that he might be turning into a homosexual, and he suffered from headaches. An old back ailment recurred which gave him fears of having contracted poliomyelitis, and he saw himself turning into a nervous wreck, a state of being far different from his former self. It was at this period that he sought treatment.

He related that he had a sister five years his junior. His parents were plain, hard-working people, and his father had worked through his lifetime at one plant, finally becoming a foreman. Unlike the patient, he was a plodding, uncomplaining person who seemed resigned to his fate. Nothing would arouse him save activities on the children's part which might disturb their mother; to these he reacted sharply, often with rage. The mother was a pious, sickly person who needed many gynecological operations which took most of the family resources; her chronic illnesses made her intolerant of noises and other household disturbances. The family knew severe financial adversities.

The patient recalled that he became very hostile and at times envious of his sister, for she would generally escape blame for the things that could upset his mother, whereas he would generally bear the brunt of the punishment. Mother would easily become "hysterical" on news of his misbehavior. The women then appeared highly valued and protected. He grew up in a tough neighborhood, and because of his small stature and belligerence became known as the "one-two punch kid." Also, because of his flair for books and learning, he was called "prof." At college he became a ferocious competitor in sports. He related that at one time his coach tried to slow him down. "The object of the game," he explained, "is to win, not to kill off your opponents." He could always be relied upon to outplay and outmaneuver his adversary.

He looked upon girls solely as sexual objects, and took great pride in the number of his conquests, but resolved to stave off any prolonged or permanent entanglement. On impregnating his wife-to-be, he felt no great moral responsibility, and would reluctantly have contributed financially towards an abortion, but did not want to go further. It was the combined pressure of the girl and his parents which made him enter into the marriage. "The disgrace would kill your mother if you didn't do the honorable thing," his father admonished. So for his mother's sake and the girl's sake, he did the "proper thing," which, he felt, was his own undoing. It was apparent that the family could not jeopardize their recently won, albeit small, social gains.

The early part of the analysis was taken up with his current plight. His marital difficulties gave him new evidence of his awkwardness in dealing with women. He always seemed to have done everything at home which was upsetting to his mother; now the same thing was happening in his marriage. Now he wanted to continue in the marriage, hoping that his wife would return, so that he could prove that he could be an adequate husband. He thought it would be a relief to be a bachelor again, but now found going out with his former chums depressing. His difficulties with his wife also raised doubts in his mind about his maleness. Might he not be basically a homosexual? This thought again gave him fears about associating with other men.

It became apparent to him that he was becoming preoccupied with bodily symptoms and obsessive hypochondriacal fears much like his mother's had been. He recalled in a casual way an operation of his own; mother wasn't the only one who was cut up. When he was six years of age, he was taken to the hospital for a tonsillectomy. On awaking later in the day, he felt a painful sensation in his lower parts. Turning back the bed coverings, he found his penis bandaged. He recalls tearing away the bandages, and seeing his bloody genitals. It was later explained that since he was already under anaesthesia, the physician had decided to perform a circumcision which the parents had privately suggested. The patient gave this as an example of it being his fate to get it at both ends. But it also augmented his identification with his mother, where genitals were repeatedly mutilated. The circumcision, requested by the parents, can be viewed in the light of an attempt to espouse middle-class mores. They wanted their boy to be "clean."

This incident, although related during the analysis as a casual memory, proved to be a severe trauma. Whereas the tonsillectomy was thought to be a punishment and correction for his oral aggressiveness (noisiness on his part in upsetting mother), in his phantasies he felt that his secret sexual aggressiveness and masturbatory activity had been detected and attended to by circumcision. The concurrent surgery in both these areas was undoubtedly felt by him as a reinforced castrative assault. His agonizing doubt was, had he been turned into a female? And, had he any rights concerning his own body? In the analysis it became apparent that there was an underlying predominant feminine identification which was successfully covered by his aggressive attitudes and behavior. His fears of poliomyelitis, for instance, represented a wish to be overtaken by a childhood disease whereby his limbs would wither, so that he would have to be carried and cared for as his father had his mother. The "withered limbs" phantasy was correlated with self-castrative tendencies, to wit: Let the job on me be finished completely so that I can receive "total disability" treatment. These feelings returned after he was forced into marriage, and his heroic defenses were shattered even further by the depreciatory attitude of his wife, who let him know what she thought of him as a husband and provider. He had resisted marriage because he apperceptively "knew" that his defenses were too fragile to withstand the vicissitudes of an attachment to another woman.

The analytic work went on successfully. He was able to leave the factory, and he upgraded his position and income. He had found satisfaction in his work as a commercial writer, using his spare time for work on the "great American novel." His wife returned, and their family had grown. However, they continued to play a "cat and mouse" game with each other wherein the wife from time to time threatened to leave because of her feeling of lack of personal fulfillment. He, on the other hand, desired to hold on and resist a break-up. Still somewhat fearful of passivity, he was free both of physical symptoms and the compensatory belligerence which had characterized him.

These two patients had in common similar ways of dealing with oedipal and pregenital conflicts. There was an intense identification with the mother: to affect denial of sexual urges toward her; to submit to, and be taken care of, by father; and to deal with the assaults of mother (real and fancied) by being like her (identification with the aggressor). Both of them had severe social disadvantages in their early life and subsequently had to learn where they belonged as well as how to act.

In both instances, the fathers were quite alike in being passive, defeated characters, capable of occasional aimless bouts of rage but not of goal-directed, assertive behavior. They were out of the race almost from the beginning, and generally suffered severely at the hands of their wives as well as unfavorable social circumstances. They could point to no personal achievements of any great merit. There was no chance for oedipal battles between father and son, because the fathers in each instance would not provoke or be provoked. The fathers had lost wives to their sons almost from the time of their birth. It was quite evident that, with the birth of the sons, the mothers lost all sexual interest in their husbands. The sons, then, had to bear the consequences of unfought victories. It is understandable that in their adolescence, and thereafter, they were constantly looking for a good fight, as if they would belatedly come to terms with a father who would stand up and fight. But later in life the women entered to "recapture the sons" and render them womanish.

In the first case the nocturnal emissions were the cause of deep concern to the patient because they represented unopposed incestuous urges. Since father would not fight, and mother was all too willing, perhaps the physician would provide a constraining influence. In the second case the double surgical procedure did represent a constraining force from the outside, and provided a punishment and threat of punishment which may have been an aid to repression. But it also reconfirmed castration fears which played so large a part in his passivity. Then it provided the impetus for the desire to give others the one-two punch.

The vicissitudes of this character structure were apparently known to both Sophocles and Shakespeare. Sophocles' *Ajax,* often considered the first full-length portrait of a tragic hero, is a paradigm for this problem. In most accounts of Ajax, he is tough, vainglorious, fearless, a man who defies the gods, and thereby brings about his own destruction.[6]

Ajax takes little heed of his father Telamon's counsel:

"Child," he said, "Resolve to win, but always with God's
     help."
But Ajax answered with a senseless boast:
"Father, with God's help even a worthless man
Could triumph. I propose, without that help,
To win my prize of fame."

Ajax was likewise contemptuous of Athena, who stood beside him in the fight urging him on:

"Go stand beside the other Greeks; help them.
For where I bide, no enemy will break through."

To both his father and Athena he showed little respect, but was boastful and arrogant. He revealed that he had

little capacity either to submit to the advice of others or to
learn from them. Later, jealous, angered, and out for revenge because he was not given Achilles' armor, he set
out to destroy the victor, Odysseus, and the Greek high
command. As he approached their tents, Pallas Athena
rendered him insane and delusional. Instead of decimating
his fellowmen, he tortured, mutilated, and slaughtered live-
stock taken as booty, thinking the animals were the Greek
chieftains. As he gradually came out of his trance, he experienced intense humiliation at seeing what a fool he had
been. He blamed Athena for her part in changing him and
causing his downfall. He was dismayed that on the same
battlefield his father, Telamon, had received honors at an
earlier date, while he suffered such defeat. His father had
clearly surpassed him.

"How my father,
Fighting here under Ida long ago,
Won with his sword the loveliest prize of all
For valor, and sweet praise at his return;
But I, his son,
Coming in my turn with a force no less
To this same land of Troy, no less than he a champion,
Nor less deserving, yet am left an outcast,
Shamed by the Greeks, to perish as I do!"

The reference to the father winning "with his sword the
loveliest prize of all" is a further indication of the oedipal
struggle for the woman (mother). The competing motives
of wanting to win, and at the same time wanting father to
win, are here discernible. Ajax's own wife Tecmessa was
spear-won. The prize, Achilles' armor, "filched" from the
hands of Ajax, may represent the phallic oedipal mother.
Odysseus, the victor, is clearly the surrogate father.

He sees no alternative to suicide, and he now prepares
himself. On learning this, his wife Tecmessa pleads with
him, fearing for the fate of their son and herself without
his protection. He appears to relent, and after reassuring
her, falls on his sword. The lines in which he seems to re-

lent have been puzzling to many critics. Some have said that it is typical cunning of one bent on suicide. By paying lip service to his wife's pleas, he thereby threw her off the track. Others interpret it as a simple change of heart. Another interpretation is here suggested, namely, that he was talking to Athena as well as to his wife, and was bitter at what she had wrought. Athena is indeed the surrogate mother, as Odysseus, the winner, is his father. These lines are:

"Strangely the long and countless drift of time
Brings all things forth from darkness into light,
Then covers them once more. Nothing so marvellous
That man can say it surely will not be—
Strong oath and iron intent come crashing down.
My mood, which just before was strong and rigid,
No dipped sword more so, now has lost its edge—
My speech is womanish *for this woman's sake* (italics
    mine)
And pity touches me for wife and child,
Widowed and lost among my enemies."

Herein is clearly a statement of emasculation: that he has become womanish at the hands of women, notably Athena. "My mood, which just before was strong and rigid, No dipped sword more so, now has lost its edge." The deflection of his aggression is seen by Ajax as castration.

There are references to Ajax's mother Eriboea. They are descriptions of how she will take the news first of his insane degradation and later of his suicide. Her grief is anticipated as being loud and dramatic. (Perhaps like the mother in the second case described above.) There is more than an intimation of insincerity. Ajax may have learned the defense of reaction formation from her.

Ajax, in preparing for suicide, anticipates that his mother will overreact:

"Poor mother! when she hears this wretched word,
How her grief's note will quaver through the town."

These lines about Eriboea are cynical in quality, again emphasizing the son's disdain. Ajax also expressed disgust for his wife Tecmessa:

"And let there be no wailing
Here out of doors; what a plaintive creature womankind is!"

Again,

"Woman, a woman's decency is silence."

And it is probably the women in his life whom he addresses when he speaks of Athena:

"But the marital goddess, daughter of Zeus,
Cruelly works my ruin."

Athena, in the *Iliad,* is no friend of Ajax. In the athletic events she unbalances him so that Odysseus, who prayed for help, wins:

"Oh now! That goddess made me slip on my feet, who has always stood over Odysseus like a mother, and taken good care of him."[7]

Athena prevents Ajax from doing the "masculine act" of seeking vengeance on his enemies. She wishes to save Odysseus and the Greek forces, and as such, Ajax's madness comes as a blessing to the Achaeans. Nevertheless, deprived of his masculine defense, nothing is left but disintegration and death.

Looking to another intuitive poet we find a similar theme in Shakespeare's *Coriolanus.*[8] The play opens with the defeat of Aufidius by the Roman hero, Caius Marcius, later Coriolanus. They had engaged in numerous battles, and each time Coriolanus was the victor. Returning to Rome after his latest victory, the radiant Coriolanus is made consul, not out of love for him but as a reward for his bravery. However, he shows only contempt for the populace. He will not show humility or mouth the platitudes which people demand. Instead he boasts of his prowess and power. Unable to hide his hatred for the rabble, he is banished from the city by them. Then, when he is ostracized, he joins up with his lifelong rival, Aufidius of the Corioli, to assault and conquer Rome. Rome is defenseless and has no leader to rally its forces. As the victory-assured army approaches Rome, Coriolanus' mother, his wife, and his child go out to him, pleading that he relent in his plans to conquer his native city and turn it over to its enemies. Coriolanus, after some resistance, succumbs to the pleas and laments of the women and turns back. This starts his downfall. When they return to Corioli, Coriolanus is quickly overpowered and killed by Aufidius.

Early in the play, something of the character of his mother is revealed. Volumnia is a Roman matron whose whole life revolves around the exploits of her son. She is frankly ambitious for him and wants him to take risks in battle. We gather that Volumnia was a woman who would have liked great personal achievement but was thwarted by the customs of her times. She prided herself on not having her son tied to her apron-strings, candidly revealing her thoughts:

"If my son were my husband, I should freelier rejoice in that absence wherein he won honour than in the embracements of his bed where he showed most love."

Here she allows herself to identify son with husband, but indicates that she would have him win her on the battlefield rather than in bed. The mother clearly approves of the son's aggressiveness, with the reservation only that it be directed toward external foes of the city. Her husband has succeeded in bed, but this apparently was not enough to gratify her overbearing phallic strivings. In her son, she would have the other gratifications. He diligently and successfully fought for himself and for her.

Here we witness the dependent personality, bewildered and paralyzed by confusing signals and commands. His destruction represents her final and complete victory over the men in her life. As she loved her son, she was envious of his power. It is she who becomes the savior of Rome. She is to Rome what Athena was to her city.

When he turned his power against Rome, she stood in his way. She caused him to sheathe his sword, rendering him a helpless victim. He became womanish, an easy mark for his old foe. Volumnia knew that her son would be destroyed; that he would have to be sacrificed for the safety of the state. Aggression toward others is acceptable, but not towards one's own people, no matter what the grievance.

Changed from the blustering, prideful hero, Coriolanus is seen again as Aufidius states:

> "There was it;—
> For which my sinews shall be stretch'd upon him.
> At a few drops of women's rheum, which are
> As cheap as lies, he sold the blood and labour
> Of our great action: therefore shall he die,
> And I'll renew me in his fall."

These are statements reflecting his new passivity, his "feminization," which led to his destruction at the hand of his foe who never before could lay a hand on him.

The similarities in the characters of Ajax and Coriolanus are obvious. These are men who remained attached to their mothers, never fought out their oedipal battles with their fathers, and developed tremendous reaction formations of implacable belligerence as a defense against their feminine identification, which, when it returns from repression, results in their destruction. Coriolanus, like Ajax, is destroyed after agreeing to listen to the pleas of his mother, his wife, and his son. It is thus that the "long drift of time brings forth from darkness (unconscious) into light" and cannot be tolerated.

Coriolanus is killed by his lifelong enemy (father surrogate) whom he had repeatedly defeated in battle until he became "womanish" by the pleas of his mother. He passively succumbs to Aufidius, his former enemy. Ajax's parents are represented by Athena and Odysseus. Odysseus and Aufidius are similarly magnanimous toward the hero after he is slain.

We recall Ajax's fight with Hector. Like Jacob and the Angel, there is neither victim nor victor. Jacob receives the blessings of the Angel; Hector rewards his adversary with his own sword. It is with this weapon that Ajax later commits suicide on enemy soil after he is deprived of Achilles' armor by the Greek high command. Ajax is thus given by his foe the sword that he did not particularly seek, but was denied by his friends the Achillean armor, symbol of leadership, for which he desperately longed. This promotes an attitude of cynicism, i.e., look to your foe for your reward and unfair treatment at the hands of your friends! Injury from one's kinsman, real or imagined, produced a particularly painful wound that provokes inexorable impulses for revenge. And yet it is not in the order of things that such impulses be fulfilled. In the *Iliad* we find when Achilles, flushed with rage, is about to assail his compatriot, Agamemnon, with his sword, Athena catches him "by the fair hair" and causes him to desist. "I have come from the sky to put an end to your *menos* (passionate impulse)."[9] Similarly, Ajax was unable to gain revenge against the Greek chieftains. He was driven mad and his sword deflected to animals just as Jehovah protected Isaac from Abraham's knife. Their aggression was spent on a scapegoat.

The lesson must be learned again and again that one cannot kill one's own, no matter what the provocation. This is the parricide barrier that must not be transgressed even at the expense of one's sanity. One can, however, strike out against the common foe, not only with impunity, but with the prospect of great rewards. Achilles' humiliat-

ing revenge on Hector for the death of Patroclus is acceptable, although desecration of Hector's body was prevented.
Achilles in his rage threatened to feed Hector's body to the
dogs after he had caused it to be torn apart by dragging it
behind his chariot. The gods wanted to prevent this desecration. Aphrodite drove the dogs back day and night and
anointed the body with "rosy immortal oil" so that it could
not be torn. Phoebus Apollo brought down a darkening
mist about the body from the sky to keep the force of the
sun from causing it to wither away. Finally, Achilles was
persuaded to give up the body for burial to Hector's aged
father, Priam. Similarly, both Ajax and Coriolanus are ac-
corded proper burial by their foes.

Coriolanus, having been ostracized by his own city,
joined with the enemy to seek revenge against it. Coriolanus was given the name of the enemy city because he
had been successful against it. The city of his enemies, not
his native Rome, was the scene of his great victories. Just
as Ajax received his sword from Hector, Coriolanus received his very name from the enemy. In each instance, an
identification with the enemy took place and kinsmen became objects of aggression.

Ajax and Coriolanus were encouraged and acclaimed, as
warriors must be, when their aggressiveness is directed toward the destruction of the enemies of the commonwealth.
Their personal actions are consonant with the values of the
group. These two warriors, however, were no longer able
to direct their hostility towards the acceptable enemy. The
pressure for revenge (parricidal impulse) became so great,
that aggression toward the external common foe no longer
sufficed. The sword had to be turned against "the family."
Coriolanus openly called himself "The Sword." We see
here a breakdown of the defense of displacement. It is as
if the individual can no longer be satisfied with slaying
enemies. The *golem* continues to kill; he knows no other
life. His impulses carry him relentlessly toward the tabooed
objects, his kinsmen. Both are destroyed because they
showed their hands.

As critics have noted, Ajax's madness really anteceded Athena's intervention. His reaction of intransigent rage after his loss to Odysseus gave evidence of the beginning of the disintegrative process. Coriolanus' incorrigibility in dealing politically with the populace of Rome betrayed a striking lack of compassion as well as adaptiveness. Aggressiveness seemed unopposed within him, and the line between friend and foe obfuscated. The *feminine* superego cannot tolerate aggression toward the family. The aggressor, confronted by threats of the superego, backs away and becomes passive, feminine. His aggression is turned against himself. With Ajax it is suicide with Hector's sword; Coriolanus allows his old foe to do him in. In both instances there occurs a passive surrender shortly after an act of violent transgression is planned but thwarted. This is consonant with psychoanalytic theory that self-destructiveness is an attempt to rid oneself of superego pressure.[10]

In Plutarch's account of Coriolanus, Volumnia succeeds in stopping her son's onslaught by invoking the claim of a debt to her as a mother. "You have punished your country already; you have not paid your debt to me." Having said this, she throws herself at his feet. After he succumbs to her pleas, he replies prophetically: "You have gained a victory, fortunate enough for the Romans, but destructive to your son; whom you, though none else, have defeated."[11]

What is the debt owed by Coriolanus to his mother? Why can he no longer go on toward his goal when she falls at his feet? We cannot miss the implication that she holds him responsible for her castration. In social terms, he, the male, was a party to the suppression of women. In falling to the ground, she revealed to him her absence of structure. She cannot remain erect, for he has destroyed her own phallic strivings. The body as penis is now limp.

Here the castration complex of the woman shows a shift from mother as castrator to son as castrator. Her genitals (phallus) were destroyed with the birth of the son. The grievance is now against her son as the symbol of civilization. He is beholden to her for having "so weakened" her. The first-born son who "splits" the mother's womb ends the expectations of the emergence of a penis of her own. Spurgeon calls our attention to the imagery of Shakespeare's Coriolanus which relates to the body and bodily ills.[12] Coriolanus himself is represented by the tribunes as a "violent disease which spreads infection which must be cut away." Coriolanus' action toward Rome is described by his mother as "tearing his country's bowels out." Coriolanus is seen as the grand inquisitor of his birthplace. He must repay his mother with his own life for the damage he has done her. He is a disease that did injury to its host and must repent. In leaving her body, Coriolanus took his mother's strength with him. He is her roving penis. Menenius argues that Coriolanus is a "diseased limb, a gangrened foot." He is a member that has become detached from its blood supply.

Adamant against all other appeals, he cannot resist the demands of his mother. He goes to a certain doom rather than defy her. Again, superego pressures appear to pre-empt preservation of the self. In the instances of Coriolanus and Ajax, perhaps the warriors succumb to the mother-god power that comes not only of superego influence but also out of the precognitive era of mother-child unity, as in Maloney's formulation in regard to theophany.[13] Theophany is defined here as the dissolution of one's will and convictions, as Jesus emptied himself of divinity in order to walk among men. Coriolanus and Ajax both are reduced to a state of helplessness by mother power, a reduction that no one else could effect.

In all we witness the conflict between those drives directed toward family, for its unity and status, and those which seek out personal achievement and ambition. Frequently they are one and the same but with Coriolanus, in particular, a choice was to be made, and family and city won out. For the male, divided in loyalty between his own search for identity and his responsibilities toward his family, the homily of "rendering unto Caesar" is not so easy in its application. Here affinity undid identity.

Although the people, real and fictional, in this chapter appeared to be torn between family and ambition, frequently succumbing in the struggle, there are others for whom the disasters appear exclusively in one area or the other. For those to whom achievement and ambition are overriding goals, failure to achieve may lead to personal dissolution. Others, who treasure family and its ties above everything, falter when the family fortunes are threatened, or are thrown into often irreversible despondency and hopelessness when some member of the family is lost through death or alienation. We can define three types of agony to which the male is heir, depending on his particular ideals—ideals which have their origins in community, national and family values: conflict between family obligations and personal ambition; conflict resulting from failing to achieve personal goals; conflicts incumbent on dissolution of family structure. Granting the gross oversimplification of this statement, this grouping appears to contain the principal challenges, and also to constitute the chief stumbling blocks to growth and development.

In marriage, one must acknowledge and respect the truths of the other. Rehabilitation, reform, manipulation, social engineering, and using undue influence discredit the integrity of a fellow human being. Within a certain range, each individual, as T. S. Eliot's Dr. Reilly says, "must seek his own salvation" in accordance with his own truths. "Truths" are those views and convictions of life which are necessary for him to live by and act upon even when these truths appear repugnant or unworthy or otherwise dystonic with the social situation. Simply put, each person must, for better or worse, work out his own reasonable destiny without the outside disturbing pressures of well-wishers and do-gooders, whether they be mother, mate, goddess, boss, or therapist. We painfully learn that there is no single truth for all men or all seasons but a repertory of truths. Each individual must find and follow his own.

NOTES

1. Richmond Lattimore, *The Iliad of Homer* (Chicago: University Press, 1951).

2. Sophocles, "Ajax," Complete Greek Tragedies, II, ed. and trans. D. Grene and R. Lattimore (Chicago: University Press, 1959).

3. F. Alexander, "The Neurotic Character," *Int. J. Psa.*, II (1930).

4. F. Alexander, "Remarks About the Relation of Inferiority Feelings to Guilt Feelings," *Int. J. Psa.*, XIX (1938).

5. G. L. Piers and M. B. Singer, *Shame and Guilt: A Psychoanalytic and a Cultural Study* (Springfield, Ill.: Thomas Press, 1953).

6. Quotations are from Sophocles, "Ajax," *Complete Greek Tragedies*, II, ed. and trans. D. Grene and R. Lattimore (Chicago: University Press, 1959), pp. 241, 242, 230, 237, 245, 235, 224, 228.

7. Richmond Lattimore, *The Iliad of Homer* (Chicago: University Press, 1951), p. 471.

8. Quotations are from William Shakespeare, "Coriolanus," *The Complete Works of William Shakespeare* (Cleveland, Ohio: The World Publishing Co., n.d.), pp. 687, 717.

9. Quotations are from Richmond Lattimore, *The Iliad of Homer* (Chicago: University Press, 1951), pp. 64, 455.

10. Otto Fenichel, *The Psychoanalytic Theory of Neurosis* (New York: Norton, 1945), p. 364.

11. Plutarch, *The Lives of Illustrious Men*, ed. L. S. Davidow (Reading, Pa.: Spencer, n.d.).

12. Caroline F. E. Spurgeon, *Shakespeare's Imagery and What It Tells Us* (Boston: Beacon Press, 1958), pp. 347, 348.

13. J. C. Maloney, "Mother, God and Superego," *J. Amer. Psychoanalyt. Assoc.*, II (1954).

CHAPTER V

FIDELITY AND JEALOUSY

"Unique and true love," said de Marsay, "produces a sort of corporeal apathy attuned to the contemplation into which one falls. Then the mind complicates everything; it works on itself, pictures its fancies, turns them into reality and torment; and such jealousy is as delightful as it is distressing."

Balzac

Love compels cruelty to those who do not understand love.

T. S. Eliot, *The Family Reunion*

The vocabulary of infidelity is almost exclusively sexual. The only type of unfaithfulness that can be reasonably communicated to others is a mate's extramarital sexual experiences. Adultery is something that everyone understands and generally condemns. The wife who complains that her husband appears more interested in his work than in her may find sympathetic ears, but this is generally never thought a good reason for drastic action. Such an abstract complaint never moves the listener, but the concrete accusation of sexual infidelity is a world shaker. Whatever the provocation or internal marital circumstance, the mate with such a complaint is clearly the righteous victim, recognized as such by the courts and society. For these reasons, many kinds of unfaithfulness in marriage have no voice, whereas sexual infidelity often assumes an exaggerated importance. As a matter of image, unfaithfulness and infidelity have suffered the pejoration of meaning "sexual" exclusively. But other acts of unfaithfulness among human beings eclipse the sexual by far. The playwrights and poets know all about this.

Jean Giraudoux wrote in *Amphitryon 38:* "You know, Mercury, most faithful wives are unfaithful to their husbands with everything except men—with jewels, with perfumes, with reading, with religion and the contemplation of Spring, with everything in fact, except a man."[1]

Women throughout the ages knew the stringent price for unfaithfulness with other men and hence went "underground." For centuries sexual promiscuity was thought to be a natural prerogative of the male; his infidelity was never severely penalized. Freedom from the restrictions of fidelity was a natural concomitant to masculine power and dominance. In this regard we are accustomed to hearing of faithful servants but rarely of faithful masters.

In *Othello,* Amelia felt that a woman's infidelity was justified if it promoted the will-to-power of her husband. "Who would not make her husband a cuckold to make him a monarch? I should venture purgatory for it." Desdemona, in her innocence, showed a virtue untouched by pragmatism. She replied: "Beshrew me, if I could do such a wrong for the whole world."[2] Amelia's position in this matter points up several debates of history. One, the age-old problem of whether the ends justify the means. This issue is for other books. However, her statement does indicate the supremacy of the male's power and achievement needs. According to her these would pre-empt the security of object relations. Is she saying that the husband would be resentful if she (the wife) gave up the opportunity of making him king by an inordinate sexual loyalty?

In his short story, "The Artist at Work," Albert Camus tells of the parents of the artist: "In Reality he thought: 'It's the same old luck.' As far back as he could remember, he found the same luck at work. He felt, for instance, an affectionate gratitude towards his parents, first because they had brought him up carelessly and then had given free rein to his daydreaming, secondly because they had separated, on grounds of adultery. At least that was the pretext given by his father, who forgot to specify that it was a rather peculiar adultery: he could not endure the good works indulged in by his wife, who, a veritable lay saint, had, without seeing any wrong in it, given herself body and soul to suffering humanity. But the husband intended to be the master of his wife's virtues. 'I'm sick and tired, that Othello used to say, of sharing her with the poor.' "[3]

The issue of fidelity can become quite abstract. Is infidelity always immoral? Can one be immoral by being faithful to another yet unfair or unjust to oneself? Chekhov's Voynitsky in "Uncle Vanya" observed of Professor Serebryakov's docile young wife: "Her fidelity is false from beginning to end. There is plenty of fine sentiment in it, but no logic. To deceive an old husband whom one can't stand is immoral; but to try and stifle one's youth, one's vitality to feel—that's not immoral."[4] The distinction made here is between fidelity as sentiment and as logic. In the former instance, the principle is followed more or less blindly for its own sake, whereas in the latter fidelity is a principle in the service of exigency.

The problem of sharing a mate with others or other interests is probably the chief source of feelings of infidelity and often pathological jealousy. This inability to share may extend to the children. An intense feeling of infidelity can result when a husband feels left out or alienated by a wife's exuberant turn toward a child. Yet the husband and also father would lose his self-respect if he verbalized or even felt such a resentment. Modern fathers cannot resort to Kronos' solution. The jealousy is displaced to other more "tolerable" areas, usually the sexual one. It is more respectable for an adult to resent the intrusion of another man than to become petulant over his wife's attention to his own child. Only the well-integrated can consciously feel and express the agony of rivalry with one's own child; for others the shame is unbearable or the intensity of disappointment too great, so that the obsession, or often delusion, of sexual infidelity is established.

What about actual sexual infidelity? Do we live in such a pristine world that adultery is a delusion? It often is the cause of marital breakup, but not as often as one might suppose, and it is not the cause of the agonies that are usually attributed to it. First of all, the cuckold is very much like the cancer victim; he is the last to know, not because he is stupid, but because he chooses to deny what he perceives. He would perhaps rather be quite gullible and a laughing-stock than confront his wife with an issue that might jeopardize what he does get from her. If he "knew" that his wife were sexually unfaithful, his pride and conventional mores would dictate that he take "some action," usually both punitive and destructive, even if he did not want to. An apocryphal tale of an elderly famous international playwright comes to mind. His friends, out of personal sympathy, came to him with the distressing news that his long-time mistress was carrying on with many men and was a whore. The seasoned man-about-town thanked them for their loyalty and replied: "Yes I know, but she is not a whore; she takes money only from me." The friends left with the agonizing feeling that they had really been trying to create some trouble.

An extramarital affair is usually a result of dependent needs as much as sexual needs. Prostitutes report that their chief business problem, a productive bottleneck if you will, is the men who want to stay and talk. One married male patient carried on an affair that was the scandal of the small town in which he lived. He provided an expensive apartment, furs, automobile, and the other accouterments required for a conventional, respectable affair. No one in that town knew, nor would they ever believe, that all that transpired between them was a discussion of books and the reading of poetry. His infidelity to his wife was a verbal one; he chose to talk to another woman. His need for this was great, yet he would suffer humiliation if it were revealed to the community that it was just that and not the expected somatic orgy. His own wife, learning of his transgression, thereupon resolved to become a better sexual partner on the theory a man turns away because of sexual dissatisfaction. She quickly put aside his confession to her that his infidelity had not been sexual as the usual lying of the errant husband. For her, she could more readily tolerate the idea of sexual ineptitude on her part than the reality that he couldn't discourse with her as a person. She then pitied herself as the suffering, righteous victim and would have none of his protestations of sexual innocence. The husband was thereafter exhausted from the now nightly wrestling matches with his reformed sexual angel, and remained forevermore mute. Likewise, his paramour, feeling dishonorable, worse than a whore for receiving so much without "doing" anything for it, packed and left town. Just as convention demands that business make a profit, that politicians gather votes, man-woman intimacies must be sexual.

Jealousy is an expected affect of living. Who would want to live a life in which one cared so little about another, or the other was of so little value that nothing he did, or who he went with, mattered? Who in the world would like to be fully trusted, fully taken for granted in every situation? If someone is precious to us, we must have a modicum of jealousy as basic cement. We should guard our freedom and prerogatives, we are told, and be jealous of them, and so with the people we love.

Jealousy is often a part of the titillation, the foreplay, between partners. Each mate takes turns in accusing the other of infidelity when they are quite sure of their devotion. In fact, it is only when they are quite sure of each other that they can indulge in this playfulness. "How come the butcher gives you the best cuts of meat?" he says. Later she might say: "No wonder you're so tired at night with that new blonde secretary at the office." However, when trust is lacking in one or the other, there is no laughter but instead the serious: "Just what did you mean by that remark?" The remarks are innocent to those able to love well, but are no joke to those whose hold on reality and to an object is tenuous at best. It is a sign of loyalty that people can share their illicit suspicion phantasies, and a sign of mistrust when everything must be concrete—no playful accusations allowed.

This playfulness is generally a part of foreplay and usually ends with sexual intercourse. In other instances these phantasies remain secret and become part of visual images that one has during the sexual act. Here the real conjugal act must be seen as unreal with one or the other partner a figment of imagination. These phantasies are quite fearful and serious in that they cannot be communicated to the mate without painful consequences. The errant images during the sexual act itself are no longer a joking matter.

Freud states that analytic work has shown that instances of jealousy reveal themselves in three classes. These are: competitive or oedipal; projected; and delusional.[5]

Normal or competitive jealousy is thought of as being compounded of the grief of losing the loved object and the pain because of the personal wound. To lose out to another reopens the old wound of the oedipal situation, where the child endures the humiliation and despair of being outdone in the struggle with his father for the mother's love. Here, it is seen on a sexual level, but now we know of the losses, defeats, and victories that go on with one parent or the other and oncoming siblings (new arrivals, new rivals) for attention, prominence, and importance in the family constellation. Here the striving for exclusiveness, for sole possession of the parent is paramount.

Tied to the above mechanism is projected jealousy, derived from actual unfaithfulness in adult life or intense repressed thoughts of unfaithfulness on the part of the subject. The subject, then, battling with his own unacceptable drives of infidelity, salves his own conscience by self-righteously "giving" them to the object. This involves a whole slew of diffuse mechanisms based on trying to assuage one's own shame in the matter. This type of jealousy has its origins in the human, albeit infantile, need to maintain an air of personal innocence.

The third and most malignant type is delusional jealousy. This, associated with paranoia and the paranoid psychoses, as illustrated by Freud in his analysis of the Schreber memories, is a construction to hide dreaded homosexuality. Here the "loved" object is really the purported intruder. Wangh has interpreted Iago's actions in *Othello* as being based on delusion jealousy with Othello as Iago's secret love and Desdemona as the rival.[6] Freud's early formulations today appear over-simplified. He did not stress the forces of the male-dominant society which have demanded inordinate faithfulness on the part of women in the roles they are forced to play. Jealousy and possessiveness, then, are as much derived from societal demands as from childhood.[24]

In clinical practice there is often seen a situation where a man is obsessed with the idea that his wife is carrying on an affair with a man who was his best friend and superior at work. He has no doubt about this and searches after positive proof for his contention. He hires detectives, feels the engine of the car to see if she's been away in the middle of the night, and examines her underclothes for telling spots. Her protestations of innocence and the negative reports of detectives are meaningless. The pleas of friends, relatives, and children are futile. They are all the more puzzled because the wife is usually a timid, reserved, church-going individual. The husband continues to work, but his whole life is now colored by his obsession with his wife's infidelity. He is said to be psychotic and delusional. But aren't psychotics supposed to construct dreams or phantasy worlds to replace the misery and agonies of the real one? If this is so, why should a husband deliberately torment himself with a new world of his own making, in which his mate of thirty or even forty years is suddenly untrue to him and going to great lengths to humiliate him with his boss? Was he not better off when he had no question about his wife? In the logic of everyday common sense, this would indeed be so. But we do not know all the facts.

In the case of one patient the circumstances of his life had changed, and the fragile equilibrium by which he lived was seriously disturbed—disturbed by events a person would ordinarily be expected to deal with. His children were now grown, contemplating marriage. Younger people were coming up in the business, and his position was becoming insecure. He was becoming short of breath, with a few dizzy spells now and then; his friends were dying of heart disease; his prowess, mental, physical, and sexual, was waning. His mental health had shown signs of strain at various points in his life but nothing had led him to seek help.

As a child he suffered night terrors and bedwetting. At puberty he became panicky at the sight of his newly growing pubic hair. In his late adolescence he had the feeling that he might have cancer of the throat. During his college years there was a period of several months of worry that his studying might lead to blindness. Several more brief periods of nervousness during his marriage occurred. Always sentimental by nature, he cried at the birthdays and graduations of his children, his babies were growing up. However, as he sentimentalized about his children, he was usually aloof and restrained in his relations with his wife.

He looked back on his childhood as completely happy, and therefore no inquiry was "needed" in this area. His parents were good to him; he had only feelings of love for his younger sister. As far as he was concerned, his chief misery started last year with his "heartbreak" about his wife and his purported best friend. There never was, and there is not now, anything wrong with his mind. Of course he is now nervous and can't sleep at night. But who would not be nervous to the point of contemplating suicide if confronted by the agony of such a conspiracy! Perhaps this man's difficulty was that he lived long enough for his destiny to catch up with him. If he had died five years earlier, he would have concluded his life a successful individual, with the praise and love of those around him. His name would have been untarnished. Now, he has run out of fuel and he is the laughing stock—a pitied creature, bringing humiliation to himself, his wife, and his children, who are both victims and witnesses of his fall.

Although brought down by the rigors of middle age, the roots of his difficulties lay in his earliest formative years. The agonies of childhood, with grave hostilities and alienation from his parents and his sister, were buried and covered over by conventional acceptable sentiments. He loved happy thoughts and covered his memories with happy, gaily colored wrapping paper. We can only speculate what phantasies of betrayal, infidelity, abandonment, and humiliation that he suffered in the "most happy" home of his childhood. Perhaps it is unfair to do this type of retrospective construction for verification of theory, as psychiatrists do, much to the chagrin of "scientists." But it would be naive to believe that a person and his troubles were born today as Santayana said: "Those who cannot remember the past are condemned to repeat it."

Now back to the question, why should he want to create a world of torment to live in, one in which he is cuckolded and rejected instead of one in which he is loved and respected? Without going into the technicalities of regression, restitution and homosexuality, suffice it to say that he, in the overall picture, gained relief from lifelong, pent-up, but personally tormenting, hostility and rage by the *deus ex machina* of delusion wherein he is cleansed to pure innocence by the complete perfidy of those who purported to love him. In his role of the complete victim of his wife and best friend, he established that the unholy alliance of woman and man now ruin his life as had another union of woman and man in the past. With such an alignment of tyranny against him, how can he reasonably be expected to function and perform with the dignity and grace of a man of responsibility? Instead, he is reduced to a position of being dependent on and cared for by others. And why not? This is small reparation for the damage done. In the course of his delusion, he is also elevated in a queer way to a position of importance which served to undo the reality of his changing work and homelife.

In the real world his importance was lessening. But how was he important in this created world of perfidy? Strangely enough, there was a feeling of personal exaltation that, of all women available, the boss had chosen his wife for his paramour! That the president of a large corporation, apparently happily married, a pillar in the community, should risk everything to carry on an affair with his wife! Even if she turned out to be a scoundrel, he now had proof that his wife, despite her age and plainness, was a choice that men of importance would run after at great risk. Even in fancied defeat, he had the satisfaction of feeling that he had lost a prize, but to the best of competitors.

Here are the words of another fading monarch, King Leontes, concerning the phantasied infidelity of his wife with Polixenes:

"Is whispering nothing?
Is leaning cheek to cheek? is meeting noses?
Kissing with inside lip? stopping the career
Of laughter with a sigh?—a note infallible
Of breaking honesty,—horsing foot on foot?
Sulking in corners? wishing clocks more swift?
Hours, minutes? noon, midnight? and all eyes
Blind with the pin and web but theirs, theirs only,
That would unseen be wicked? is this nothing?
Why, then the world and all that's in't is nothing;
The covering sky is nothing; Bohemia nothing;
My wife is nothing; nor nothing have these nothings,
If this be nothing."[7]

It is an old observation that tyranny begets tyranny. Man apparently must depreciate and humiliate those against whom he sins.

Our dreams regularly show extensive sexual infidelity even if we try to deny its existence in waking thoughts and daydreams. It has been observed by Freud and others that sexual dreams are rarely if ever with one's mate. Some people become disturbed by these nocturnal lapses and would like to feel that their dreams come not from themselves but from some capricious god who imposes this phantasmagoria to plague or test them. The dream allows for fanciful indulgences and excursions into immorality and transgression that generally go against one's wakeful integrity. To some observers, this has been an indication that our morality is but skin-deep and is subject to strong pressures from an inner life which would overthrow those values we consciously prize dearly.

Psychoanalysis, along with poets and dramatists, has uncovered the conflictual nature of man in regard to the opposing forces of orderliness and disintegrative chaos. The great struggle, as Freud defined it, is between the pleasure principle, which would seek gratification without much thought about consequences, and the reality principle, which would measure gratification of an impulse in terms of present and future variables. Under the reality principle one would then take into account both self-preservation and altruistic considerations. In dreams, the pleasure principle often prevails. Dreams help keep us goal-directed in our waking hours by draining off in harmless nocturnal phantasy those asocial and wanton acts of sexuality and aggression, so that in our waking hours we may act and play properly. But dreams reveal what we hate to admit in our conscious state, that the past is very much with us and may haunt us in ways not usually clear to us. Dreams regularly reveal intense sexual desires toward members of one's own family.

For instance, fathers, in dreams, see themselves in sexual situations with young daughters. Mothers find their sons or brothers as lovers. These family romances are almost "organic" in their persistence and power in the lives of all of us. Fortunately, in most instances, they are relegated to, and perhaps partially handled by, the dream drain, and this allows us to live rationally the rest of the time. In many instances they are not "contained" by dreams and spill over into the day where they are apt to be most disruptive of important object relations and personal aims. These errant sexual thoughts from infantile life may interfere with conjugal sexual behavior. Because sexuality has become tainted by its association with "unnatural" objects, i.e., family members, etc., it becomes a forbidden act even where normally and legally permitted. Some, then, act as if sex with a mate is incest, with all the revulsion and disgust that such violation of basic social rules would entail. Thereupon, there can ensue a search for objects outside the home or the social group, where the taint of family sexuality can be obliterated. This escape from the incest horror is a frequent motivation for a search for more gratifying and safer sexual objects. Getting someone from another world might eliminate the incestuous plague. But most often, because the "disease is within," the new fresh objects become contaminated with the old affects and they too, becoming tainted, cease to satisfy.

Freud's discovery that the oedipal complex (mother as the first sexual object with concomitant rivalry with father) is a dominant overwhelming force in the development of every individual, has brought the realization of the long history of sexuality in each of us. As indicated in Chapter I, mating is an old story, not springing from "legal" marriage as our social convention would have it. Because of this long history, those who design simple explanations and even solutions to sexual problems, as if they are solely current and contemporary "problems of living," are most unrealistic. It is for this reason that efforts at marriage counseling, mental health advice, punitive legal measures, by professionals and do-it-yourself devices, such as trial marriages, affairs, switchings, polygamy, etc., have offered very little to distressed people. There are no panaceas and no substitutes for the work and agony involved in the confrontation of one's history. In seeking these ersatz and makeshift solutions, an individual most often commits his greatest infidelity; he becomes faithless to himself. With all our science, we must not be above the wisdom of certain aphorisms of our heritage. In this instance, we can profitably quote Polonius in his farewell speech to Laertes: "Above all, to thine own self be true." The turning away from one's origins, from one's history, the denial of impulses and relationships, are attitudes of deception about one's own being. They are the greatest infidelities of which we are capable.

Not the least amongst these auto-infidelities is that to one's work. Here, often using the rationalization of adapting to reality and expediency, we may make compromises that chip away at the ideals which are the source of life-sustaining hope. The distinction between right and wrong becomes obfuscated, so that thereafter anything goes. And if anything goes, so may life itself, and one is reduced to a humanoid state where the only goal that remains is getting by. Work, however, is not as merciful as one's mate; it cannot talk back, gives no warning such as: "You have been unfaithful to me; you have been flirting with whores; you are jeopardizing all that is valuable to you." Work has been cuckolded more than any mate has, at inestimable injuries to self-esteem, leading to aimlessness, with its attendant cynicism.

The alienation and dehumanization of man in relationship to his work as well as to the societal institutions have been well documented by writers such as Kafka in "Metamorphosis," more recently by William H. Whyte in "Organization Man," and Paul Goodman in "People or Personnel." In Kafka's idiom human beings are often reduced to cockroaches by the betrayals of others in work as well as the compromises against fidelity which we are often forced to make. If love and work are the two basic sources and sustainers of man's reality, fidelity to both appear vital for the maintenance of the human spirit.[8]

The literature of our civilization is replete with descriptions of consuming jealousy. In Greek mythology Hera, wife of Zeus and goddess of storm, was known for her intense jealousy and was said to have made life pretty miserable for the highest god, at one time nearly succeeding in shackling him. On the other hand we are told that Zeus became morbidly jealous and distraught because his queen had produced a child all by herself. Not to be outdone by Hera producing Hephaistos parthenogenetically, he himself gave birth to Athena.[9]

The Old Testament describes the disturbed King Saul's jealousy of the incumbent David. And, of course, Shakespeare's *Othello* is a classical study of jealousy.

Some historians believe that jealousy as we know it in marriage is an outgrowth of the patriarchal monogamous system. Before that, in the neolithic days of matriarchal polyandry, because any woman could choose any number of lovers she pleased, natural jealousy could hardly have existed. If the historians are correct, then jealousy may be looked upon as another by-product of male-dominance.[10]

The play, "The Guardsman," by Ferenc Molnar, deals with a jealous husband. Briefly, an Actor, married six months, is compelled by suspiciousness to test the faithfulness of his wife. The Actor explains to his old friend, the Critic, that he is certain that his wife is tired of him and is looking for a new interest, a new friend. He proclaims that this would be unendurable to him because "I've never really been in love until now. This time it is the last, the greatest, the most torturing love, the love that exhausts my innermost power of feeling—the richest in beauty, the richest in pain." In order to test the fidelity of his wife (and to display his acting ability), he disguises himself as a Guardsman with the idea: "I will make her love me again."

The Critic asks the Actor what he hopes to get out of this, and he replies: "Either she will yield, or she will not. If she does not, then I will be very happy. For I will know that she is true to me. If she does yield, then I will be very unhappy—but at least I will know. . . . But anyway, I will have had one sincere kiss from her."

In the ensuing seduction, the Guardsman suffers some success which leads him to remark: "Pity the husband, but congratulate me."

The climax comes when the Husband-Guardsman reveals his identity but the wife indicates complete intelligence. Yet the husband and the audience are left mumbling, "Did she or didn't she?"[11]

This farcical plot brings forth many questions. First of all, what was the origin of the suspiciousness? After six months of seemingly pleasureful relations, what provoked the need for the test? Why the disguise? Why is the Actor compelled to go into competition with himself, intent on succeeding in his seduction? Here is a manufactured triangle, obviously serving some purpose for the Actor. That this purpose is in the nature of gratification is evident in the intensity of the feelings experienced by the Actor in the laying and executing of the plan. Psychologically, one is immediately impressed with the idea that this is a manifestation of the oedipal triangle. The Actor attempts to work out his conflict as an actor might, through drama.

One suspects that the Guardsman is the son trying to steal mother away from father. The fear that the woman is succumbing to the "other man" may be the wish that mother should do this, the other man being, in truth, the son himself. The wish is revealed in the test. The mechanism finds its full expression when the Actor-Guardsman says: "Pity the husband, but congratulate me." The son has won over the father. This general idea was pointed out by Freud as the nuclear complex. He stated: "The lover with whom the mother commits the act of unfaithfulness almost invariably bears the features of the boy himself, or to be more correct, of the idealized image he forms of himself as brought to equality with his father by growing to manhood."[12]

Amphitryon 38 by Jean Giraudoux is a play expressing the same mechanism with the essential elements of "the test" and "the disguise."[13] Jupiter reveals to Mercury his love for Alkmena, the faithful wife of the mortal Amphitryon. Jupiter aspires to win Alkmena, not as he has won so many others in the past, but as a mortal man. He poses the question: "Faithful to herself, or faithful to her husband. . . . You know, Mercury, most faithful wives are unfaithful to their husbands with everything except man—

with jewels, with perfumes, with reading, with religion, and the contemplation of Spring, with everything, in fact, except a man. The difficulty with these virtuous wives is not to seduce them, but to persuade them that they may be seduced confidentially."

The two gods deduce that the only possible way Jupiter can realize his aspiration with Alkmena is to be her husband, to appear to her as Amphitryon. The two conspirators then descend to earth, and Mercury arranges a war so that Amphitryon is called to duty. Consequently, Jupiter gains entrance to Alkmena's chambers, although she is able to see through the disguise. Again, Jupiter is both triumphant and chagrined by his conquest. In reply to Mercury, Jupiter states: "What do I want? What every man wants! A thousand contradictory desires! That Alkmena should remain faithful to her husband and also give herself to me. That she should remain chaste under my caresses and yet that desire should flame up in her under my very sight. That she should know nothing of the intrigue, and yet that she should connive at it with all her might."

The play continues in a series of mixed identities and feelings among Jupiter, Amphitryon, and Alkmena, later including Queen Leda. Again, the woman is being tested for faithfulness with quite ambivalent feelings on the part of the disquieted male as to whether he seeks success or failure in his venture. Jupiter's above-quoted speech could easily be that of the son in the oedipal situation.

In cases of pathological jealousy, the teasing and playfulness are not present. The patient is very seriously preoccupied and distressed by the infidelity of the mate. The idea cannot be dispelled by reassurance; all evidence is transformed to suit the concept of unfaithfulness and sexual looseness. The idea has the strength of a delusion. These instances of malignant jealousy have nevertheless the same underlying motive in the normal relationship. However now there is no pleasure, but instead agony.

A twenty-two-year-old male student presented himself for psychiatric treatment because of extreme depression characterized by frequent crying spells, agitation, and somatic symptoms of anxiety. He related that he had been seeing a young girl with whom he was deeply in love and was debating the issue of marriage. The obstacle as he saw it was the fact that he had knowledge of her previous sexual experiences with other men. This thought tormented him in spite of the fact that he himself had intercourse with her. This jealous thought could not be dispelled by all the "broad-mindedness and tolerance" that he could muster; he tried to break away from her but always returned. The fact that she was of a lower economic and social status was not the determining factor, he thought. He could not "tolerate" the idea of her previous sexual promiscuity. Yet his own sexual activities were not of a limited nature. Further exploration revealed another mechanism.

As therapy continued, he brought out that he had always been fascinated by "loose women," always preferring their company. He would become intrigued by gossip about them and always sought intimate details as related by other boys. In the present instance he was overtly consumed with jealousy about his girl friend. He had to learn from her and from male acquaintances a full inventory of her past sexual experience. He found himself inextricably involved; he could not marry her because of her "promiscuity," yet would not leave her. He always came back, as he described it, "crying in her lap."

This individual came of a family of moderate means. There was an older brother with whom he fought continually. The father was described as "quick-tempered, unreasonable and stubborn; a man who pushed his children to achieve his own end." Mother, on the other hand, was described as an emotional person, "basically sentimental"; mother was overprotective and restrictive, always fearful that her children would get hurt. Extremely reserved in her attitude and behavior, she saw danger in everything.

The idea of the woman with clandestine sexual experiences was discussed. In his early childhood he had thought much about the circumstances of his parents' marriage.

They had eloped, an unusual occurrence in a religious family such as theirs. Later he wondered if his mother had been pregnant so that she had to get married quickly and quietly.

The origin of the idea of woman being sexually promiscuous was speculation about mother. Yet in the beginning the daydreams about mother were of a pleasant nature. It was only later, with the mother substitute, that the suffering manifested itself. No longer could the conscience allow pleasure to be experienced with these incestuous thoughts. It was replaced by gloom and despair.

Another situation, similar to the one described early in this chapter, was that of a fifty-four-year-old male who had been urged toward a psychiatric consultation by his wife. Life had become unbearable for them because in the last four of their twenty years of marriage, he had successively accused her of infidelity with three male acquaintances of theirs. He was quick to notice little gestures that his wife made, and he had thought of many devices to "catch" her. Through these devices, although he had no concrete evidence, he felt without doubt she was untrue to him. And he was apparently tormented, anxious, and extremely despondent. He felt that life was no longer worth living with the situation as it was. Somatic symptoms appeared, fear of heart trouble, cancer, etc. He felt deep sorrow for his eighteen-year-old son who would have to live with the embarrassment of an immoral mother. He contrasted his own home life; his mother had the respect of all who knew her. Never had a disparaging remark been made about her; her character was impeccable. Needless to say, he was a devoted son to his mother. Because of this deep understanding between them, no overt gestures of affection had to be displayed, so he stated. There was another brother, with whom the patient had always quarreled; for the last five years they had not spoken to each other. Father appeared to be quite a passive individual, about whom the patient had little to say.

At the age of 34, the patient had severe misgivings about

marriage, even though he stated he was madly in love with his bride-to-be. He had the feeling that she really did not love him but married him because he was well off financially. Before the marriage took place he demanded and received a letter from a gynecologist attesting to her virginity. Early in the marriage suspiciousness of a benign nature began to show itself. He always teased her with, "I know that your heart is somewhere else." Up to this point, this might be delusional jealousy with repressed homosexuality as the underlying mechanism, i.e., identification with mother, demand for virginity (the Virgin Mother), accusations of infidelity with male friends, etc. However, another more pertinent and basic mechanism seemed to be the underlying psychopathology.

He told, in the nature of a confession, that for many years, in spite of her overt decorum, he had visualized his mother affectionately embracing and having sexual play with a younger man, not his father. In recalling these thoughts, he stated that they were absolutely insane because he had never seen his mother display affection toward any man, including his own father, brother, or himself. During his adolescence, these thoughts about his mother began to disturb him but he said he dismissed them from his mind.

The daydream of this patient appeared to be corroborative evidence that he identified, not himself, but his wife with his mother. The patient was identified with his father. The delusion of jealousy in this instance is actually a wish that mother should be loose sexually and that she should have an affair with another man—the other man being, of course, the patient himself.

So, again, the fear is actually the wish. It is most significant in these cases that the mother in each instance was very reserved, modest, and restrictive in attitude. These phantasies betray the desire on the part of the son that she be otherwise—that the illicit and clandestine seduction of the son should proceed.

In everyday life the teasing by suspicion is based on a

desire of the individual to have his mate free sexually—with him. On the oedipal level, it is a similar feeling toward mother.

The depreciation of the unfaithful mate is always a concomitant feature of malignant jealousy. This degradation as explained in 1912 by Freud again serves to disguise the mother and at the same time to allow "sexualization" of her.[14]

Now the question of the extreme suffering and anxiety of the jealous patient must be answered. If the jealousy seems to fulfill a wish for sexual freedom with mother, why should patients become so disturbed about the infidelity? This cannot be answered with direct evidence at this time, but it seems from these cases that the subjective symptoms are based on guilt feelings because of the incestuous wish. The fears accompanying jealousy, i.e., fear of breaking up the home, fear for the reputation of the family, fear of insanity and general physical breakdown, so often expressed, are most likely in the nature of castration fears because of the tabooed wish in the phantasy and delusion. In the beginning the phantasy is most pleasureful; only later does a hypertrophied conscience demand its price and obfuscate the original gratification.

Clinically, the jealous person resists reassurance; on the contrary, he comes to therapy for substantiation of his phantasy. He will not easily give up the gratification inherent in this mechanism of jealousy.

Although the more dramatic and communicable problems of marriage have to do with "low" fidelity, a subtle form of imitation is high or exaggerated fidelity. In this there is a devotion and obeisance that can be oppressive, stifling and enraging. One mate may become a puppy-dog to the other, following, imitating, obeying with such obsequiousness as to drive the other mad. A major part of the maddening process of this relationship is that it is very difficult to lodge a complaint. In this world of cruelty, alienation, and abandonment, how can one tell a judge that "my mate loves me too much"? Yet our poets and damatists have told us the vagaries of loving unwisely. If, for some situations, love may not be enough, for others it can be too much. The observer soon sees that servile love is a sign of immaturity in the giver and an act of oppression to the object. It is a "killing with kindness" syndrome, really a grave insincerity which hides behind the euphemism of devotion.

This sort of "devotion" led one woman to seek psychiatric help. Her chief complaint was that her husband spent his time following her around the house. His overriding preference was to be with her every moment that he was home from work. Her company pre-empted all social and recreational activities. His home was his castle; he seemed to have no other needs outside of it; he knew no one on the outside with whom he would rather be than the woman whom he had chosen and loved. At parties and social gatherings, her presence and conversation were always the most attractive and most stimulating. What friends they had were ones whom she had "found"; he was grateful that she assumed this social responsibility. Similarly, he relinquished his ties to his own parents and siblings, and seemed to prefer his in-laws.

The most oppressive aspect of his uxorious devotion was the imitative component. He liked to follow her in her interests and hobbies. When she signed up for a course in adult education, he immediately thought this would be a good idea for himself and matriculated. When she undertook to play a musical instrument, he dusted off his adolescent violin. He similarly took his cues about political, religious and moral issues from her. She appeared to be, to say the least, like an overbearing wife and perhaps the promotion of this image was one of his underlying motives. Ultimately she would play Jezebel to his Ahab, or so it would appear. Although she was gratified to some degree by her husband's seeming compliance with her wishes, she was also distressed by having too much of a good thing. She, in her own right, had never sought or demanded this sort of authority in the home. As a modern woman she cherished what she considered a reasonable degree of autonomy for herself but showed no particular lust to possess the will of her mate. This he seemed all too freely to relinquish; for her this was no valuable acquisition, but indeed a tiresome burden. He wished to effect a fusion with her in hope of gaining needed support, but for her this was a severe threat to her own boundaries and integrity.

The observer could see his behavior as reminiscent of a boy tied to his mother's apron strings—a manifestation of exteme dependence on a woman, eclipsing needs to maintain the conventional image of the male as independent, strong, outgoing, and self-sufficient. Yet, in his own mind, he was nothing but loyal and loving. He was deeply hurt when she was annoyed with his behavior. Could he help it if he loved her so dearly? What he was unable to see was that in giving himself over to her, he was performing a religious act of adoration—one that should be reserved for one's Deity. Or, again using the idiom of religion, he emptied himself of his own identity in the manner of theophany, and became a devotee. He hoped thereby to obtain for himself the blessings that accrue to what might appear as unselfishness but which was really selflessness.

Ironically, the above type of devotion may be normal conventional expectation for a woman. Her "theophany," her emptying herself of all personal goals when she marries, is looked upon as perfectly normal, and her docility is viewed as a prime virtue. When a male does it, it becomes a clinical case! Indeed, part of the above female patient's confusion was that her husband was acting out the role that would be expected of her. She was suspicious that he was indulging in parody, displaying womanish character traits perhaps to goad her into relinquishing, or at least feeling guilt about, the autonomy she had secured. Rarely, if ever, is there the complaint that a wife is too docile, too submissive, too much at home. She may without danger become her husband's devotee. We might conclude that "high" fidelity on the part of the male is considered highly "unnatural" for him and at best looked upon with a great deal of suspicion. Conversely, the usual expectation of fidelity on the part of the woman is part and parcel of her docility, submission, and consequent dependence on the authority of her husband. Biblical Ruth's credo to this day largely defines woman's destiny.

Montaigne's admonition in the 16th century is still largely ignored. He wrote: "We have not made a bargain, in getting married, to keep continually tied to each other by the tail, like some little animals or other that we see, or like the bewitched people of Karenty, in doglike fashion. And a wife should not have her eyes so greedily fixed on the front of her husband that she cannot see the back of him, if need be."[15]

Fidelity as a sentiment as opposed to logic, as a function of the superego, was explained by Chekhov in the play alluded to above "Uncle Vanya." This is expressed by the oafish character Telyegin in the following: "Voynitsky: 'Because her fidelity is false from beginning to end. There is plenty of fine sentiment in it, but no logic. To deceive an old husband whom one can't endure is immoral; but to try and stifle one's youth, one's vitality, one's capacity to feel—that's not immoral.'

"Telyegin (in a tearful voice): 'Vanya, I can't bear to hear you talk like that. Come now, really! Anyone who can betray wife or husband is a person who can't be trusted and who might betray his country.'

"Voynitsky (with vexation): 'Dry up, Waffles!'

"Telyegin: 'Excuse me, Vanya. My wife ran away from me with the man she loved the day after our wedding, on the ground of my unprepossessing appearance. But I have never been false to my vows. I love her to this day and am faithful to her. I help her as far as I can and, to bring up her children by the man she loved, I gave all that I had. I may have lost my happiness, but my pride has been left me. And she, poor soul, her youth is over, her beauty, in accordance with the laws of nature, has faded, but the man she loves is dead. . . . Now what has she left?'"[16]

Fidelity thus becomes a rigid virtue unrelated to integrative functions. It is for the mind that must operate through authority and command that would not trust a logical approach. As such it is a strait jacket into which one comfortably fits oneself. It is with such mentation that one returns to the side of the volcano, and it never takes part in change protest or to speak of revolution.

E. M. Forster conceptualizes a hierarchy of loyalties in which interpersonal relations would claim his highest feelings. In an oft-quoted, if unlikely, credo, he states: "If I had to choose between betraying my country and betraying my friends, I hope I should have the guts to betray my country."[17] This may be a fine democratic sentiment but is a luxury which few have in this world. And it is a highly theoretical and abstract position. We really do not know how he would act in this reality.

The question of his loyalty may be out of his hands because loyalty in such situations may be influenced from above. And the issue of loyalty cannot be divorced from the power that one has or the power that can be exerted on one. Lord Acton might tell us that those with power may exempt themselves from the very loyalty and fidelity that they can impose on others. One generally hears of loyal servants or subjects, rarely of loyal masters or rulers. This can be applied to aspects of faithfulness in marriage where the rules of conduct as far as infidelity are concerned are much more stringent and condemnatory for the relatively powerless woman than for the man. Therefore, in the male-dominant society the infidelity of the male is generally excused whereas the woman's lapse has severe consequences. This well-known double standard has been rationalized and vindicated in the fiction that the male of the species is basically polygamous, and therefore his transgressions are a part of his basic nature; whereas the woman's is a moral fault. This is another instance where power can write its own favorable rules supported by an ongoing mythology. We might have to agree with the cynic when he says that if one is powerful enough one does not have to be sexually faithful and yet at the same time can demand unswerving loyalty from another. The best safeguard for mutual fidelity may in the end be a healthy balance of power. There is an overwhelming amount of evidence that seems to confirm Lord Acton's wisdom. Power always does seem to corrupt. Let even the most moral man then be confronted with possible penalties and adverse consequences. Virtue thrives on consequences.

The problem of fidelity was for a long time dealt with by psychoanalysis as an "id" problem, based on the oedipal complex and its variegated offshoots. Fidelity as an ego entity awaited explication by Erikson. He did this in an adroit re-examination of Freud's analysis of the famous Dora case. She, the adolescent girl, was sent to Freud by a distraught father because of her general rebelliousness as well as hysterical symptoms. Freud uncovered at that time as the chief, but not only, source of her troubles a conflict over a love situation with an older man, Herr K, who was the husband of her father's nurse and paramour. She in turn was taken into the unsolicited confidences of her parents and the K couple about the confused interfamily relationship but always with half-truths and circuities. Freud felt that Dora, with her budding but Victorian sexuality, "fell ill" from the exacerbation of an unresolved father complex now reactivated by Herr K's seductive behavior.

Erikson added, with no contradiction of Freud's earlier formulation, that Dora, concerned with the structuring of convictions and values, as adolescents must be, was brought to a premature crisis in her life by the circumstances of family problems—in particular the behavior of her father with his nurse. His example and explanations served as a crushing blow to any ideal of fidelity that she might have been constructing inside herself. Erikson in effect stressed the importance of fidelity as an ego need. Never discounting this later need from factors of earlier development, he nonetheless, at the risk of taking a narrow moralistic stand, spelled out fidelity as more or less basic for the developmental process.[18]

Erikson wrote: "If fidelity is a central concern of young

adulthood, then her case appears to be a classical example of fatefully perverted fidelity. A glance back at her history will reveal that her family had exposed her to multiple sexual *infidelity,* while all concerned—father and mother, Mrs. K and Mr. K—tried to compensate for all their pervading *perfidy* by making Dora their confidante, each burdening her (not without her perverse provocation, to be sure) with half-truths which were clearly unmanageable for an adolescent."

Again, Erikson: "Dora needed to act as she did not only in order to vent the childish rage of one victimized but also in order to set straight the historical past so that she could envisage a sexual and social future of her choice; call infidelities by their names before she could commit herself to her own kind of fidelity." For those investigators who view the formulation of conviction, ideas, and values of adolescence of no less importance than earlier events, Erikson's interpretation is a welcome leap forward.

If Dora was the victim of hypocrisy and double talk, her destiny was sealed finally by the greatest act of infidelity of all committed by her father on her by turning from her to her brother. Erikson writes of Dora: "A vital identity fragment in her young life was that of the *woman intellectual* which had been encouraged by her father's delight in her precocious intelligence, but discouraged by her brother's superior example as favored by the times, she was absorbed in such evening education as was then accessible to a young woman of her class. The negative identity of the *"declassée" woman* (so prominent in her era) she tried to ward off with her sickness: remember that Mr. K, at the lake, had tried to seduce her with the same argument which, as she happened to know, had previously been successful with a domestic."[19]

This disloyalty of fathers to their daughters in first valuing them as bright young people and then in adolescence viewing them as nothing but "homo sexualis" is a most prevalent disease. As fathers do it, so do husbands who, although promising to love and honor, most often end up by only loving. And as we have been reminded love is not enough. If Giraudoux is correct in saying that "most faithful wives are unfaithful to their husbands with everything except a man," it may be truer that fathers and husbands are unfaithful to their women in everything except sex. And it is the sexual role that they faithfully and unambivalently assign to their women. Men seem all too happy to place women in strictly biological roles whether that of nursing, feeding, love making, etc. This is an ongoing, unrelenting perfidy of our civilization which is sealed by the mythology of "naturalness."

We can affirm that fidelity with its partner, trust, is a necessity for harmonious social relationships. Without it, no family, no community, no nation can long exist. Fidelity, although born in the family, permeates all subsequent relationships and understandings and must be prominent in the hierarchy of commitments from marriage, to business, to profession, to church, to country.

"Fundamentum enim est justitiae fides," said Cicero. Fidelity is the foundation of justice.

Simone de Beauvoir has expressed with candor the question of fidelity as it arose between two "liberated" people. Although unmarried, she revealed the same problem of preserving basic faith, and at the same time the maintenance of autonomy of the individuals involved. Even with a great deal of abstract philosophy and high-sounding intentions, she reveals plenty of banal hurt feelings, anxieties, and suspicions when Sartre related his feelings for M. As an overall philosophy for their relationship, she writes:

"Often preached, rarely practiced, complete fidelity is usually experienced by those who impose it on themselves as a mutilation; they console themselves for it by sublimations or by drink. Traditionally, marriage used to allow the man a few 'adventures on the side' without reciprocity; nowadays, many women have become aware of their rights and of the conditions necessary for their happiness; if there is nothing in their own lives to compensate for masculine inconstancy, they will fall prey to jealousy and boredom.

"There are many couples who conclude more or less the same pact as that of Sartre and myself: to maintain throughout all deviations from the main path a 'certain fidelity.' 'I have been faithful to thee, Cynara, in my fashion.' Such an undertaking has its risks—it is always possible that one of the partners may prefer a new attachment to the old one, the other partner then considering himself or herself unjustly betrayed; in place of two free persons, a victim and a torturer confront each other.

"If the two allies allow themselves only passing sexual liaisons, then there is no difficulty, but it also means that the freedom they allow themselves is not worthy of the name. Sartre and I have been more ambitious; it has been our wish to experience 'contingent loves'; but there is one question we have deliberately avoided. How would the third person feel about our arrangement? It often happened that the third person accommodated himself to it without difficulty; our union left plenty of room for loving friendships and fleeting affairs. But if the protagonist wanted more, then conflicts would break out."[20]

Finally, something should be said about the word opportunity—so disdained in sophisticated psychological circles. It is easy to say that moral behavior is overwhelmingly determined by internal needs, defenses, prohibitions, and values. We hear that the sound person will respond ethically to all and any temptations. Even if it is true that the morality or lack of it in any individual may be predictable, we can say so only with the qualification of "more or less." Only belief or illusion has absolute certainty. If it is so that we can say that a person will be "more or less" faithful, we must then take into account unpsychological factors such as proximity and opportunity. With lack of opportunity, the worst scoundrel would have to be a saint. As Goethe said: "Opportunity makes connections as it makes thieves."[21] Taking into account drives, ego needs, and the vagaries of opportunity, one is justified in speaking of fealty in human terms of *more or less*—that the relationship without blemish is not to be condemned as rigid or compulsive. Nor is a lapse or two to be interpreted as a sign of deep and unalterable corruption of character. Inconstancy is not necessarily infidelity. It was the genius of Freud that turned away from unalterable positions in favor of conceptualization in terms of fluidity—of progressions and regressions. Freud never did accept the vision of man's unswerving and unfaltering propulsion to heaven. One can be deemed faithful if he is more or less faithful in spirit and body.

The issue of certainty as a human quest has already been alluded to in Chapter I. The question of fidelity and jealousy that arises is inextricably tied to man's basic wish for the absolute, for the unalterable and infallible. Jealousy in a sense is the by-product of the breakdown of belief in another human being. His belief system has been shattered not only by actual infidelity but by the inherent incapacity of his fellow human beings to sustain and imitate the model of God.

As indicated above, certainty is found only in religion and does not characterize the world of reason. Jealousy therefore never requires of itself that it have a real or provable basis. Love gives the illusion of certainty and therefore becomes precious in a world built on doubt and probabilities. We can again gainfully quote Balzac: "Certainty is the basis for which human beings crave, for it is never lacking in religious sentiment; man is always certain of being fully repaid by God. Love never believes itself secure but by this resemblance to define love. . . . To believe in a woman, to make her your religion, the fount of life, the secret luminary of all your least thoughts—is not this a second birth? And a young man mingles with this love a little of the feeling he had for his mother."[22]

Years later another perceptive Frenchman, Albert Camus, was to write in the rhetoric of existentialism the following: "A faithful love—if it does not impoverish—is one way for man to maintain the best of himself to the greatest possible degree. It is thus that fidelity is re-established as a value. But this love is outside the eternal. It is the most human of feelings with all the word includes both of restriction and rapture. That is why man only realizes himself in love because in it he finds in a dazzling form the image of his futureless destiny (and not, as idealists say, because it approaches a certain form of the eternal). The type: Heathcliff. All this is illustration of the fact that absurdity has its formula in the opposition between that which endures and that which does not. It being understood that there is only one way of enduring which is to endure eternally and that there is no middle term. We are of the world that does not endure. And everything that does not endure—and nothing except what does not endure—is ours. Thus it is a question of recovering love from eternity or, at least, from those who disguise it as an image of eternity. I see the objection already; the fact is that you have never loved. Let us leave it at that."[23]

NOTES

1. Jean Giraudoux, *Amphitryon 38,* adapt. S. N. Behrman (New York: Random House, 1938), pp. 18-19.

2. William Shakespeare, "Othello," *The Complete Works of William Shakespeare* (Cleveland, Ohio: The World Publishing Co., n.d.), p. 1007.

3. Albert Camus, "The Artist at Work," *Exile and the Kingdom* (New York: Penguin Books, 1958), p. 84.

4. Anton P. Chekhov, "Uncle Vanya," *Chekhov: The Major Plays* (New York: Signet Classic, The New World of Literature, Inc., 1964), p. 171.

5. Sigmund Freud, "Certain Neurotic Mechanisms in Jealousy, Paranoia, and Homosexuality," *Collected Papers,* ed. Ernest Jones (London: The Hogarth Press, 1949), p. 232.

6. Martin Wangh, "Othello: The Tragedy of Iago," *Psychoanalyt. Q.,* XIX (April 1950), p. 202.

7. William Shakespeare, "The Winter's Tale," *The Complete Works,* ed. W. J. Craig (New York: Oxford University Press, n.d.), p. 375.

8. William H. Whyte, *Organization Man,* and Paul Goodman, *People or Personnel* (New York: Random House, 1965).

9. Charles Seltman, *The Twelve Olympians* (London: Pan Books, Ltd., 1952), p. 60.

10. *Ibid.*, p. 26.

11. Quotations are from Ferenc Molnar, *The Guardsman* (New York: Boni and Liveright, 1924), pp. 50, 56, 131.

12. Sigmund Freud, "Special Types of Objective Choice," *Collected Papers*, IV (London: The Hogarth Press, 1950), p. 199.

13. Quotations are from Jean Giraudoux, *Amphitryon 38*, adapt. S. N. Behrman (New York: Random House, 1938), pp. 18, 19, 101.

14. Sigmund Freud, "Contributions to the Psychology of Love," *Collected Papers*, IV, ed. Ernest Jones (London: The Hogarth Press, 1949), p. 203.

15. Donald M. Frame, "Montaigne. A Biography," *Sunday Herald Tribune Book Week* (Nov. 21, 1965), p. 19.

16. Anton P. Chekhov, "Uncle Vanya," *Chekhov: The Major Plays* (New York: Signet Classic, The New World of American Literature, Inc., 1964).

17. E. M. Forster, *Two Cheers for Democracy* (New York: Harcourt, Brace & World, 1938), p. 68.

18. Quotations are from Erik H. Erikson, "Reality and Actuality," *J. Amer. Psychoanalyt. Assoc.*, X (July 1962), pp. 459-60.

19. *Ibid.*, p. 459.

20. Simone de Beauvoir, "The Question of Fidelity," *Harper's Magazine*, CCXIX (Nov. 1964), p. 57.

21. J. W. Goethe, *Elective Affinities*, trans. Elizabeth Mayer and Louise Bogan (Chicago: Henry Regnery Co., 1963).

22. Honoré de Balzac, *A Study of Woman* (New York: P. F. Collier & Son, 1839).

23. Albert Camus, "A Writer's Notebook," *Encounter*, XXIV (March 1965), p. 29.

24. As every anthropologist knows, the sexual jealousy and possessiveness we see so much of in our culture is by no means universal. For instance, amongst the *Irigwe* of Nigeria (see footnote Chap. I) in their system of *primary* and *secondary* marriages, marital partners leave for others without engendering hostility and rancor.

CHAPTER VI

IS ANATOMY DESTINY?

Women are the universal depressed minority group which is why they are looked down upon, exploited, patronized, and resented. I thought everyone knew that.

Emile Capouya

The psychoanalyst must turn to Mill, not Freud, for the heuristic statement about the problems of women in our civilization. The disappointment with Freud in this matter is all the more distressing since psychoanalysis cut its eye teeth on the psychic illnesses of women patients. The *Studies in Hysteria* by Breuer and Freud dealt with women exclusively. Preoccupied with psychosexual matters, they missed the opportunity to illuminate the psychosocial factors which, as Erickson was to point out later in the Dora case, were more consequential. This error of psychoanalysis, unfortunately, has resisted correction in the mainstream of orthodoxy. How one would have welcomed in Freud something similar to the opening statement of John Stuart Mill in his essay, "The Subjection of Women": "That the principle which regulates the existing social relations between the two sexes—the legal subordination of one sex to the other—is wrong in itself, and now one of the chief hindrances to human improvement; and that it ought to be replaced by a principle of perfect equality, admitting no power or privilege on the one side, nor disability on the other."[18]

Rumor has it that Freud was concerned about the social inequity of the sexes but his outlook, it is reported, was less than egalitarian. R. V. Sampson in his exciting book, *The Psychology of Power,* writes: " 'There must be inequality,' Freud is reported to have remarked in a conversation with Dr. J. Worthis on the subject of the relations between the sexes. And since this inequality must prevail, 'superiority of the man is the lesser of the two evils.' There is no reason to doubt that this aptly summarized Freud's own relations with his wife. The adored Gretchen of courtship is wooed tenderly and ardently in order to be raised subsequently to the respected position of matriarchal *Hausfrau.* The husband remains devotedly loyal, but distantly so in terms of emotional involvement."[23]

We are being told in essay and novel today that womanhood is an atrophic disease rather than an identity.[6] These writers, for the most part, are convincing and can be read to great advantage. On the other side Phyllis McGinley extols the virtues and pleasures of domestic chores.[16] However, as a Pulitzer Prize-winning novelist, she herself is not exactly a typical housewife or homemaker. Her wonderful accomplishments elicit from us great admiration for her as a person, but these same achievements make us doubt her sincerity and objectivity as an adviser on these matters. Those who reside on Parnassus have no difficulty recommending simple pleasures for the non-literati.

Woman's status in the world today, even in the United States, where it is better than most places, is grossly unequal to that of her sexual counterpart.[32] Most women, apparently succumbing to the euphuistic prose and poetry about sweet femininity and domesticity, do not seem to know or care about the grossly inferior place to which they have been relegated. As a matter of irony, women themselves, in a form of self-hate, generally condemn members of their own sex who strive for something better. As an indication of woman's snail-like progress in gaining recognition as a person one recent news item is enlightening. It was reported in the *New York Times* that for the first time certain nuns and leaders of Catholic women's organizations would be admitted as "auditors" of debates of the third session of the Ecumenical Council known as Vatican II. Pope Paul VI's statement is commendable but somewhat cautious and perhaps overdue: "We believe that the day has come in which it is necessary to place in higher honor and greater efficiency feminine religious life."

This is gratifying progress and certainly a step toward justice. It is also a reminder of just how ignored and suppressed womankind has been. Even though she has been the bulwark of religion in every country through the ages, and has steadfastly upheld and promoted religious belief and practice—as even in Russia today—even in the face of scoffing and rebellious males, she has been excluded from any authoritative role in central church activities and given pitifully little honor. It is therefore laudable if somewhat overdue that women for the first time in two thousand years may be allowed in the ecclesiastical chambers to observe, giving hope that someday they may even be participants in what is now an all-male conclave. The records of other major religions on this score are no better. Religions are habitual laggards in the major moral issues. The church traditionally has been run on male homosexual libido. Margaret Brackenbury Crook, holder of a Certificate in Divinity, hopes that in the future it will be otherwise.[33] The progress here, as she freely admits, is somewhat slower than a snail's pace.[3]

Women gain little from the messages about them found in our heritage. Graves and Patai say: "Hebrew myths treat women as fields to be ploughed and sown by godlike heroes —passive and thus necessarily guiltless if the wrong farmer should enter."[10]

The Talmud in its parable about the origin of woman was all too prescriptive in tone: "God deliberated from which part of man to create woman. He said, 'I must not create her from the head that she should not carry herself haughtily; nor from the eye that she should not be too inquisitive; nor from the ear, that she should not be an eavesdropper; nor from the mouth that she should not be too talkative; nor from the heart that she should not be too jealous; nor from the hand that she should not be too acquisitive; nor from the foot that she should not be a gadabout; but from a hidden part of the body that she should be modest.' " (Genesis Rabbah 18:2) The woman who has a feeling for autonomy and involvement might question whether there is anything in the above for her.

The renegade psychoanalyst, Otto Rank, writes: "Although the role of the Jew in human civilization epitomizes on a world-historic scale the psychological paradoxes of human nature and behavior, there is still another story of symbiotic assimilation much more profound in its basis and much more significant in its effect on human nature, because it does not concern the perpetuation of culture throughout the ages but the very core of life: the perpetuation of the human race as such. We are referring to the matter already discussed at length—the position of the woman in this man-made world, and her position as ascribed to her by man and accepted by her as an imposition from without. In this sense, woman's place in life and her psychology has often been compared to that of the Jew, inasmuch as she has been subjected throughout history to the treatment a slave is given, has been persecuted periodically as the scapegoat for all human evils (medieval witchcraft), in fact, was pictured as the 'cause' of evil itself, a curse which the Jew took from her not only by becoming the scapegoat but by inventing the first psychology as an explanation of evil in the human being."[21a]

Perhaps a step up from the woman as field (Graves and Patai) is Claudel's metaphor of woman as plant in his novel, *The Satin Shoe*. "The husband of Dona Prouheze, the Judge, the Just, as the author regards him, explains that every plant needs a gardener in order to grow and that he is the one whom heaven has destined for his young wife."[5]

Shakespeare's Rosalind, disguised as a male, tells Orlando: ". . . but indeed, an old religious uncle of mine taught me to speak, who was in his youth an inland man, one that knew courtship too well: for there he fell in love. I have heard him read many lectures against it, and I thank God, I am not a woman, to be touch'd with so many giddy offences as he hath generally tax'd their whole sex withal."[25]

It is the old story that, once they have gained it, men and institutions rarely give up power without pressure to do so. In the case of women, the pressures have been minimal because they have dutifully "known their place" and made virtues out of submission, docility, and inferiority. "Facis de necessitate virtutem." They become ecstatic over the niggardly crumbs handed to them. In public matters, theirs is a role played from the balcony as in synagogues of old. They are generally resigned to this role and have taken it as being "natural," rather than man-made. The difficulty here is that all those tasks and roles assigned to women are principally in the realm of biology, the having and feeding of children, the care of the lean-to, and a variety of things that a self-respecting male would consider demeaning and would stalk off the job if asked to do. Even at work away from home, she is the secretary, not the boss; laboratory worker, not scientist, teacher but rarely principal; social worker but never director of the agency. Nursing is about the only profession where women control their own house, supplying both the executive and working force. According to statistics, there were in 1969, 26 million working women. But the vast majority are working at very menial jobs. When the *Harvard Business Review* attempted to make a survey of women's executive opportunities, they gave up in despair, the barriers being so great that there was scarcely anything to study. The percentage of women in the professions has actually declined since the 1930s.

There is tragic irony in the generally held belief that women are strongly "narcissistic." This term is applied to them because of their well known habits of preening and other self-attending activities. The importance they place on their clothes, mannerisms, and other attention-getting devices as well as their so-called propensity for hypochondriasis and psychosomatic disorders have led many erroneously to feel and write that women have a high level of narcissism in them. The opposite, of course, is the case. It has been observed that self-love, as far as the female is concerned, is grossly wanting. It is both scarce in women and poorly tolerated by society when it exists. Lionel Trilling's words are perceptive indeed. "There is a great power of charm in self-love, although, to be sure, the charm is an ambiguous one. We resent it and resist it, yet we are drawn by it, if only it goes with a little grace or creative power. Nothing is easier to pardon than the mistakes and excesses of self-love: if we are quick to condemn them, we take pleasure in forgiving them. And with good reason, for they are extravagance of the first of virtues, the most basic and biological of the virtues, that of self-preservation. But we distinguish between our response to the self-love of men and the self-love of women. No woman could have won the forgiveness that has been so willingly given (after due condemnation) to the self-regard of, say, Yeats and Shaw. We understand self-love to be part of the moral life of all men; in men of genius we expect it to appear in unusual intensity and we take it to be an essential element of their power."[30]

Freud recognized this absence or diminution of self-love in women. However, he characteristically attributes this quality to anatomy rather than to society. He states that the girl "is wounded in her self-love by the unfavorable comparison with the boy who is so much better equipped. . . ."[28, 29] Clearly then for Freud anatomy is destiny. Freud, however, might have pondered whether the girl is victimized by the equipment she is born with or by what she is later denied. Clara Thompson wisely pointed out that the girl's envy of the boy could be adequately explained in the gross cultural inequities that do exist. Unfortunately her voice has not received the attention it deserves. By demonstrating the frustrations and renunciations that generally held for the female in the patriarchal society, she eclipsed Freud's anatomical theory. Similarly, Karen Horney was in the forefront of exposing the social aspects of woman's plight. Her treatment at the hands of mainstream psychoanalysis is a sad chapter in the history of that science.[34] Freud's was a hard act to follow.[8, 9]

It is generally agreed that one has to search far and wide for female geniuses in science or in the arts. This has been used as evidence of cerebral inferiority or at least psychological inhibition or inadequacy. Psychoanalysis, following Freud, tends to explain the woman's seeming lack of creativity on the nature of her being and on psychological ontogeny. Greenacre postulates that the woman's creativity becomes absorbed in her biological function of producing children. And in a strange twist of values, she seems to indicate that because a woman creates children, she would therefore have no need to express herself creatively in other ways.[11] And there are those in psychoanalysis who hold that man's creativity results from his frustration at not being able to become pregnant, i.e., he is reduced to having brain children. Although quite poetic, this simplistic formulation regarding creativity in the male and female is unconvincing.

On the contrary there is evidence to indicate that the factors of opportunity and salutary climate play decisive roles. The most pertinent and perceptive statements on the subject seem to come from those outside of psychology and psychoanalysis. For instance, in the matter of woman writers, Madeline Chapsal finds the dearth of women novelists is due primarily to cultural restraints. She states: "The act of writing, a hyperindividualistic act, would seem to be incontestably linked to social condition, that is, to the degree of individual freedom with respect to the group and to the society as a whole—the society itself having to be not only free, but economically 'developed.'" She also writes: "For centuries, and especially in the 19th century, the one thing forbidden to girls above all, just as it was to married women, was freedom of speech, which was suspected of leading—and we see how right they were—to freedom of thought, then of action."[1]

The above statements appear to be more logical in their explanation of the woman's lack of artistic production than the focus on her biology. Without in the least knocking the value and delights of having babies, writing books would seem to be another thing again. The picture might be quite different if her spiritual freedom went hand in hand with her child-producing license.

Today there are great actresses although it is only in recent times that they have been allowed on the stage. In spite of their successes on the stage, their struggles for achievement are still quite difficult. The unconscious (?) prejudice against them shows no sign of abating. It has been observed that although we have outstandingly talented actresses, very few playwrights write substantial parts or plays for them. Harold Clurman, in an article called "Our Neglected Women," writes in this regard: "The reason for this is not simply that production in the theater has so painfully shrunk in the past 20 years. That of course is a major factor but beyond this is the failure of our dramatists to provide truly interesting parts for women. During the years of decline only Williams, Inge and Arthur Laurents have consistently written central roles for our actresses. Only in *After the Fall* has Arthur Miller leveled his sights to the feminine (independent of the purely maternal) sphere of life and that from a largely male point of view—which indeed is one of the points of his play." Mr. Clurman, admittedly straying from his thoughts in the theater, goes on to say: "Women today are free but the stage neglects them. We are all crazy about them, but do we love them? They are rarely seen for and in themselves. They are seen as babies or brides who need protection, monsters from whom we must protect ourselves, martyred saints, mothers who stifle us, thorns in the flesh, solace to broken men. Even as the cause or excuse for outrageous passion they have become almost obsolete. At their most enthusiastic, dramatists see them as destroyed persons, victims. And so in a sense they are. Ibsen's *A Doll's House* is now held to be outmoded. And it is: Nora doesn't have to leave the house and slam the door; she is virtually pushed out. But once she's out, where, humanly considered, does she go?" He blames this on the harassment of modern-living rather than deliberate oppression. "There is no personal villain to this story. The pressure of our society on its men folk (the prosperous as well as the poor) is so great that they have little time, patience or energy except for partners in business or in bed and hardly ever for true companionship. The moral and emotional stature of men has contracted; women suffer from this diminution; and the stage offers them insufficient opportunity to realize themselves. . . ."[2] If Mr. Clurman's existential analysis appears to exclude the factor of personal psychology as well as the demiurge of bias, it at least highlights the problem of women in society in human terms. And, sadly enough, he shows how little actual progress toward equity has been made.

One statement of Mr. Clurman warrants emphasis and is applicable to areas of involvement other than the stage. He indicates the training, willingness and freedom of the woman today but the lack of *opportunity*. There is no place for her to go. She is shut out by design or bias from all but the menial and routine jobs. Unfair to those already in the market, the real damage is done to the will and hope of the young who are deprived of models to emulate. Thus a malignant constraining force is produced which diminishes the options and alternatives for the young girl. This may account for the stampede toward marriage and the relinquishing of educational opportunities.

Mr. Clurman says that there are no villains here. There doesn't have to be, for as in other instances of prejudice and persecution, the dirty work is done by the institutions, the silent coalescence of man-made and man-dominated systems of education, religion, business, government, and "psychology" which effectively does the job of exclusion and diminution. So effective has this work of attrition been that chastity belts need no longer be applied—women have been reduced to insuring their own modesty.

It is this depreciatory attitude toward their daughters that largely accounts for the hostility that daughters feel toward their parents—especially their mothers. The mother characteristically looking to her son for the fulfillment of her own frustrations, relegates the member of her own sex, her daughter, to second-class status. This is felt by the daughter as a horrible betrayal and disloyalty. Psychoanalysis, routinely finding this rage in daughters toward their mothers, has attributed it to the sexual rivalry between women for the father's love, the classical Oedipus triangle. In addition, the concept of the castration complex has been invoked to explain further this antagonism. This complex in women is derived from the daughter's alleged phantasy that mother *had* taken her penis away when she was an infant, i.e., has castrated her. On this basis, the daughter's rage against the mother is irrational—a figment of her imagination and a derivative of her "unreasonable" penis envy.

Professor Andrew Hacker at Cornell writes: "It is the fate of . . . girls not to be taken seriously by their parents. After teaching young women for a dozen years, I never cease to be depressed over the low level of expectations that most parents . . . set for their daughters. Even the most up-to-date mothers and fathers persist in thinking of Judy and Carol as sweet, scatterbrained young things to be dutifully raised and ultimately married off in a white gown at the neighborhood church."[12]

These anatomical and bio-sexual explanations have proved to be oversimplifications. For as Hacker points out above, "the castration" of the girl in her childhood and adolescence does in fact take place via the lack of serious consideration that is afforded her. Therefore the daughter's phantasy of "being cut off" is not an irrational phantasy—but a social reality. She is in fact cut off from the world that we have always defined as being most meaningful and relevant. The castration complex is no myth as psycho-analysis would have it.

Yet much of the injury to women is self-inflicted. They have succumbed to the culturally-directed penis awe and fully cooperate in the apotheosis of the male. Ask a woman for whom she would rather work and most often she will say "for a man." In seeking out a physician or a lawyer, most women would say they would have more trust in a male regardless of matters of training, competence, skill, etc. Just as many Negroes are "Uncle Toms" in the civil rights movement, most American women would rather be docile and cooperative than fight for their self-respect. In this process, they hate women who do seek out other than the traditional destinies. It is most difficult for them to understand that they indulge in self-hate when they heap ridicule or scorn upon those of their own sex who may attempt to break through some of the male-female shibboleths. These are the Marthas of the world who, having to wait and serve, deeply resent the positions of the worldly and wisdom-seeking Marys. To the former the words of Jesus of Nazareth, Rudyard Kipling notwithstanding, are still appropriate: "Martha, Martha, you are anxious and troubled about many things. . . ." It was Mary's position that he defended. Theologians today seem to have forgotten this.

Again, the progress that is made, such as woman suffrage less than fifty years ago, or the Federal equal-pay law in 1964, is welcome but really serves to highlight the extent of the lag and newness of bare recognition of the inequity. It took until 1964 for the basic element of justice to be proclaimed whereby two persons of equal skill and competence and productivity should be similarly rewarded. But the public aspirations of women have always been lightly taken, as evidenced in Presidential news conferences where the Chief Executive would handle a question about women's rights with a quip that would bring down the house: "I thought women always ran everything." Similarly, Mrs. Margaret Chase Smith's entry into the Presidential primaries of 1964 lent a humorous note to an otherwise very serious competition of giants. Treated kindly and lightly by solicitous gentlemen, she was openly scorned by her fellow-women.

Because women are traditionally bossy around the home, permitted a great say in inconsequential matters, there has arisen in America, the mythology of the matriarchy. Everybody seems to know and remember that Mother appeared to run everything; nothing is further from the truth. (In the so-called American matriarchy, seven states do not give mothers equal control with fathers over their children.) There was a joke a few years back concerning a harmonious marriage. When asked the reason for their harmony for thirty-five years, the husband replied that there had been an agreement to divide the authority and decision making. The husband made the major decisions and his wife the minor ones. The husband was then asked if he would give examples of what constituted the major decisions. He answered this way. "The decisions about NATO, relations with the Soviet Union, our activities in Vietnam, and the missile build-up are left to me. My wife takes care of the rest. We have never had a quarrel in thirty-five years." This sounds like the typical condition of the American "henpecked" male in which harmony can be reached only by abrogation of all say in his life and family. However, there is tremendous irony in this joke. For in reality the consequential and crucial decisions of the destiny of Americans are in the hands of the males. There are no women in the National Security Council, rarely in the President's cabinet, and never in significant numbers in legislative positions. Women are given a say in their families perhaps as a compensation for their almost total exclusion from influence in public matters. And this compensatory authority in the home (and we know in life and clinically) is often less than salutary to powerless children. Mothers often "identify with the aggressor" and bludgeon the children to degrees of their own exploitation as people. That boys grow up feeling that their mothers have castrated them comes as no surprise. Similarly, girls, who find their mothers inadequate models for themselves, feel that they have been betrayed. For them the bossy and overbearing mother is not somebody whom one could profitably and honorably emulate. This is if anything a pseudo-matriarchy system—with all the ill effects of responses that accompany chronic subjugation, hypocritically called equality and even dominance.

There are differences between men and women and, as the French say, long live the difference! Yet it was a Frenchman, Gregoire, who wrote: "Respect for women is the test of national progress in social life." It is the highest attainment of human mentation to acknowledge and accept differences between man and woman, the gifted and the dull, black and white, Christian and Jew. This does not mean that deliberately cultivated differences or inequities are to be similarly tolerated or respected. The words of Dr. John Paul Mather, President of the American College Testing Program and former President of the University of Massachusetts, are germane to this subject and are most welcome even though it is discouraging that they are presented as a discovery in the year 1965. The *New York Times* reported his remarks at a symposium at the University of California Medical Center as follows: "He declared that 'rapidly advancing research-directed, computerized, automated civilization' would offer increasing chances for women 'to meet their family commitments and at the same time find positions, challenges, exciting and productive outlets outside of the home.' 'Indulgent parents,' Dr. Mather said, 'have soothed daughters, troubled by fractions or algebraic equations, with the admonition that women aren't supposed to be able to keep a checkbook in balance or figure out a bank reconciliation. And the daughters have listened, even when they had real ability, and quit trying.' Actually, he asserted, many women have a flair and capacity for mathematics and 'constantly demonstrate ability to be more careful, more accurate and more imaginative than men.' He foresaw growing opportunities for top and middle management career women, particularly those who have finished the child-bearing, child-rearing phase of their lives."[19]

The concept of "equal but separate" roles for male and female is to a degree a necessary one and a *sine qua non* for the merger known as marriage. There must be a division of work and responsibilities and this dichotomy must be responsive to the all-important biological needs served by women. Theirs is to bear and nurture and there can be no adequate substitute for this—nor should one be sought. Childbearing and the rearing of children do not take second place in importance to anything the husband accomplishes. Granting these irreducables, one must then carefully examine whether womanhood has been encumbered by many labors of unlove which are the result of the male-dominant society. The dictum, separate and equal, too often suffers pejoration wherein those with power take unto themselves more and more, to the attrition of the other. Molière was correct in saying: "Du cote de la barbe est la toute-puissance." (All the power is with the sex that wears the beard.)

The male has always been and must be more than a husband or a father. If that is all he aspires to, we know that he is destined to fail, for one can be nothing before there is identity as a person with goals of personal development and achievement. Unless he has such goals and some measure of success with them, he will fail miserably as a husband or a parent because he will expect his wife and children to provide the gratification which should come, must come, from his own achievements. Furthermore, unless he has some modicum of creativity, he brings very little of enrichment to the family other than his biological presence.

What of the woman? Strangely enough, she may be censured if she aspires to anything more than mother and wife. There are many voices in the land, who, witnessing the general discontentment of women today, have seriously advocated a new and separate college curriculum for women. Note the recommendation of Dr. James J. Rue, director of a "marriage clinic," before a national psychological association, reported in the *New York Times*. The article appeared under the rubric, "Rise in Divorces Laid to Education":

"Los Angeles (Religious News Service)—A blistering attack on the American educational system that trains women to become men's competitors rather than companions was made recently here by Dr. James J. Rue at the eighth annual meeting of the American Catholic Psychological Association. "Dr. Rue, director of the St. Thomas More Marriage Clinic here and president of the Southern California Association of Marriage Counselors, blamed the skyrocketing ratio of divorce in the United States and marital unhappiness in millions of homes on the materialistic concept of a 'part-time wife,' for which the present educational system prepares women, instead of the 'old-fashioned wife and mother.'

"To save the family structure in America, he said, the entire educational system must be reoriented toward home economics to teach women how to be wives and mothers and to teach men how to be good husbands, tasks that the average American is no longer performing.

"Only after these fundamentals are achieved can American women afford the luxury of intellectual pursuit and careers, he added."[20]

Instead of liberal arts and the sciences, which are taken in classes with boys, women, they say, should be taught a separate curriculum to prepare them for wifedom and motherhood. This would become an all-embracing education for life in a private world and would avoid education which gives the female a feeling that her mental abilities, capacities, and performance are at least equal to men. Encouraged in these beliefs and being witness to comparative results in the academic world, she finds it difficult to remain in the house watching the division of work and roles evolve in which her husband just *happens* to be able to use his education effectively and participate in worldly affairs, to be stimulated by contacts with other minds, and on the other hand finds herself immersed in activities about 180 degrees opposite. Instead of having stimulation, opportunity, rewards, etc., she is witness to her lack of opportunity, inability to use her skills (which are gradually lost through disuse), and sees herself reduced to the menial labors of the day which she is told are feminine.

It is a paradox of our civilization that even the deprived peasant women of Europe and Asia were more than mothers and wives; they were indeed expected to do the work of the fields and the community. (Gabon and Libya are among the developing countries with laws guaranteeing equal pay for men and women, something achieved in only 30 states of the United States.)[35] Yet the American woman, often highly educated and sharp-witted, is supposed to be able to turn her back on what she has learned, and accept her period of education as a happy interlude to be recalled but never put to the test. It is said that being a wife and a mother are full-time jobs and of inestimable importance; for, of course, the hand that rocks the cradle rules the world. But a mother before she is anything else must be a person with self-respect, assured of her own worth, and, more importantly, must feel that she has not paid an inordinate price for motherhood in terms of her personal striving and aspirations. If she has, her motherhood will produce sour milk and the offspring will know there is something horribly wrong.

If, as we are told, love is not enough for children, it is equally true for parents. For a woman, as for a man, to be loved by husband, by children, by family, is not enough in the quest to be whole. Meeting the biological needs of one's self and of others, as important and as basic as these are, cannot alone sustain either man or woman. If love is not enough, neither is bacon from the male or milk from the female sufficient to make life worthwhile. Being a decent model for a child is a most worthy objective, but one can become a worthwhile model for a child only if one feels himself worthwhile. And there must be some confirmation of "worthiness" from other people than those who love you or who depend upon you. This entails performance, use of skills, professional confrontations, and varying degrees of competition in the market-place of talents not found at the supermarket.

When a woman is able to find the formula that successfully combines personal and family fulfillment, her comfortable level of self-esteem makes family life actually easier. For one thing, she does not feel "gypped" and does not look upon her husband and children as burdens or persecutors. She can also enrich the family with the example of achievement that she sets and the worldly knowledge that she can bring back with her. But finding that formula, striking that happy balance, is a most difficult task, attained often only after agonizing appraisals and prodigious soul-probing. It is a task that a man has simplified for him in that he rarely has to make a decision between being a father and making a livelihood; he has a built-in stimulus and opportunity for personal achievement.

Is work a cure? If it is used as one, beware! Women who get married or have babies to solve deep intrapsychic problems are destined for disappointment or worse. Similarly, "going to work" as a solution for longstanding personal conflicts will be found a weak reed for both men and women. "Going to work" should never be considered a cure for neurosis, or a usually good thing, or a submission to a contemporary fad, or some heaven-directed categorical imperative, but rather a derivative of one's own truth. Yet Freud indicated that work has a greater effect than any other technique of living in the direction of binding the individual more closely to reality; in his work, at least, he is securely attached to a part of reality, the human community. However, did he have only men in mind when he made this statement? Or are women to look elsewhere for reality-finding devices? It would be consistent with truth for a dependent and aimless person to seek shelter and not meddle with situations too fearful and too complex for his capacities. So, too, those who have goals within the realm of achievement, by reason of training, skill, and personal investment, would be untrue to themselves if they turned their back on, or were blocked from, pursuit of them. Therefore a "back-to-work" movement as a cure for unhappy or discontented women has a built-in self-destroying mechanism. No one can or should work unless adequately prepared and honestly motivated.

This motivation has to do with the ego ideals—those internalized images of worthwhile goals, which we value highly and think worthy of our own maximum efforts. These internalized ideals give direction as well as stimuli. Generally speaking, it was once assumed that these ideals differed sharply between man and woman. For the man it was work, success, achievement, fatherhood. For the woman, it was marriage, motherhood, being a helpmate to a loving husband. And as some have said, "God may have created women to mollify men." We now realize that this neat abstract dichotomy is not and probably never was, as clearly defined as the dualists would like to have us believe. We are now coming to accept the idea that the differences are not as great or as important as we were led to believe, or wanted to believe.

In Shakespeare's *Cymbeline*, when Imogen is to disguise herself as a male, she is advised by the servant Pisanio of the necessary changes, revealing in this advice the inconsequential and superficial difference between the sexes. It was Shakespeare's genius that he saw through the folly of these artifacts.

"Pisanio: 'Well then, here's the point: You must forget to be a woman: change Command, into obedience. Fear, and niceness (The handmaids of all women, or more truly Woman its pretty self) into a waggish courage, Ready in gibes, quick-answer'd, saucy, and as Quarrelous as the weasel; Nay, you must Forget that rarest treasure of your cheek, Exposing it (but oh the harder heart, Alack no remedy) to the greedy touch of Common-kissing Titan, and forget Your laboursome and dainty trims, wherein You made great Juno angry.' "[26]

The ideals of many women in their own development are not solely homemaking. They often share the goals of their fathers and brothers. These ideals which may be commonly shared with their brothers should not be labeled "masculine" or "feminine," but perhaps "family" truths. Whether the one sex or the other succeeds in the propagation of this inheritance depends on a myriad of complex circumstances, including luck, opportunity, and social tolerance. As some substantiating evidence for this statement, let the reader recall that, until the turn of the present century, women had not been thought of as having the wisdom to cast a political ballot. In Switzerland, women to this day are not given the right of franchise. Imagine the circumstance that Eleanor Roosevelt or Margaret Smith would be considered less competent to vote at the polls than the crudest male imbecile. This was the case in this country a few years ago!

Anatomy may be destiny, just as skin color or religious background play an overwhelming force in determining one's destiny, but it must be remembered that these circumstances of anatomy or destiny loom as large or small as the social rules of society make them. If these rules place a great premium on, say, the penis, then anyone without one will be looked on as a reject, a cripple, and inferior. There is a great tendency in humanity to fear differences, and an equally great tendency to find excuses to relegate the subjugated to inferior roles. Women have been the subjects of men and have been badly exploited. They have been, paradoxically, victims of cultivated inequalities. They have never made a real protest because they have been sold a bill of goods that their "assigned" role was a "natural" one and to protest was to go against nature. The words of Goethe seem quite appropriate: "No one is a greater slave than he who imagines himself free when he is not free."

Women have been called the defeated sex probably from

the time when men learned that women could not produce children by themselves. Stripped of this magic, woman was thereafter placed in a secondary role in human society. To keep her subjugated, she was "endowed" by men with unfavorable and demeaning characteristics. Eric Fromm writes: "The war between the sexes has been going on for several thousand years, and men's propaganda about it is just as silly as war propaganda. Men say women are less courageous; it's notorious that they are *more* courageous. That they are less realistic; it's notorious that they are more realistic. Women are more concerned with the question of war and peace than men are."[13]

Let her strive for excellence in almost any field and she will be called "masculine."[36] And at one time, we recall, it was considered against nature that she be given an anesthetic for childbirth and against nature that she vote. The doctrine of natural law has had an infamous history of being invoked to vindicate all types of subjugations and suppressions, but nowhere more flagrantly than in the treatment of women. "Quam multa injusta ac prava fiunt moribus." How many injustices and wrongs are enacted through custom. Separate-but-equalism has worked as badly here as in race relations, because the power to give or withhold and to balance is reserved to the dominant group. It results operationally in the accretion of the one and the attrition of the other. How could a woman attain the wisdom of a bishop or a cardinal if until today she was not permitted to audit their dialogues? And to those who would say that women are not fit for high religious duties, religion must ask itself about its own responsibilities. Perhaps they should ask, with Balzac's M. de Valois, "whether stupid women take naturally to piety or whether piety, on the other hand, has a stupefying effect on an intelligent girl."[4]

The woman who seeks a professional identity in the world is faced with many hazards. They arise not only from a hostile and resentful environment, but also from her own inner doubts about what she is doing. Even when she reassures herself or is given support that her stand is proper and justified, she frequently manifests a feeling of guilt about not being in her proper place—the home. As a result she distorts her character into shapes which are often quite grotesque and unappealing. She may appear not as "mannish" but, regretfully, "apish." One result is a pseudo-aggressive stance wherein she constantly seeks to prove, and usually finds, that she is being unfairly treated. She may thereby divert most of her energies and time to a personal "civil rights" issue which makes her an anathema in any office and generally loathed by those who otherwise might accept her talents. She is soon diagnosed as not really productively working but primarily interested in a life-and-death struggle with men. This type frequently earns a male "backlash"; the men reaffirm their basic prejudice that women belong in the home. Behind the facade of bravado, these women are usually very fearful of their new roles and overreact. Their difficulty in adjusting, their perpetual grievance-hunting, contain a hidden appeal to be sent back to the kitchen from which their liberation has been specious. They hurt their whole "race" thereby.

A twenty-four-year-old woman became a junior executive in an industrial firm, having been graduated from a school of engineering. Her attitude was that she would neither ask nor give any quarter. She was most serious in every project she undertook, brooked no levity, and resented any flirtatiousness, even though in spite of her austere manner she was quite attractive. No slight, real or fancied, passed her by. At certain social affairs of the company, when invitations to "employees and their wives" were sent, she would reply with a long and biting letter that this was indeed the 20th century and routine form letters have to be altered to acknowledge the existence of female employees. She studied the salary scales of the men and women and brought the inevitable inequities under the nose of her employer. She also ranted and bellowed about the inefficiencies and stupidities of the men around her who appeared to have little interest in their work other than paychecks and automatic promotions. Her general behavior made her male associates very happy with their own wives. She brought that ray of darkness into their working lives that made their homelife appear that much brighter. She was married but disdained anything about her own home and had made an agreement with her husband that there would be no children until she was well along in her career.

As she worked in this manner, she came into heated controversy over policies with her boss. She threatened to go to the stockholders about the terrible state "management" was in. She was fired in this clash of personalities. Although her competency was never in question, her adaptability was zero.

After her dismissal, she became distraught. For a while she railed against her former employer, against men in general, and against civilization that sanctioned injustices. But she appeared to lose interest in work as if mortally wounded and made no attempt to find other employment. Instead she preferred to stay at home and lick her wounds like Philoctetes on Lamnos. She too could not be induced to return to the wars; instead she withdrew into herself. Her condition of distress manifested itself now by severe phobic reactions whereby she became completely housebound, needed the constant presence of her husband, and was obsessed with losing her mind. If she tried to cross the threshold of her front door, she was stopped by feelings of dread. All the shopping as well as communication with the outside world had to be done by her husband. She appeared too fearful to answer a doorbell or the telephone. Here was a transformation of a person as complete as could be imagined. Anyone who had known her in her former state of independence and arrogance could not recognize her now. They postulated that either she had been undone by rank injustice (that a man in her job might have been dealt with with more respect and would have been more tolerantly listened to) or that her "aggressive" behavior had been a manifestation of an incipient mental illness.

This question is indeed difficult to answer. We could never say that extreme frustration and disappointment could not destroy a person. Yet her nature was such that she ignored the need for adaptability. Who can say that she was wrong in wanting equality, in acting directly, and in not submitting to the circuitous and hypocritical modes of behavior that are expected of inferiors? In defense of her employer, it may be said that he felt a personal sense of nobility in hiring her against the advice of others who worried about allowing a woman to enter the managerial level. He then looked upon himself as her benefactor and expected her gratitude and loyalty, if not obeisance. Instead he got the opposite and had to suffer the humiliation of the attacks from her and the smiles of his confreres. These, however, are the foibles of the *transition,* the period when both sides are unsure that what they are doing is right. They then are apt to overreact, make fools of themselves, and swear "never again."

Another type, equally insecure, is the woman who must exaggerate her femininity in the so-called masculine world. She wants to do a reasonably successful job, but runs from any accusation of being competitive with men. She dresses consciously in the "feminine" mode, usually on the sexy side. She takes every opportunity of appearing helpless and never relinquishes those aspects of etiquette traditionally due a woman. Unlike the woman described above, she overlooks inequities and tries to defer to men as much as possible. At critical points, she appeals to their strength and ultimately may proclaim that line of Americana, "But I'm only a woman!"

In line with this posture is her vulnerability to the reawakening of the adolescent "crush" syndrome—falling in love with some man she is working with who has given her aid or has promoted her cause in the office over the resistance of others. He then appears like her true knight in armor, performing the rescue mission she has always dreamt of. In this he eclipses her husband, who is usually in no position to promote her career in more than a passive way. Her enthrallment with her new benefactor may lead to phantasied or overt marital and sexual disloyalties which may wreck her household. In her anxieties about her new role, she reacts with imprudence and may destroy both her homelife and career.

An example of this hazard was the case of a thirty-six-year-old woman, mother of three, who decided to return to her field, experimental psychology, after fourteen years of marriage and professional inactivity. She felt that her children no longer needed as much care as formerly and that she could profitably pick up her career. She returned to work on a part-time basis with the general approval of her family. She was filled with enthusiasm and hope, in spite of the many years of being away from her field of endeavor. Being an affable and attractive person, she was well received in the laboratory. She was given extensive briefings by co-workers and was praised for her enthusiasm if not competence. She was a delight to have around because of her good nature. She expressed her gratitude frequently and asked that her shortcomings be tolerated until she could learn the required techniques. She came under the tutelage and supervision of a senior male psychologist who appeared especially attracted to her. He patiently introduced her to the new techniques, and they set up a research project. They became a research team, or partnership, as they preferred to call it. With him, she attained a degree of competency which led to having several scientific papers accepted and published. She began to become known in her field.

Her husband and children joined her in the pleasure of her accomplishments and continued to encourage her in her pursuits. Seemingly not loving her husband less, she had deep affection for her research partner, who had been largely responsible for her success. Her husband's benevolent attitude had afforded her the opportunity to achieve in her field, but it appeared that his role was eclipsed by the active help that the senior psychologist gave. In the course of two years at work, the friendship and teamwork of the two led to feelings of deep love for him. He, on the other hand, felt deep affection for her but never moved to indicate that he desired a relationship other than friendly professional.

But he was also attractive to others. His work had become highly thought of, and he was offered a chair at a leading university, which he accepted. On learning of this change, she, at first joyful over his good fortune, privately became despondent. Her life and personal success had been intimately tied to him and his presence. He had been her rescuer and was about to desert her. She had no confidence that she could function on her own or could cooperate with the others in the laboratory without his kindly intervention. Her despondency became overt; she could no longer tolerate her husband or her children; she felt now that she had been victimized but did not know her oppressor. In a depressed state, she attempted suicide but was saved by a thoroughly perplexed husband. No longer able to work or relate to her family, she asked to be hospitalized. Her adventure had brought ruin on herself and her loved ones. Who or what was at fault? The husband for being cooperative? She, for wanting to pursue her career? The psychologist for wanting to be a helpful friend? Let the reader decide. It was my personal impression that the fault belonged to no one of them, and yet a little to all. Unpreparedness, imprudence, and lack of perspective were the predominant shortcomings.

The suddenness of her success and the strangeness of the "downtown" environment clouded her judgment and threw her value system out of balance. Her freedom was a fresh new penny and she became penny-foolish to the distress of all. Yet this evident failure should not provide a moral to prove a "basic" weakness of femininity or naturalness of this or that role. Rather, it should point up the complexities and challenges of woman's struggle for intellectual survival. This woman suffered a "cultural shock"; hers was a problem of re-entry no less difficult than that which is encountered in space exploration.

A man usually handles this problem with more aplomb because he has tradition and experience to guide him. It is all new for women, and they often succumb to the onslaughts of a hostile environment as well as inner distortions. These failures, and they are frequent, become living ammunition for those who preach that such roles are unnatural for women; much is always made of the mess they make in any but their divinely directed life of domesticity. For the patient observer, these instances, far from proving feminine inferiority, or biological or divine determinism, point up inherent problems of *transition* which will eventually be resolved, as both sexes accommodate to new and more equitable modes of behavior.

Many women who sincerely possess strong convictions about the value of their professional work find that married life and the pursuit of traditional feminine expectations are quite impossible for them. Dr. Alice S. Rossi, at an assembly of women at Cambridge, Massachusetts, adroitly observed: "Hence women who enter the more demanding professions may remain unmarried, not simply because they are not chosen by men but because they find fewer men worth accepting, and because marriage is not an exclusive life goal. It is also the case that marriages among professional women are slightly less apt to 'succeed' in the conventional demographic sense of persistence."[14]

Those who find solutions to problems of all women through work and competition in the "outside" world are highly unrealistic. There are basic psychological obstacles today that make this step most difficult, if not impossible, for an overwhelming number of women. First of all, there must be some tradition or example in her own family—a tradition that stamps approval on such activity for a woman. A mother or an aunt who has successfully achieved business or professional goals can reassure a woman that similar goals for her are "morally" right. In this, as in many other facets of living, it is difficult to be a pioneer, proceeding into the unknown and mysterious without some familial ideal. She must have an example of success within her own kinship orbit, showing that a woman can achieve without being considered mannish, or apish.

If a girl in her development has no other than the image of a woman in the domestic role, this image will be internalized and become her principal knowledge of what a woman is and does. It forms the basis of her morality, and behaving differently sets up a moral conflict. In spite of later worldly education, the earliest lessons come from all-powerful, life-giving and sustaining giants—parents—and they stick. This learning is, then, the education of how to please, how to be loved, how to survive. These earliest lessons from kin take priority and can be overcome only by vigorous self-purging efforts. The little girl who sees her own mother and aunts and grandmothers invested completely in household matters and disdainful of women who are active in the world will feel that any but the attitudes and roles of her female relatives are unnatural and immoral. She is getting her definition of femininity, and will thereafter "know" what a woman should properly do. Contrary to the expectations and demands of reformers, human growth is never acrogenic.

Even though it is very high-sounding and presently popular to claim that the chief goal of living is to be or become "a person," very few individuals have the strength to overlook or transcend their sexual identities. No woman will treasure any fame or glory she may achieve at the price of being called "unfeminine." This below-the-belt blow sends most women into despair. Therefore, we see that the doubt cast on sexual identity is another great deterrent to worldliness.

The problem of sexual identity, never absent in everyday living, may become particularly acute and distressing because of personal developmental experiences. One woman in her childhood had the misfortune of losing her mother through an acute illness. She, along with three brothers, was thereafter raised by her father and transient housekeepers. There was no woman with whom she could identify. She was exposed to a masculine world and for a while enjoyed being "one of the boys." In her late adolescence, however, she became acutely conscious of her different attitudes and modes of behavior. Now the youths shunned her even as they had played with her earlier in her life. She wasn't feminine! However, she would do something about it. In college she asked for help from her roommate about how to dress, how to use cosmetics, how to behave on dates. Yet it all came to her with great effort and unnaturalness. She did begin to date but continued to have grave doubts about what she really felt and who she really was. In her conscious effort to be feminine, she rushed into marriage, forfeiting her educational goals. She married a man with two children by a previous marriage. This, she felt, would keep her feminine and motherly. She became a good mother, endured financial hardships that plagued her husband, and was generally successful except for recurrent periods of mental depression. She felt, however, that she would have to stick it out to prove that she was feminine after all. She raised "his" children and had "two of her own."

In later life, when her children were grown, she resumed her education. She did very well in her studies and was faced with the issue of working at her interest. She now had severe misgivings about going out into the world, even though both her home situation and outside opportunities were conducive to her doing so. She was faced with her old dilemma of identity. Was she now to risk the emergence of her old "masculine" ways if she were to work and compete with men? She had spent years proving that she was feminine and now was on the threshold of placing her "acquisition" in jeopardy. At this point in life, on the threshold of achieving worldly goals, she began to have obsessive thoughts that her body was changing, turning into a man. If she were to work, it would mean to her that this was what she had wanted all along—that her motherhood was a sham, that she was really one of her brothers all along. She was beset not only by the external problems of a middle-aged woman seeking a place in the world, but also by the internal issue of identity that was a recurrent source of anxiety for her. As it turned out, she could not risk the doubts of her femininity that working might bring, and she relinquished her ambitions.

As if serving the expiatory needs of a male-dominant society, physicians are now telling American women that the distress of their lonely and alienated middle years is due mainly to an internal hormonal imbalance to which all women are allegedly heir—no less than 85 per cent of them—the other 15 per cent miraculously escaping by dint of a fortuitous and still unknown biological factor. Furthermore, the women have been told that both the imbalance and resultant distress are readily cured by proper medication. Although the cause and the cure are subject to question, the proportions of women's agony are here acknowledged and documented. We cannot fully trust the gynecologist's eye view of the world in these matters and must ponder about forces other than internal biological ones that may be consequential in the destiny of American women. There may indeed be an imbalance—one that the physicians care not to see, for it might entail healing themselves, not their patients.[31]

Whether or not psychoanalysis, used in a doctrinaire fashion, has also contributed to modern woman's dilemma, as Betty Friedan suggests, is an interesting issue.[37] The argument is that psychoanalysis, by stressing the importance of motherhood and the early infant-mother relationship, has kept woman in the home for fear of imparting mortal damage to her offspring. Allusion has also been made to psychoanalysts' loosely used male and female character classifications, and their purported jubilance when an analysand marries, a woman's acceptance of her "feminine" role, etc. Psychoanalysts are indeed responsive to conventional expectations (although less so than most).

The psychoanalyst in theory does not tamper with the ego ideal of the analysand. This is strictly his or her business. Admission for therapy requires that the ego ideal be reasonable, be within the frame of reality. However, the analyst never seeks to interfere with—much less destroy—the convictions and aspirations of the fellow human being before him. It is instead the analyst's job to help an individual pursue his goals more effectively. Whether these goals are "masculine" or "feminine," as convention sees them, should not concern either analyst or analysand.

The success or failure of therapy is based mainly on whether an individual is able to reaffirm and act effectively on those inner truths which he deems most valuable and important to himself. The issue in analysis is whether the analysand can free himself of the doubts and ambivalences wrought of experiences throughout his life. If a woman wants to become an atomic physicist like her father, the analyst does not seek to change her mind. Nor is the analyst apt to extol the virtues of marriage and motherhood to her, as some critics have intimated. He is more likely to hear her aspirations with the attitude of one who would fiercely resent any tampering with his own.

We have seen that the ego ideal of the male is generally a confluence of breadwinner, husband, parent, and achiever, and that these are more or less compatible. On the other hand, for the female the ego ideal as achiever may sharply clash with ideals connected with her womanhood. She cannot easily be a "good" wife, mother, and homemaker and at the same time aspire to "soul-satisfying" goals. There is set up for this more complex woman a conflict of goals or ego ideals which she somehow must integrate. Today it is past saying that women ought to be brought up or educated with only the one ego ideal, that for which she was biologically built. Her task is most difficult because she is made to feel guilty if her other aspirations impinge on her role as a mother. Therefore she needs help not only from an exceptional mate who genuinely understands her struggle and provides a proper milieu and opportunity for her fulfillment, but from society, which needs a reorientation on the male-female question similar to the one it is attempting in the racial issue. It is not a question of educating women; they take to that themselves and usually out-perform the men here. They must be given full opportunity for the expression and use of their skills without discrimination and condemnation. The idea of masculine professions and female jobs should be done away with. All of these should be done by qualified people without regard to sex. In this there might have to be legal protection—stronger laws and a bit of militancy on the part of those who are oppressed. Change of attitude would be nice, but unfortunately, as the Negroes have learned, this is unlikely. Human nature being what it is, a group does not relinquish its power unless forced to. Contrary to the euphuisms of some "realistic" politicians, morality generally has to be legislated.

If a woman is allowed to accomplish the more difficult task, her shame about loss of identity will be lessened, and she will be more apt to accept her children as developing human beings rather than despising them as burdens, or clinging to them as toys or as parts of her own body. If ever there is a schizophrenogenic mother, it is the one whose aimlessness causes her to cling to her children with the desperation of a drowning person. The child is never allowed to test reality on his own, never learns his own boundaries, often fails to distinguish between the animate and inanimate. He treats the world as a "thing," just as he has been treated by a mother who has no thing. A mother who has something is apt to behave quite differently. Although it is a vast oversimplification to attribute mental illness to one cause, we are becoming aware of social forces that filter down to the family and mother-child unit. The effects of a male-dominant society on "mothering" cannot be overlooked as potentially and actually disintegrative. Justice and equality for women may pay the dividend of more stable male offspring and females with a more hopeful model to emulate.

Men have never wanted to compete with women, whether on a tennis court or in a court of law.[38] The prospect of being bested is altogether beyond toleration. Misogyny throughout history is well documented. The historical phenomenon of the witch and witchcraft, perhaps the all-time low point in man's intellection, bears evidence of the hatred and depreciation that the male was capable of toward woman whom he purportedly loved and loved to protect. He simply placed the blame and burden for his impotency on her. If she couldn't be cajoled into returning his powers to him, then she had to burn. This was all backed to the hilt by the judgment and morality of the church hierarchy, which had no women in it. The irony of this blackness is that to this very day the word witch is used to characterize a bad female; there is no word at all for bullies whose delusioned creations they were. Some very serious psychiatric historians have come up with a new phantasy, diagnosing these women as mentally ill. In their scientism and misogyny they seem to overlook the fact that witches were pure delusions in the minds of men. If mental illness was involved (and if it was then we must indict all of humanity for periods of hundreds of years including the writers of the Bible, where witches are floridly described), it was the illness of those harboring the delusions, rather than the victims of this projection.

If all this was in the past and over with, if it was just an object lesson in foibles of which man is capable, then we should content ourselves with being happy historians and leave it at that. But just as McCarthyism did not die because it was roundly condemned, the fear and daemonization of women is not alien to contemporary mentation. In the dark years of each man in the desperation of facing his inadequacies, whether moral, political, ethical, economic, social, or sexual impotence, he can even today find it within himself to place the blame on his wife. This is not to say that women are incapable of bitchery, and they have done their share of harm in the subtle and circuitous ways open to them. They too share the heritage with their sexual counterpart of aggression, demonolatry, and destructiveness. Yet the sexual imbalance, blatantly evident today, is the responsibility of the power structure which prefers to maintain it that way. Power corrupts, we are told, and it also perpetuates itself. A great deal of the ignoble in women can be viewed as an excretion caused by the pressures directed against them. Much of what has been decried as malignant and irrational and "feminine" can be explained as resultant distortions. She gossips because she is excluded from meaningful communication; she chatters because she is deprived of a voice; she is hysterical because she is not taken seriously; she is indecisive because she is left out of any decisions of importance; she is a spendthrift because she can't earn much; and she is petty because her life has no aim. Would there be chaos if women were allowed equality?

Marya Mannes adroitly observed: "Most men of our society, although they claimed to be interested in women are not interested in Woman. What concerns them is not what a woman is but what she is to *them*. Their interest even their affection is still relative rather than absolute."[15]

To achieve sexual balance in quotations, the following is offered. Jules Feiffer, who can be listened to with great advantage on most social issues, under the rubric "Men Really Don't Like Women," wrote in a popular magazine: "The American woman is a victim. She is unique, as far as victims go, in that she has been trained to be ill at ease admitting it. Her trouble is that she is doing comparatively well as a victim—making a buck, running a family: and then, too, there are so many more *imposing* victims around."[21]

Great men are expected to transcend throughout their lives all the banalities of their environment. In his own green years, Freud spoke with the same male condescension and euphuistic drivel that would be expected of *Untermenschen*. In a letter to his fiancée, Martha Bernays, answering an inquiry of hers about the startling new expositions on the feminine problem by John Stuart Mill, Freud wrote: "It seems a completely unrealistic notion to send women into the struggle for existence in the same way as men. Am I to think of my delicate, sweet girl as a competitor? After all, the encounter could only end by my telling her, as I did seventeen months ago, that I love her, and that I will make every effort to get her out of the competitive role into the quiet, undisturbed activity of my home. It is possible that different education could suppress all woman's delicate qualities which are so much in need of protection and yet so powerful with the result that they could earn their living like men. It is also possible that in this case it would not be justifiable to deplore the disappearance of the most lovely thing the world has to offer us: our ideal of womanhood. But I believe that all reforming activity, legislation and education, will founder on the fact that long before the age at which a profession can be established in our society, nature will have appreciated woman by her beauty, charm, and goodness, to do something else. . . . The position of woman cannot be other than what it is: to be an adored sweetheart in youth, and a beloved wife in maturity."[17]

Here Freud reveals the typical attitude of his day toward women, that they should be there for the needs of man.[39] They have to be meek, docile, weak, dependent, not because these qualities are good for them, or necessarily promote their own feelings of worth and identity, but because all of these serve "our ideal of womanhood." This is the rhetoric of the Southern racists in our own times who cannot give education and suffrage to Negroes because it will take away their carefree, irresponsible nature and possibly their love of folk singing, and shatter the social-comforting ideal of white supremacy.

In fairness to Freud, with the wisdom that, hopefully, comes with maturity and being witness to the circumstances that women, including his own beloved daughter Anna (and none of his sons), contributed to the new science of psychoanalysis disproportionately to their number, he wrote quite differently in later scientific papers.

In 1932, Freud recanted and advised against equating any particular psychological trait or characteristic with either masculinity or femininity, even such opposites as activity and passivity, which had been solidly ensconced in all psychoanalysis as male "nature" and female "nature" respectively. He wrote, speaking of the bisexual problem: "In recent times we have begun to learn a little about this, thanks to the circumstances that several of our excellent women colleagues in analysis have begun to work at the question. The discussion of this has gained special attractiveness for the distinction between the sexes. For the ladies, whenever some comparison seemed to turn out unfavorable to their sex, were able to utter a suspicion that we, the male analysts, had been unable to overcome certain deeply rooted prejudices against what was feminine, and that this was being paid for in the partiality of our researches."[7] And in the last paragraph of this chapter, Freud admits that psychoanalysis has occupied itself mainly with the woman in so far as her nature is determined by her sexual function. Then, in a concession that may become an all-time paradigm for niggardliness, he wrote: "It is true that that influence (sexual function) extends very far; but we do not overlook the fact that an individual woman may be a human being in other respects as well." Finally Freud succumbed to the wisdom of the inadequacy of his own appraisal, and perhaps the invincibility of his own prejudices, and advised: "If you want to know more about femininity, enquire from your own experiences of life, or turn to the poets, or wait until science can give you deeper and more coherent information."

Psychoanalysis continues to drag its feet in understanding the plight of women. Even our "liberal" psychoanalysts have an inaccurate understanding of how it really is. One of these, Marmor, writes:

"One need not assume that motherhood and a fulfilling life in the outside world are incompatible, any more than fatherhood and such a life. In contrast to men, however, who are *expected* to combine these two aspects of life, women have alternatives now; they may or may not choose to combine them, and the choice is theirs."*

There is no truth in what Marmor says. When he says men are *expected* to be out in the world and a father, he makes this sound like some imposed hardship like saying Nixon is expected to be Commander-in-Chief of all the armed forces as well as Chief Executive of all the people—poor fellow has no alternatives! Furthermore, Marmor's statement that women can *now* do both or have a choice sounds like a liberal telling about the great advances of the Negro in America! Has Marmor seen statistics of women in academe, the professions, in business? Apparently not. Even a cursory investigation would show that their number in public life are actually decreasing. The sad reality is that women do not have a choice—they are *given* a choice but a choice so weighed with inequities that they stay home. Today women are allowed into the world only if they do not take what they do *seriously*. That is, in no, even trifling, way jeopardize their marriage and/or their image as a wife or mother. She is tolerated as a working person only if she is ambitiousless and steers clear of decision-making areas. After all, who likes a woman who is not "feminine"?

The job by the male on the woman has been so well done, using every important social institution—religions, schools, law, medicine, psychology—in his own behalf, that he has been successful in extinguishing even the *wish* of women to have equality with the male in those matters which stamp the value of a human being. She has bought the bill of goods about the determining effects of her biological nature. "Anatomy is destiny; anatomy is destiny," they repeat until there is no room for the examination of any other dimension. Thankfully, the female is different,

* *The Marriage Relationship, Psychoanalytic Perspectives*, Edited by Salo Rosenbaum and Ian Alger, Basic Books, New York, 1968. Judd Marmor, "Changing Patterns of Femininity: Psychoanalytic Implications," Chapter 3, pp. 31-44.

but because she is different, she should not be hated and despised and deprived of those opportunities for self-development and accretion which men have always considered their God-given and "natural" rights. Men have not shown proper respect for differences—sexual, academic, racial, or religious.

Man's fear of differences has made him reluctant to extend opportunity to those who are different. In the unconscious of men as found in psychoanalysis, there is a deep-seated fear and loathing of women. All the songs of love do not dispel this underlying contempt for those "unfortunates" with gaping wounds where a penis ought to be. It is the loathing of differences that encourages and maintains the male homosexual culture from which females are regularly excluded. And the culture embraces infinitely greater numbers than the handful of so-called "queers" who parody society in general by their flagrant behavior. Men's preference for their own is seen in any gathering and in most living rooms where people may come together for sociability and conversation. It is not only the Church or the Army, as Freud alleged, that are homosexual institutions, but also big business, science, law, and almost everything else of importance. Men just are not comfortable with women unless some degree of flirtation is involved. The issue of intellection and even passion between the sexes is largely dismissed. It is an old story. Kenneth Rexroth writes: "To judge by primitive song, legend and epic, romantic love has commonly existed between members of the same sex, and seldom in the institutionalized relations between men and women until those institutions pass through formalization to etherialization, as in the court circle of *The Tale of Genji*."[22]

In a treatise, surprisingly late in coming for something so obvious, sociologist Tiger confirms the strong affinity (and bonding) men have for one another in both public and private endeavors.* No argument against this verity.

* Tiger, L. *Men in Groups,* Random House, New York, 1969.

However, Tiger reaches the conclusion that this is quite salutary and attributes civilization's major advances to it. For those (women) automatically excluded from the most creative and exciting aspects of their community and must experience these vicariously, if at all, such successes might seem pyrrhic, just as black people might not be particularly enthralled by white America's progress. There are many who justify white racism because "our way of life" has achieved so much. But for whom? Some might consider Tiger's conclusions as derived more from self-serving, male chauvinism than from "science."

Our present society, based on male dominance as it is, most reluctantly accepts women for positions of authority and/or possible leadership. Women are different, but most of their purported differences are cultivated in the minds of men in order to justify oppressing them. Then, men have interpreted women's aimlessness, which results from this oppression, as intrinsic and natural to them. Women, then, must be kept down because they are not trustworthy. They must then be loved and protected because they are too stupid to fend for themselves. Unfortunately, we cannot turn to most women for statements confirming this oppression, for, as indicated above, for the most part women have fully succumbed to the propaganda against themselves. Yet they do not know why they are so bored, restless, hysterical, hypochondriacal, and too often mentally stunted.

However, some women have made direct and forthright statements. The impotent rage of Shakespeare's Beatrice in being unable to act in the injustice done to Hero is shown in the following:

"Beatrice: 'Is a' not approved in the height a villain, that hath slandered, scorned, dishonoured my kinswoman? O that I were a man! what, bear her in hand, until they come to take hands, and then with public accusation uncovered slander, unmitigated rancour? O God that I were a man! I would eat his heart in the market place.'"

Later she laments the poor job that the male is doing

with his power. Lacking the power herself, grieving over the loss or injustice is all that is left to her. She states: "Princes and Counties! surely a princely testimony, a goodly Count, Count Comfect, a sweet gallant surely, O that I were a man for his sake! But manhood is melted into curtsies, valour into compliment, and men are only turn'd into tongue, and trim ones too: he is now as valiant as Hercules, that only tells a lie, and swears it: I cannot be a man with wishing, therefore I will die a woman with grieving."[27]

The corroding effects of the unfair use of power at each level of existence from interpersonal to international, is the theme of a recent book by R. V. Sampson. We know of the corrupting as well as self-blinding effects of power and its disabling effects on the person in subjection. We have recognized these in international and political spheres but have been reluctant to see them in the structure of family life. Sampson's words are most instructive: "To the extent that the forces of power prevail over the forces of love, domination and subjection characterize human relations. The former is good and leads to human well-being; the latter is bad and leads to human suffering and strife. The struggle between these dialectical forces is always the same. No one may contract out of it, however much he may wish to do so. For of necessity, everyone at all times and in all positions stands on a relation with other men which will be predominantly of one category or the other. In this sense, what happens in the world, what happens in history, inevitably reflects the contribution, active or passive, of everybody who participates in the vast web of human interrelations. There are not diverse planes of reality to be judged by different stands. There are no separate, insulated planes of the cloister and the Chancellory Office. Jesus Christ and Adolf Hitler belong together to the common plane of our single human experience. It is merely that they represent extreme polarized positions within our common moral spectrum."[24]

It may be argued that the quest for equality is Utopian and that, as Freud purportedly said, there must be a leader in every social unit. If this is indeed so, that marriage can be based on no other than a dominance-submission model, then let us at least face the reality to which our sisters, wives, and daughters are to be subjected instead of invoking the euphemisms of love and devotion to cover up what is nothing else but servility. Then, if servility is all that is wanted or can be hoped for, so be it. At least women will not have to bear the burden of guilt when, as is happening in ever increasing instances, they rebel against their assigned role of inferiority and subjugation. Furthermore, if their basically unjust treatment is recognized, men will no longer be puzzled and dismayed by the atrophy of mind and emotions that befalls their daughters and wives that inferior status inevitably brings. Men will then be able to understand the zombie-type apathy of those who have totally submitted and the Medea-like frenzy of those women who have nothing remaining but intransigent desires for revenge.

Love conquers all, we are told. Yet if it does, there must be concern for protecting the vanquished. Until now, the defeated party in love and marriage has been the woman. Therefore, if love is to have the transcendent meaning we purportedly hope for, Buber's "I and Thou" must prevail. Can we reach the level of human relations wherein loving the other includes concern for her well-being apart from the pleasure and services she can provide? Let us not ignore "Love's Body" but, hopefully, therein can also be tolerated an intact soul.[40]

NOTES

1. Madeline Chapsal, "Feminine Plural, Present Tense," *New York Times Book Review*, Sec. 7, March 12, 1967, p. 5.

2. Harold Clurman, "Our Neglected Women," *The World Journal Tribune Magazine*, New York: March 12, 1967, p. 25.

3. Margaret Brackenbury Crook, *Women and Religion* (Boston: Beacon Press, 1964).

4. Honoré de Balzac, "The Old Maid," *Great French Short Novels*, ed. F. W. Dupee (New York: Dial Press, 1952).

5. Simone de Beauvoir, *The Ethics of Ambiguity* (New York: Citadel Press, 1962), p. 138.

6. Simone de Beauvoir, *The Second Sex* (New York: Bantam Books, published by arrangements with Alfred A. Knopf, Inc., Aug. 1961); Betty Friedan, *The Feminine Mystique* (New York: Dell Publishing Co., Inc., 1963); Edith de Rham, *The Love Fraud* (New York: Potter, 1964), p. 319; Judith Heiman, *The Young Marrieds* (New York: Simon and Schuster, 1961); Ann Helming, *A Woman's Place* (New York: Coward-McCann, Inc., 1962).

7. Sigmund Freud, *New Introductory Lectures on Psychoanalysis* (New York: Norton & Co., 1932), p. 116.

8. Sigmund Freud, *New Introductory Lectures on Psychoanalysis* (New York: Norton & Co., 1933), p. 172.

9. Sigmund Freud, "Some Psychological Consequences of the Anatomical Distinction Between the Sexes," *International Journal of Psychoanalysis*, 8 (April 1927), p. 133.

10. Robert Graves and Raphael Patai, "Hebrew Myths," *The Book of Genesis* (London: Cassell, 1964).

11. Phyllis Greenacre, "Woman as Artist," *Psychoanalytic Quarterly*, 29 (1960), pp. 208-27.

12. Andrew Hacker, "How You Got Your Jewish Son-in-Law," *The World Journal Tribune Magazine* (New York, March 26, 1967), p. 4.

13. Richard Heffner, "An Interview with Eric Fromm," *McCall's*, Oct. 1965, p. 216.

14. John Lear, "Will Science Change Marriage?", *Saturday Review*, Dec. 5, 1964.

15. Marya Mannes, "What Every Male Should Know," *Sunday Herald Tribune Book Week*, Feb. 14, 1965, p. 2.

16. Phyllis McGinley, *Sixpence in Her Shoe* (New York: Macmillan, 1964).

17. John Stuart Mill, *Letters of Sigmund Freud*, selected and ed. Ernst J. Freud (New York: Basic Books, 1960), p. 76.

18. John Stuart Mill, "The Subjection of Women," *Three Essays* (London: Oxford University Press, 1912), p. 427 and p. 522.

19. *New York Times*, Jan. 25, 1965.

20. *New York Times*, Sept. 27, 1964.

21. Jules Feiffer, "Men Really Don't Like Women," *Look Magazine*, Jan. 11, 1966, p. 60.

21a. Otto Rank, *Beyond Psychology* (New York: Dover Publications, 1941), p. 285.

22. Kenneth Rexroth, "Sappho—Poet and Legend," *Saturday Review*, Nov. 27, 1965, p. 27.

23. R. V. Sampson, *The Psychology of Power* (New York: Pantheon Books, 1966), p. 47.

24. R. V. Sampson, *The Psychology of Power* (New York: Pantheon Books, 1966), p. 2.

25. William Shakespeare, *As You Like It*, ed. G. B. Harrison (New York: The Shakespeare Recording Society, Inc., 1963), pp. 50-51.

26. William Shakespeare, *Cymbeline*, ed. G. B. Harrison (New York: The Shakespeare Recording Society, Inc., 1963), p. 58.

27. William Shakespeare, *Much Ado About Nothing*, ed. G. B. Harrison (New York: The Shakespeare Recording Society, Inc., 1963), pp. 64-65.

28. Clara Thompson, "Penis Envy in Women," *Psychiatry*, 6 (May 1943), p. 123.

29. Clara Thompson, "The Role of Women in this Culture," *Psychiatry*, 4 (1941), pp. 1-8.

30. Lionel Trilling, *Beyond Culture* (New York: The Viking Press, 1955), p. 38.

31. Robert A. Wilson, "A Key to Staying Young," *Look Magazine*, Jan. 11, 1966, p. 66.

32. Faith A. Seidenberg, *The Wave of the Future — NOW*, in The Cornell Law Forum, vol. 21:2:1969; also by the same author, *The Submissive Majority*: Modern Trends in the Law concerning Women's Rights, Cornell Law Review, vol. 55:262: 1970.

33. That Cynthia Wedel was elected president of the National Council of Churches in December, 1969, is certainly an indication of a greater consciousness that women will have a voice at the decision making level. Hopefully, this will lead to equality of participation for women as part of the clergy. In this regard, Mrs. Betty Schiess of Syracuse, New York, is now completing her training at the Rochester Center For Theological Studies with the prospect of becoming the first woman to be ordained as priest in the Episcopal Church.

34. There is, however, ample evidence that mainstream psychoanalysis continues to view women as an inferior breed. Here are the written words of an eminent analyst, Dr. Judith S. Kestenberg: "Feminine integration is completed when woman learns to adjust to her role as wife and mother. In this she can succeed only if she is teachable and can accept her husband and children as organizers of her femininity" (Page 485). Again, she explains: "Women who are teachable, but unsuccessful in meeting and attracting men able to teach and assume

domination (sic) in a relationship, frequently adapt to habits, neurotic attitudes, and unconscious fantasies of the men they do find." (Page 479, in the *Journal of the American Psychoanalytic Assoc.*, July, 1968.) From what Dr. Kestenberg says, not only is a woman to be dominated, she will be made neurotic if she is not! I can think of no other instance in human relationships or social or political life, outside of brutal totalitarian societies, where domination becomes an imperative for "health" —a proud goal to be sought after, a *sine qua non* for the good life, a described condition for survival. Dr. Kestenberg herself leads an active professional life and is, from all reports, an excellent teacher of men and women in psychiatry and psychoanalysis.

35. The much heralded American instinct for utilitarianism apparently does not extend to women. O'Neill writes: "Whether they know it or not, American women are an exploited sector of the work force; they contribute in measurable terms far less to society than their education warrants: and their objective position is generally inferior to that of women in other developed countries." (O'Neill, Wm. L., *Everyone Was Brave, The Rise and Fall of Feminism in America*, Chicago, Quadrangle Books, 1969, p. 347.)

36. Stoller has made a contribution in reminding us of the distinction between *sex* and *gender*. Sex is, of course, a biological given, whereas gender is largely socially and historically determined. It follows then that someone on earth decided what is masculine and what, feminine. (Stoller, R. J., *Sex & Gender*, New York, Science House, 1968, part 1.)

37. One cannot deny that psychoanalysis has been no friend of feminists. O'Neill writes: "The jargon of psychoanalysis gave the old charge that feminists were 'unnatural' a more sophisticated appearance. Of course, it is also true. When society decrees that a woman's place is in the home, the woman who leaves it is by definition aberrant." (William J. O'Neill, in *Everyone Was Brave*, Chicago, Quadrangle Books, 1969, p. 290.)

38. Seidenberg, Faith A., *The Woman Lawyer*, in Case and Comment, vol. 74:30: May-June, 1969.

39. Freud's statement on the importance of *work* for a person has been widely quoted by social scientists. Freud wrote: "It is not possible within the limits of a short survey to discuss adequately the significance of work for the economics of the libido. No other technique for the conduct of life attaches the individual so firmly to reality as laying emphasis on work; for his work at least gives him a secure place in a portion of reality, in the human community. The possibility it offers of displacing a large amount of libidinal components, whether narcissistic,

aggressive or even erotic, on to professional work and on to the human relations connected with it lends it a value by no means second to what it enjoys as something indispensable to the preservation and justification of existence in society." (Freud, S., *Civilization and its Discontents,* New York, W. W. Norton, 1962, p. 27.) Does this apply to women as well? How is the housewife to "test reality in the human community?" And unto whom is she to displace *libidinal components?* Freud's statement adroitly defines the role of work (professional, he says) in keeping one's identity, integrity, yes, sanity. It is a valid and salutary prescription, if not an imperative, for both sexes.

40. The inequalities in what is advertised as the ecstasy of love lead not only to the degradation of the victim but to the inevitable corruption of character of the dominant male who gains ascendency and power through "inheritance" and custom rather than earned worthiness. This corruption erodes morality in the same manner that white racism has corrupted Caucasians. John Stuart Mill long ago told us of this; it is as relevant today as then: "All the selfish propensities, the self-worship, the unjust self-preference, which exists among mankind, have their source and root in, and derive their principal nourishment from, the present constitution of the relation between men and women. Think what it is to a boy, to grow up to manhood in the belief that without any merit or any exertion of his own, though he may be the most frivolous and empty or the most ignorant and stolid of mankind, by the mere fact of being born a male he is by right the superior of all and every one of an entire half of the human race: including probably some whose real superiority to himself he has daily or hourly occasion to feel; but even if in his whole conduct he habitually follows a woman's guidance, still, if he is a fool, she thinks that of course she is not, and cannot be, equal in ability and judgment to himself; and if he is not a fool, he knows that, notwithstanding her superiority, he is entitled to command and she is bound to obey. What must be the effect on his character, of this lesson?" (18)

In order to "love" as he professes, the man must overcome his historical privilege of dominance, abhorring the role of master as he would that of the slave. To do this, he must transcend the dictates of custom as well as the seeming compliance of the subjected. Marriage should encourage bonds but not bondage in which the identity of one is all but submerged. (Even her name goes—an anonymity that sadly presages her destiny.)

CHAPTER VII

BONDS AND BODY

> After all, what is the mean which marriage expresses
> between the pneumatic and the psycho-somatic?
>
> Sóren Kierkegaard

Psychosomatic

When words cannot be used between people, a type of
charade is substituted for conventional language which
may involve not only gestures and movements but also the
use and cooperation of the tissues and systems of the body.
This phenomenon is in the province of psychosomatic medicine, that catchall for poorly understood occurrences.
There may be pseudocyesis—the make-believe pregnancy
that "befell" Honey in Albee's *Who's Afraid of Virginia
Woolf?* (to be discussed in Chapter X). Honey typifies
the woman with classical hysteria—the actress par excellence who can play the role so well that she pressed her
own cells into the service of the performance. This type of
control and direction are part of a body language that has
the purpose of both an appeal for help and a desire to
keep one's problem obscure. The ultimate hope is that
some parental wisdom will understand the distress and give
the relief without the ambiguities and dangers of verbal
demands. Hysteria was, albeit wrongly, thought to be a

female disease, perhaps because it was so prevalent in women. However, its use by women can perhaps be understood because, although they are purportedly great talkers and chatterboxes, they have had very little *voice* in matters of importance.

The following two cases illustrate phenomena of direct yet uncanny body participation in mental conflicts having to do with the vagaries of relationships in marriage.

One type of hyperhidrosis (excessive sweating) has been called mental or emotional by dermatologists and neurologists. They have noted that a profuse, cold, clammy sweating occurs on the palms and soles, or in the axillae (armpits), during mentally stressful activities. It is always bilateral and usually unrelated to external temperature changes or internal diseases. Often the palms and feet are involved together, but the condition can be confined to one or the other. The sweating in the axillae appears to be independent of that in other areas.

Kuno noted that thermal sweating appears universally over the general body surface, whereas "mental" sweating appears over the palms, soles, and axillae.[1] He postulated that moistening the surface of the palm would increase the friction between it and objects with which it comes in contact. Consequently every sort of muscular work would be facilitated not only for this physical reason, but also because the sense of touch becomes more acute when friction increases. Therefore, palmar sweating would provide a better adhesive surface for grasping and doing work. On the other hand, axillary sweating was thought to be for sexual purposes.

Sulzberger and Herrmann indicated their agreement with Kuno when they observed that "practically any activity, e.g., the lifting of an object, attentive listening, conversation, etc., is, in certain persons, sufficient to elicit profuse sweating in the areas of pre-dilection." They also noted the severe vocational and social handicap that is caused.[2]

Since sweating has always been known as a sign of

anxiety, it is surprising that this condition has received so little attention in the psychiatric literature. Hyperhidrosis was a common condition among the anxiety cases of World War II. "Sweating it out" is an overworked phrase today. The material following may be of some value to readers in understanding certain mind-body occurrences. It demonstrates the unique way prior ties and linkages affect adaptations. The concept of early ties and connections has been alluded to in Chapter I.

A coy, attractive woman of twenty-seven came for treatment because of marital difficulties. Married for two years, she felt no love for her husband and wanted to leave him. She could give no tangible reasons for her disenchantment. She only knew that the relationship could not continue. Both of them were German nationals, recent emigrants from West Germany. He had lived here for a short while before this and had met her on a business trip to his native land. They had known each other several years before. She had no enthusiasm about marrying him and coming to this country, but her mother finally convinced her that this would be a good opportunity for happiness and security. Always prone to be submissive and obedient to her mother, she consented to the marriage.

After arriving in this country, she found employment in a job commensurate with her education and also made a fair social adjustment. However, much as she tried, her marriage relationship progressively deteriorated. In the beginning she tried to be amiable, but found that intimacies had become completely repulsive to her. Her husband was a good provider and seemed to have the ingredients for a good husband, but these did not endear him to her.

Her husband and several close friends who were familiar with the situation suggested that she might seek psychiatric help. She herself saw no reason for this move but felt obliged to try. It was her feeling that the only solution to her problem was terminating the marriage. In the course of history-taking, she indicated that she had a lifelong "physical" problem—that of excessive sweating of her hands, but of no other part of her body. She had had this affliction since the age of eight, and it had become progressively worse. There was no familial history of this condition. She described her hands as literally "dripping like a faucet" on certain occasions. Nothing she could do ever gave relief, although the sweating did diminish for certain periods of time.

She often wore white-cotton gloves, which would become soaked. She recalled that at the age of eight, she took piano lessons. Whenever she practiced, the keys would become so wet as to make impossible further attempts at playing. As she grew older, she became aware that anticipation of any activity involving the hands would immediately cause them to become wet. Shaking hands in particular became a nightmare for her. Eating in public was difficult, for the silverware and tablecloth near her would become wet. This condition did not involve the feet or axillae.

Her father was a well-educated, taciturn person, the superintendent of a coal mine in the Ruhr. Absorbed in his work, he left the household and care of the children strictly to his wife. For example, after perfunctory greetings in the evening, he would retire to his library and become occupied in his reading and business work. She recalled that she would accompany her father each Christmas to the mining area, where he would shake hands with each miner and wish him a Merry Christmas. Witnessing the handshaking made her own hands wet. She recalled seeing the Russian prisoners brought to work in the mines during the war. She and her mother would take them bread. She was extremely close to her mother and antagonistic to her only sister, three years senior.

She had been told that as an infant she was a chronic headbanger. This activity ceased as she grew older, but she remained a "difficult sleeper." For example, her sister could not sleep in the same room with her, for she noisily thrashed about, turning her head abruptly from one side to the other. She still has this problem at night. She also has difficulty in falling asleep and in arising in the morning. At the age of twelve, she reverted to bedwetting. She felt that this was caused by nightly bombing attacks on their city by the Americans. Because of the bedwetting, she could not be evacuated with the other children to a country school. Therefore she remained through the war years with her parents. She claimed that the bedwetting ceased four years later, concomitant with the cessation of the bombing raids. The father died shortly after the war, and she remained with her mother. The sister teased her a great deal because of her bedwetting and other "childish" traits. During her adolescence she shied away from dates and parties, turning her back on youthful boy friends whom she had known since childhood. Instead, in her late teens, she became enamored of several older men. These were men in their fifties, married, all quite prominent in the field of music and the arts. She had sexual affairs with them, but also liked their fatherly attitude toward her. Boys her own age always seemed to be "ugly or boorish."

She grouped her husband with the younger men. Although she tolerated sexual relations with him, kissing was especially repugnant to her. Because of her coldness towards him, her husband accused her of being a Lesbian. She felt that this was not true because she had had strong feelings toward older men in the past. Disclaiming any gross nervousness or, for that matter, any problems, she had a phobia about dirt. She was very fastidious about personal cleanliness and expected the same in others. She was particularly disdainful of other girls in the office who did not correct sweating under their arms. Another fear that she recalled was of earthworms. She would not touch them and would become upset if she actually stepped on one. She avoided going to classes in biology when worms were studied; she said that they were cold and slimy. It was also "eerie" the way you could cut them in two and each end would continue to live.

During her early adolescence she was a shy person, closely attached to her mother. She attributed her shyness to her "hand problem," for it was the custom in Germany to shake hands before and after any social encounter. (Although far from being enchanted with the United States, she was happy to find that handshaking is not so common a practice here.)

Shortly after coming to this country, she received news of the death of her mother. This came as a severe and unexpected blow to her. Now she had no one of her own family except an indifferent, and often hostile, sister. This added fuel to her resentment towards her husband, for, in taking her to this country, he had deprived her of being with her mother during her last days.

She was employed at a nearby university as an assistant in the training program for air force personnel. Was she resentful of the country and air force which bombed her native city and brought terror at night? "No," she replied, "that is all in the past. I hold no grudge against anyone." One day she reported being at a graduation of the air force candidates. She stated that she suffered when she witnessed the Chancellor shaking hands with them. On watching his her own hands began to "drip like a leaky faucet." She was very happy that it was the Chancellor and not she who had to do the handshaking.

She had many cultural interests, especially classical music. Beethoven's Ninth Symphony was her favorite. Whereas good music was soothing to her and often lulled her to sleep, noises, especially sudden ones, were disturbing to her. The pop of a wine-bottle cork, the sound of an icicle falling, an unexpected cough, children shooting toy pistols in the streets, caused her hands to become wet immediately. It is important to note that she reported the effects of these disturbances as being directly on her hands. She did not indicate the presence of panic or fearfulness. She did not say that she was fearful of being injured or that she would lose control.

She looked upon treatment as another intrusion, a type of conspiracy to keep her in an untenable marriage. "Is a person crazy because she does not love her husband?" she asked. She disclaimed being nervous and felt that the sweating of her hands might be a physical condition. It became apparent that the prospect of a psychological exploratory treatment, with the concomitant relationship that had to be made with the therapist, was a grave threat to her. When it was indicated to her that therapy might prove beneficial to her excessive sweating, she replied that she had recently heard of a new operation which might be immediately corrective. In spite of obvious causes and reactions, she could not accept psychological treatment for herself. She did, however, participate to some degree.

Having heard somewhere that dreams might be helpful, she mentioned the following dream. "A little boy friend appeared that I knew when I was six or seven years old. We played together. The dream was quite vivid. I even recall the house. His sister was there too." To this dream she associated the following: "I don't know why I dreamed of him. I haven't seen him in ten years. We played together as children. I admired him at that age but when I was a teenager, I didn't like him—but he seemed to like me. Sometimes I dream of people I never think of."

The age that she saw herself in this dream was shortly before the onset of her hand symptoms. It was the therapist's hypothesis at the time that she was communicating an intensely stressful situation in her life which had undergone repression without adequate resolution. The playing with the boy and his sister being present might have indicated the oedipal conflict. There were also indications from her associations that during her adolescence, when fulfillment was possible, she had to turn her back on heterosexual feelings that would result in a close tie with an eligible male. Also, by identifying herself as "six or seven years of age" in the dream, she may have been indicating that this was the time of severe stress for her, a time of life when postoedipal phobic reactions are prominent. The onset of her symptoms was about at the age of eight. It can be hypothesized that the usual resolution did not occur, but in its stead there occurred faulty repression with symptom formation. From her history it became apparent that strong preoedipal forces operated to make a resolution at the higher level most difficult.

A second dream presaged her termination of treatment and gave further insight into the genesis of her symptoms. "I was on the street. I looked up and there five stories above was a man washing windows with a wet sponge. As I watched him, the strap by which he was attached to the building broke loose and the man was hurled to the ground below. I immediately went to him. He was a mass of blood but he was not as yet dead. He lifted his head and reached for me as if he had something to tell me, but he slumped back dead." For her this was a terribly sad dream. She was always sympathetic toward people who had to risk their lives in order to make a living. She recalled the miners who were killed and the tragic sight of their families. There was once a wounded flyer who fell from the skies and was killed. She herself could not see how window cleaners could trust the meager connections they had to the building while they worked. It made her happy that she was a woman and would not be exposed to such occupational hazards.

The dream was a signal that she was forced to break away from treatment, as she did several sessions later. Then she indicated that this type of treatment now seemed senseless for her under the circumstances. Her husband and the marriage were the sources of her immediate difficulties, and her money would be better spent on a divorce and possibly for fare back to Germany. However, in the above dream and the associations, one can detect an identification with the fallen workman who had something he wanted to say but could not get it out. Instead he slumped back in silence (death), a solution which the patient decided was best for her. In fact, she had effected a denial of any personal problems or conflicts of living, excepting perhaps a bad decision in her marriage. Indeed, she was even able to deny to herself that she was anxious!

Because contacts and attachments had come up so frequently in regard to her hand symptoms and in her general conversation, the symbol of the workman cleaning windows and being attached to the building was thought to be very significant.

During the interviews it was difficult to assess the day-to-day change in the sweating pattern. After the first few sessions, during which no interpretations were made, she reported a marked improvement. She recalled, however, that this diminution had occurred on previous occasions, i.e., during her first contacts with the older men in her life. As the treatment relationship progressed, with concomitant interpretive work, she became increasingly perturbed. She had envisaged a friendly, protective, erotically tinged union but now was faced with the prospect of work involving painful self-reflection and exposition of infantile needs. (Note the dream of the fallen window cleaner.)

Thereafter, she reported that her sweating was as bad as it ever was. She became visibly disturbed by noises in and around the consultation room, i.e., the ring of the telephone, doors banging, and street noises. They elicited the dripping-faucet type of sweating of her hands. She was distrustful of the linkage with the therapist, whom she now saw as an agent of a hostile, intrusive world. Certain cultural problems undoubtedly played a prominent role here, too.

Here is an individual who has effected an almost complete separation of ideational content from emotions and responds to indifferent stimuli. In addition, as noted above, she has no awareness of the presence of anxiety. There is, therefore, not only a repression of ideational content but also of a major component of affect. This accounts for a relatively "painless" existence. As a result her hand sweating appeared to her, and might to an observer also, as a casual autonomic response or, if not casual, then related to external stimuli which had nothing to do with intrapsychic forces. From her history we see early preoedipal difficulties, i.e., headbanging and sleep disturbances. Bed-wetting, which recurred at the age of twelve during the war years, indicated an ease of ego regression. Her choice of objects showed a propensity for parental figures rather than for individuals her own age with whom she would have to deal on a more equalitarian basis. Are we dealing with a vegetative neurosis?[3] In favor of this concept, we see a response unquestionably mediated through the autonomic nervous system. However, it is not a generalized reaction, but is largely confined to the hands. Is there a symbolic meaning to the sweating hands? Can this be conversion hysteria? In favor of this diagnosis is the repression of ideational content and the typical "belle indifference." We could give free rein to speculation about the affected hands and with further study it might be shown that they symbolize certain displacements, etc. One can readily see how the hand can be eroticized or connected with aggression.

There is an alternate explanation that embodies the "organic" aspect of the vegetative neurosis and at the same time encompasses psychological considerations. In addition, one could avoid the dubious concept of autonomic system regression. (Organ or system repression seems to be biological and "extramental," and therefore outside the frame of inquiry for the psychological worker.) This is found in the concept of linking or linkage as already discussed in the psychoanalytic literature by Bion, Ostow, and myself.[4] Briefly, linking is the concept relating to the ties that an individual may have to external and internal objects both past and present. These ties can be represented in oral, anal, or genital terms. The archetype for this would obviously be the umbilical connection, but no claim is made here that an actual memory of this attachment exists. The links, real and fancied, are those made during the individual's development. In later efforts in human relations, there are struggles to break away and also to become connected. Often there are feelings of love and a deep need for the object and also a desire to destroy and incorporate it. One sees a need to break the link from one object in order to become attached to a more favorable one. Also, an in-

dividual may face a conflict between linkages to internal
and external, as well as animate and inanimate, objects.
There can be conflict between linkages to the past and to
the present.

The patient under study here has shown a great deal of
difficulty in making and breaking connections. We may
look again to the second dream, which preceded her
breaking her connection with treatment. In this dream, she
described literally the cord which broke, causing a personal disaster. Her only constant tie was to her mother.
In her late adolescence she became fascinated with older
men, but these relationships were ephemeral, for they
were married and tied to others. In her marriage she was
intent on dissolving the bonds as quickly as possible. It is
of interest here that she abhorred kissing, an oral tie, more
than any other contact with her husband. Also, she had
an "eerie" feeling about the idea that both ends of an
earthworm could live after a disconnection. This woman's
linkage to an internal object—the mother—competed with,
and precluded, any attachment to external objects. This
conformed to the well-known formula: everything inside
is good and clean; everything outside is dirty and wicked.
Yet at the same time she would reach out for older men,
i.e., external objects, but never for permanent attachments.

Hands are for grasping and holding. Sweating is the
anticipatory response to these. Excessive sweating here
could indicate anxiety concerning the prospect of grasping,
holding, and being connected. Although some sweating increases friction to facilitate this, an excessive amount prevents a favorable connection from being made with the
object. It appears that her difficulties in the hand-object
(animate, inanimate) connection are a representation of
her ever-present fearfulness in the general area of object-
relatedness. The excessive sweating may be viewed as a
primitive bodily expression of overwhelming anxiety about
forming adult, mature ties and connections. Preferring
what she thought to be a safe, a symbolic relationship

with an internal image, she fought off disturbing external ones.

This woman, no common garden variety in either her make-up or destiny, brought many problems to her marriage which were insurmountable. Furthermore the union and intimacy which marriage demands were detrimental to her welfare. Her unique psychosomatic expression of conflicts became aggravated as she was stampeded into a closeness that was completely dystonic with her internal identity.

Outwardly she was a woman who supposedly was taught the docility and servility that every good *hausfrau* must have. Brutalized by war, separated from loved ones, she could trust nobody. It was as if she had to separate herself from the rest of humanity, for they meant her no good. She had to get married to fulfill her mother's needs and to follow the pattern that society demands. There could be no verbal protest or rebellion; her upbringing precluded this type of behavior. There remained, however, body language which was occult and mysterious for which she could have little responsibility. Her body language indicated her distrust of contacts, linkages, and intimacies, and at the same time effectively broke those bonds which were so threatening to her.

Marriage is psychosomatic in that it is supposed to bind people together in intimacies which promote and gratify bodily feelings. The behavior of the sexual organs is the elementary example, the original paradigm for psychosomatic phenomena. The sexual act in marriage was abhorrent to her because it expressed something directly opposed to her own drive for isolation and separation, whereas her own psychosomatic symptoms, taken from her youth, made her slippery to effect escape and disengagement. This was not the lubrication to receive that a woman typically secretes. Without going overboard in imaginative speculation, we can postulate that she had taken her sexual psychosomatic mechanism in her own hands (sic); she displaced it and indeed reversed it. Distrustful of a world of cruelty which she knew in her childhood and adolescence, she had no trust, basic or otherwise, in others. Certainly the male of the species had given her no evidence that her fate would be safe with him. Union meant fusion for her; this was incompatible with her survival. Her hope lay in separation, even isolation from the purported benefits of human relations. From her experiences she "knew" that even the heavens were dangerous, for they spewed fire and bombs; the heavens proved as untrustworthy as the earth which gave way under her feet.

Her husband was innocent, even a rescuer from the horrors of Europe. He took her to a new world—the promised land—sanctuary in, of all places, the land of her enemies! He married the woman he was in love with; he planned to care and provide for her, expecting the usual responses of affection and gratitude. His expectations were in no way unusual; therefore his shock and disturbance were understandable. He ingenuously believed that he was doing nothing different from a million or more other men in similar circumstances. He did not know that in this union he was indeed taking on the problems of the world in microcosm. Who would marry if he knew he was taking the world to bed!

This woman could not trust the therapy and therapist any more than other "helpers" and institutions. Therapy was talk—perhaps smooth talk designed to direct her into doing what the "system" thought best. She was suspicious of words because she had learned to distrust anyone's word. Words were vehicles of betrayal. When she was reassured with words that everything would be all right, it never turned out that way. Instead she wished to end her embarrassing symptoms through surgery—severance of tissues and nerves, mutilation. This was closer to the violence she grew up with. This was the tragic irony of her existence, that the terror of her childhood was the only sensation she could understand and trust. Her nightmares were the safest remnants of her memories.

Another woman suffered mental conflicts which were

translated into symptoms referable to her mouth. There are things we may and may not do with our mouths, depending on age, sex, occupation, social status, etc. In infancy there are few prohibitions of oral activity, except perhaps biting and thumbsucking. Enthusiastic suckling, eating, and noisemaking are usually most gratifying to parents. Biting is generally poorly tolerated; thumbsucking may be accepted or prohibited, varying with class status and occupation of the parents. Generally in the lower classes, it is fairly well tolerated, whereas in the middle and professional classes it is borne poorly by the parents.

Thumbsucking in adults is generally not tolerated. Nailbiting in adults does not provoke censure except in professional groups. Among these, facial tics and stammering are also taboo. Lipbiting is quite general and is accepted as a mannerism denoting concern. Tonguelicking of the teeth and oral mucosa are deemed private activities, and nothing much is said about them.

Much has been written concerning oral habits, the dynamics derived mainly from the libido theory. Nailbiting has been described as providing gratification and atonement, satisfying a desire to bite and be bitten. It has also been looked upon as an integrated release of aggression, denial, and self-punishment by biting at the claws, particularly favorable because of the element of reversibility—the nails grow back, unlike other mutilations.[5]

Pouting can be a distinctly acceptable coquettish mannerism in a woman but is not tolerated in an adult male. One researcher found it an infantile mode of expression, representing an oral conflict when persisting in adult life. "The thrusting out of the lips seemed to be a literal reaching out for the breast and milk." He concluded that pouting represented a regressive wish to return to a state of satisfactory maternal contact.[6]

Blathering is a less familiar activity. It is a rapid, noisy, recurrent protrusion and withdrawal of the flattened relaxed tongue through moderately relaxed lips and jaws. Dr. Clifford Scott found it in an adult female patient. He related it to "taking in" and "going into" the object fed upon, referring to the rapid tongue movements of the infant during the act of feeding.[7]

Freud described lipsucking and tonguesucking, along with thumbsucking, as manifestations of infantile sexuality. Here the tongue may become a substitute for the breast, thumb, or other external object.[8]

The use of the mouth as a sexual organ is influenced by both cultural and psychological factors. For instance, a prostitute took almost puritanical pride in that she did not "do it the French way," like some of her sisters in trade. On the other hand, the daughter of a clergyman repeatedly performed fellatio instead of genital intercourse so that she could remain a virgin. Oral activity in foreplay seems to differ among the social classes (it is more prominent in the upper).

There is a stratification among homosexuals based on predilections for the anal or oral routes. Homosexuality has both sociological as well as psychological determinants. Proust thought of homosexuals as a persecuted minority group, a race accursed. He wrote: "Just as there were no Jews before the death of Christ, there was no such thing as homosexuality in the epoch when it was customary and befitting to live with a young man as nowadays it is to keep a ballet dancer; when Socrates, the most virtuous man there ever was, cracked jokes about two youths sitting side by side as we might about a nephew and niece who make eyes at each other—so that the sin of homosexuality dates its historical origin from when, having lost its good name, it did not conform."[9]

In the matter of the ubiquitous kiss or buss, we are aware of the role of social custom. (It is illegal to kiss in public in some communities.) The kiss has been codified by the acting profession. In the movies and on television, the kiss as an act of passion is freely enacted and shown to an accepting public. However, there persists a squeamishness about saliva.

Recently, the coquettish open-mouthed female with

quivering lips has received wide acceptance in movie-going circles. However, the male who keeps his mouth open is deemed an idiot.

Food idiosyncrasies of children and adults are well known to us. Besides the fads, medically sanctioned diets (pertaining to cholesterol regulation, etc.) have become popular. Religious rituals regarding food are present in almost every sect. Orthodox Jews demand extensive precautions to see that only bloodless meat touches their lips, yet the twentieth century gourmet will send the steak or roast beef back to the kitchen if it is not minimally broiled.

The most prevalent oral social habits in our western culture are smoking and drinking. Drinking, at least for the majority, is a mark of sociability and probably masculinity. Smoking is advertised as pure pleasure, alcoholic beverages as the great social catalyst. On the other side, moralists have been joined by medical science in claiming the somatic and social destructiveness of both.

As yet, with some notorious exceptions, women confine their smoking to cigarettes. Smoking habits vary according to occupation. Many business offices prohibit working girls from smoking on the job, although it is freely permitted in the executive offices. Cigar smoking in airplanes is generally prohibited because of the offensive odor, just as, along with the pipe, it may be restricted in individual households. The recent cancer scare has added a medical dimension to the cigarette smoking habit. This has placed women in quite a quandary. They cannot easily switch to cigar or pipe as men can.

It is part of the etiquette of the medical profession in the United States that physicians abstain from smoking during an interview, examination, or treatment of a patient. It is of interest that psychiatrists and psychoanalysts do not follow this custom and thus in this respect divorce themselves from the medical model. Psychoanalysts, generally, seem to be heavy smokers and may smoke in the treatment room while prohibiting the analysand to do the same. One possible reason for this is that Freud, like Winston Churchill, never appeared in the flesh or in photographs sans cigar. Social custom dictates that lawyers may smoke with clients, but not in court; and those working with children, i.e., teachers, etc., are not expected to smoke during their work.

There have been strong reactions against smoking habits in the form of social, political, religious, and medical prohibitions. Abstemiousness has been adopted by many religious groups, i.e., Methodists and, more rigidly, Seventh Day Adventists. Abstinence becomes the other side of the coin. To abstain, then, aids morality and tends to promote individuality. One's superiority is demonstrated by the ability to resist the "evil" to which the majority has succumbed. Interestingly enough, such people now receive a bonus for their abstinence from medical science, which attributes a myriad of diseases and degenerative processes to chronic alcohol and tobacco usage.

We see that both addiction and abstinence may be used as adjuncts to social adjustments. It is therefore not surprising that we find attitudes about smoking and drinking communicated by patients either directly or via symptoms. Such is the case with the patient whose history follows.

A fifty-six-year-old school teacher was referred by a physician from a rural community. He indicated that he thought she was suffering from a nervous condition which had not responded to tranquilizers or a course of electroshock treatment. He now felt this woman might be helped if she had "someone to talk to," although she had "no" apparent problems.

A pale, emaciated, sickly-looking woman appeared, accompanied by a corpulent husband who looked like an ex-prize fighter. He was, however, quite meek in manner. When I motioned her into the office, she had difficulty arising from a chair and staggered across the room with a loose-jointed, wobbly gait, supporting herself on adjacent furniture. She pointed to reddened sores on her lips and corners of her mouth. She indicated that these sores were causing all her difficulties. They were very painful, making it impossible for her to eat. She lived on liquids, but really had no desire for food. As a result of this, she had lost thirty pounds in the last year. The lesions had not responded to any of a myriad of medications, both local and systemic. She and her doctor now felt that it might be due to "nerves." Because of the appearance of her mouth, she would not appear in public and would not teach in the last school year. At the same time her dentist observed that there seemed to be an increase of tooth decay. In spite of the incapacity due to the ataxia, she made no reference to this symptom. Only on direct questioning did she reveal that her difficulty in walking appeared concomitantly with the lesions of the mouth.

Her "nerves" seemed to be centered in her mouth. Whenever she "got upset," she tensed up in this region. She described a behavior like pouting but also tightening of her lips in purselike fashion. She would vigorously press her tongue against them. This would invariably produce the lesions. She knew this but could not help herself in this behavior.

She had heard of psychological treatment, but concurred with her family physician that she was a happy person with no family or social problems. Her husband, a retired policeman now convalescing from a heart attack, was devoted to her and met her every need. Her two children, one a school teacher and one a teacher in training, were respectful and of excellent character. The younger, a son, was still at home but completing his education. The daughter had been married for five years and had one child.

Her nervous symptoms first appeared at the time of the daughter's marriage five years previously. However, she admitted that she was of a general "nervous temperament," taking sleeping medicine every night since her own marriage. Although happy about her daughter's forthcoming marriage, she had been overcome with concern as to how the couple would make ends meet on the meager income of an apprentice teacher. (Her son-in-law was also a teacher.) She had been insistent that she would not have a wedding reception for them because of the expense. She said that she had nothing against the boy and no reason to feel snobbish about him, but she "knew" how her daughter had been brought up. They were not wealthy, but she had inculcated in her children a high sense of honor and dignity. However, the fact that they both followed her in the teaching profession did not reflect undue influence on her part, she said.

She was extremely proud of her children because they resisted the temptations that other young people appeared to be succumbing to. As they entered their adolescence, they both took religious pledges that they would neither drink nor smoke. She was proud that they had done this on their own; it was not a "command." Her husband had his "plebeian" habits, which she had not been able to do much about. She felt it was not her right to deprive him of his smoking (although it "dirtied and smelled up the house"), his beer drinking, and his Thursday night bowling. She "wished" she could smoke like the rest of them; it might "settle her nerves." Beer always tasted terrible to her, although she had drunk it occasionally during courtship. She had some concern about her son-in-law, but he proved to be abstemious like herself and her own children.

She came, she said, from "shanty Irish," who were, however, devout in religion and respectable in social conduct. Her father and two older brothers worked on the railroad. They were largely illiterate. The patient wrote reports for her father as needed on his job. Two of her uncles had died early of alcoholism. Her mother consequently made her children take religious pledges to abstain. The older brothers had little education, in contrast to the patient and the younger brother, both of whom became teachers. She stated that she was constantly pampered by her brothers who, characteristically, treated her as the family baby. However, she helped her younger brother through college and remained closest to him. Her mother was constantly on guard against the drunkenness and irresponsibility in the largely immigrant community where they lived. She was extremely proud of her two younger children, who broke away from the pattern. The patient was married in her late twenties. Her husband was below her educational level, but she stated that he pampered her as her brothers had. As noted above, she started taking sleeping medicine on the day of her marriage.

As for the "sores" which had first erupted when her daughter was married five years before, the patient was at that time admitted to a specialized clinic and hospital where she received an intensive work-up. During the course of the tests and examinations, the lesions cleared up completely within one week, and she was restored to health without any specific treatment, whereas the remedies of her local physician had had no effect. The lesions reappeared two years later, and again disappeared after three days of hospitalization. They developed again two years after that, and she was put under the care of a psychiatrist in a nearby town. She was immediately given a course of electroshock treatment, without relief; and since that time her state of health had deteriorated consistently. She was unable to teach or even leave her house.

She expressed great hope of being helped by someone with whom she could talk. She was quite impressed with the fact that she had to wait a long time for an appointment. She was also reassured by her local physician that no electroshock treatments would be used. Her one concern was that she did not know why she needed help, since she had always lived a virtuous life and really knew of no personal problems. She could not understand any reason for an emotional illness, since everyone was and always had been good to her. The children had been moral and respectful. She had a kind and devoted husband and children who gave her a great deal of respect and pride. True, they were not wealthy and had survived hard times, including the loss of all their possessions during a flood several years before. She felt that "nerves" caused her mouth lesions.

At the end of the hour, it was agreed that she would

return in one week to discuss her problems further and to see what else could be done. She expressed gratitude and promptly wrote out a check with a very shaky hand. To the suggestion that she might wait for a statement at the end of the month, she protested that she did not want to "owe anyone—always paid bills on time."

At her next appointment she walked in briskly and the lesions around her mouth had completely disappeared. They had cleared up three days after her initial visit. She could not explain how it happened; but it seemed to re-affirm her doctor's confidence—that all a woman like her needed was to talk to someone, rather than be subjected to shock treatments. She had begun to eat and now was able to go shopping, which she had previously been fearful of doing. She felt that she could return to her job as a teacher; she subsequently did and was able to teach for the next year. Although she felt that she had recovered from her difficulties, she wanted to continue on a weekly basis to insure her "recovery."

She continued "talking" about one year. During this time she came accompanied by her husband, who generally slept during the hour in the waiting room. She asked for frequent changes of time and days of appointments, which were granted in the beginning. She had the feeling she was being accommodated, and she responded to such spe-cial treatment. She brought her problems of school to the sessions, and these revealed her intense rigidity. She now taught the first grade, having transferred from the fourth grade because she felt the younger children would be more cooperative. She stated that she got along well with the children, but it was the parents who upset her by their misunderstanding of the role of a teacher. She said that this was entirely different from the early days of teaching, when people had respect for the position and authority of a teacher. Now all that was changed; the parents seemed to take no responsibility for the children. She became fear-ful of giving low grades to the children lest the parents should think that she was being unfair.

One day, while she was taking the pupils to the cafeteria, the dietitian told her that she was five minutes behind schedule. This brief remark completely unnerved the patient, causing her to feel depressed for the following three days. She lamented that it was not her fault, and she was going to explain the whole matter to the principal. At home she was annoyed with the drinking and smoking of her husband, but she tolerated it as best she could.

As treatment continued, changing the hours was refused, and she was not allowed to pay at each session. However, after statements were sent, she became delinquent in payment. She felt very hurt about this new treatment, but then explained it by saying this was a way of "testing" her.

About a year after she started treatment, her oral lesions and anorexia returned. This was in a setting of three concurrent situations: a less indulgent attitude on the part of the therapist; the end of the school year, when she would be left to face a summer vacation; the graduation of her son from teaching college and his leaving home to take a job in another city.

The patient stopped eating, complained bitterly of her lesions, and could not go out on the street any more. Her husband and son felt they could not manage her in the household. It was also quite apparent that the office visits were not providing the proper magic at this time. Therefore, she voluntarily admitted herself to the local psychiatric hospital.

She entered on Friday, and by Monday her symptoms again disappeared. By Wednesday of that week, she was gleeful over her quick recovery, and had effusive praise for the young intern who had been taking care of her and had spent so much time with her. She was grateful for having a special room. (This was not true.) She also claimed that she was very interested and compassionate about the other patients around her. She felt particularly fortunate in having come upon doctors who were skilled and who were interested in her. Her doctor (the intern) was young but seemed to know his business. She was in the hospital for approximately three weeks, during which time she had her husband visit her daily, making a trip of 150 miles from their home.

It is to be noted that during her hospitalization she greatly antagonized the medical students and some of the junior staff members. Perhaps this was because she lacked humility, asked for special considerations, desisted from going to occupational therapy with the other patients, etc. She immediately identified herself with the doctors and not with the patients. She was discharged from the hospital and continued to be in "good health" and to teach with somewhat lessened rigidity. Her initial symptoms did not reappear, and she gained weight steadily.

The internist's general impression had been that her oral lesions, including a dry, red sore tongue, were manifestations of a vitamin deficiency; but he was unable to see how a well-nourished woman on a well-balanced diet could develop such a deficiency.

It is quite apparent that, with middle age, this woman found it increasingly difficult to deal with her changing situation. In her work, she could no longer compete with the younger teachers in the field and had to compensate through becoming more authoritarian in her class. At the same time she was in constant fear of what she called "dirty notes" from parents who might not like her handling of the children. At home, she found competition from her children whom she was no longer able to dominate. She found herself in more contact and greater intimacy with her husband, now retired and dependent, whom she had always secretly felt was inferior to herself. On a psychological level, one may understand her symptoms as an oral regression that displayed her rejection of the situation in which she found herself.

However, it was felt there was another component in her symptomatology which could be understood only in terms of a particular social interaction. In her haughtiness, she betrayed her fears and contempt for the people with whom she had been associated, past and present. She had

known of drinking, fighting, and other barbarities. She felt
that she had risen above this and demanded strictness in
the members of her family. It is significant that her daughter, at seven years of age, became obsessed with the idea
that she had sinned. The daughter had been taken to a
counselor at that time. Later in life the patient demanded
that her children abstain from drinking and smoking.

Viewed in this social context, her symptoms take on a
more specific meaning. These are the people she had
known in her childhood, the men who reeked of sweat,
tobacco, and alcohol. Her father was illiterate and blustering. She saw her uncles with blotchy, swollen faces, and
ataxia, dying of alcoholism. She had struggled against this
way of life and, along with her younger brother, had succeeded in elevating herself. Yet her husband, although
neither illiterate nor alcoholic, showed lower-class habits
and attitudes. At school, she had to contend with the rude-
ness of the janitors and cafeteria help, as well as the
"country-bumpkin" parents of her children who sent "dirty
notes" complaining about marks and the general handling
of their progeny. With her oral symptoms and staggering
gait, she was identifying with the drunkenness and low
nature of the "contemptible" individuals she felt were
around her. At the same time she was displaying her own
repressed oral cravings. She then became, in the phantasy
of the symptoms, the "mealy-mouthed drunken bums" she
had seen around her. This was like the parlor game of
charades—a pantomime. Freud at one time likened hysterical symptoms to a pantomime.[10] Thus an identification
with the contemptible object or objects is effected. (Identification with the aggressor is a well-known psychoanalytic
concept.)

In regard to her speedy recovery on contact with new
therapists, it is not appropriate to use the term "transference" in this connection. The phenomenon here was in
the nature of an instant identification. She gained a great
feeling of importance in being interviewed by specialists;
she would not respond to an ordinary doctor. Her con-

stant dread was of being "ordinary," a state of being she had tried to avoid most of her life, but which she was now slipping into in her postclimacteric period. When she could be made to feel like someone special, she was able to overcome her bitterness and forego her mimicry of the "immoral," orally addicted, internal objects. This immediate response was evident in each instance of recovery.

This case demonstrates an exquisite compounding of social and psychological forces at work. It highlights the oft-neglected social representation of symptoms. About the production of lesions around the mouth, one can only speculate. Undoubtedly there are complex psychological and biological factors involved. However, it was apparent that this woman indulged in intense pouting, as well as tongue-sucking, and thrusting her tongue against the mucosa of her mouth and lips. It may be that the synergy of this constant physical trauma, plus bacterial pathogens, combined to produce the lesions. The evidence for this speculation is her immediate recovery when she was able to stop her psychical-oral activity. On the other hand, her staggering gait was purely hysterical, without any physiological or organic components.

Her symptom complex appeared to be the opposite of what one might consider acting-out behavior, for in acting out an individual generally expresses internal conflicts via social behavior. However, this individual, through mimicry, expressed her social feelings through psychological mechanisms. This woman might have shown her protest by acting out behavior, such as becoming an alcoholic or an excessive smoker. In doing this, she would have behaved like the contemptible objects, i.e., her husband, father, uncles, railroad workers, shanty Irish, etc. The advantage of her autoplastic defense was that, via the mechanism of the pantomime instead of the deed, she was able to be expressive and yet retain, or even enhance, her virtue. This may be called "acting in," a term already used by Zeligs.[11]

The competition of ties in the present against those in

the past is intrinsic to the human condition. Gulliver knew that one could be as helplessly and as securely bound by a thousand microscopic strands as by the gross chains which encumbered Prometheus. Gulliver's experience is more germane to human existence because the imperceptible ties in the unconscious are the significant and determining ones. The thick umbilical cord, as everyone knows, is cut at birth—no problem there! In living there is nothing so unsophisticated as the Gordian knot which succumbed to one well-placed blow. In human relations, therefore, the therapist soon learns that changing, or turning a new leaf, or "letting go"—in Philip Roth's idiom—is never a simple matter. The middle-aged school teacher described above was suffering the consequences of the sequences of generations, and dramatically and pathetically attempting to undo her social inheritance—struggling to deny the ties which linked her to a sinful past.

Until recently, the existence of social classes, with their attendant struggles and tensions, was America's best kept secret.[20] In England, yes, but not in the land where all men are created equal. You were to be judged by your morality or your accomplishments—no one was to be excluded or resented because of his birth, social class or job status. Everyone knew that people married for love—the song that confirmed this was: "I Found My Million Dollar Baby in the Five and Ten Cent Store."

Psychoanalysis did nothing to demythologize this belief. Freud rarely mentioned social class as relevant to any of the problems he dealt with. His main concession to the acknowledgment of social differences was that psychoanalysis as treatment was limited to "wage earners." He was to deal with "eternal truths" that transcended class, race or sex. Marx, with his emphasis on alienation and disaffection because of the vicissitudes of class struggle, was totally ignored by Freud and most of his followers. This denial of the relevance of social class resonated well with American tradition. Freud, not Marx, gained ascendancy in the United States. Yet the acknowledgment of social classes and their vicissitudes had to come and with it its relevance to emotional problems.

This writer, trained in the Freudian tradition, nonetheless has found that social class tensions, as exemplified in the case under consideration, do play a crucial role in the "psychopathology" of individuals. These anxieties, long overlooked, play a central role in symptom formation. Psychoanalysts in America have noted a "disappearance" among their patients of the grosser and more flamboyant symptoms such as paralysis, ataxia. They attribute this to increased sophistication as well as knowledge of more bizarre psychiatric syndromes. The more literate people somehow are able to avoid these. More to the point is that symptoms themselves may reflect the habits and predilections of social classes to begin with. The "disappearance" of these symptoms may reflect the non-appearance of poor and low-income patients in general in the clientele of psychoanalysts. It seems reasonable that the more literate classes would have psychological symptoms of an "intellectual" nature; the poorer classes on the other hand, whose primary concerns are the biological problems of getting enough to eat and a roof over their heads, would have psychological symptoms, not of an intellectual nature, but those related to biology and bodily functions. The bizarre conversion symptoms are less frequently seen in affluent areas than amongst the rural poor where physical deprivations are the greatest. Furthermore, these symptoms are apt to appear, not in the steady state of poverty and despair, but in situations where there is some change imminent, even an improvement in living conditions with which an individual, rendered inelastic by cultural alienation and physical deprivation, cannot cope. The writer recalls the instance of a woman who developed a hysterical paralysis of all her limbs when her slum dwelling was demolished in an urban renewal project. The prospect of better housing for her in another area had little appeal;

her community as she knew it was gone, along with its
sustaining qualities. She had no resiliency for a new adventure, even for so-called improved living conditions. Yet
this was impossible to express in any but body language.
She was taciturn to begin with; an expression of her panic
about moving might reflect an ingratitude to the "generous" people who insisted on helping her. Total paralysis
was her reply.

To return to the case of the ataxic woman, the traditional psychoanalytic interpretation would most likely emphasize genetic problems—those of earliest childhood, to
which she had regressed. No one can deny that this
woman's psychic structure and its particularity had their
origins in oedipal and preoedipal phases of her life. Yet
these postulates do not explain the occurrence of such
symptoms at her age. Only when these genetic factors are
combined with existential ones can an intelligent analysis
be derived. The patient was very conscious of her past and
similarly conscious of the social present. Psychoanalysis
speaks of the regressive tendencies to infantile levels of
psychic organization. True. But equally pertinent is this
woman's struggle with forces, real and fancied, which
would cause a status regression with a husband who em-
barrassed her with his low-prestige job and manners and
with children who might stray from her ideals of moral
impeccability and possibly bring disgrace to her. These ambitious strivings and anxieties could not be directly expressed or admitted; in fact they were to be strongly denied.
They came out as the opposite; namely, love, concern,
and humility. Her symptoms communicated and expressed
her anxieties of not being able to maintain the upward
social mobility that she had initiated. Threatened by her
own failing physical self (aging) and faltering mental acumen, she "feigned" physical disability to warn her kin of
what a drunkard looks and acts like and at the same time
through her symptoms attempted to mobilize the attention
and power that are due to an ailing but self-sacrificing

mother. Textbooks in psychiatry are quick to diagnose hysterical symptoms as attention-getting mechanisms. This is usually true but is only part of the larger gestalt in which the frantic appeal for attention is vestigial to disappearing influence and authority. The attention-getting mechanism connotes failure and slippage—the bathos of a defeated person.

The world has not yet arrived at a state where competition, power, and dominance have been entirely eliminated from human aspirations. This woman, like the deceased mother in Philip Roth's *Letting Go,* felt that she had married someone who was her inferior, in social class and education. It is part of societal pressure on young girls that they make compromises in order to avoid being spinsters. They are told that a girl must not be too particular, for there are only a few opportunities. "He isn't so bright but he'll make you a good husband." With this advice, women have married men for whom they not only have no love but of whom they are ashamed. They feel that they have been betrayed and sold as slaves by worried parents. And in an unconcerned society, a woman of this sort at best must lead a life of resignation mixed with desperation. She rues the day of her female birth and feels that the penis was wasted on her husband. She feels that she might have accomplished so much had she been granted the unearned position of the male. Such frustration in the ataxic patient led to contempt for her inept husband who was an obstacle rather than a help in elevating the family position.

Shakespeare wrote of such frustrated, ambitious women. He would have been able to diagnose this woman's oral symptoms. Volumnia, in *Coriolanus,* embittered by the banishment of her son, states: "Anger's my meat; I sup upon myself, and so shall starve with feeding."[12] And could not the woman in this protocol have spoken the words of Lady Macbeth: "Come you spirits/That tend on mental thoughts, unsex me here,/And fill me from the crown to the toe, top-full of direct cruelty"?[13]

Somato-psychic

Nothing with a blemish was acceptable to the Lord. The
Bible contains no fewer than sixty references to "blemish."
Only animals without blemish were to be sacrificed to the
Deity. No man with a blemish or deformity could carry
offerings to the Lord. ". . . Whosoever *he be* of thy seed
in their generations that hath *any* blemish, let him not
approach to offer the bread of his God. For whatsoever
man *he be* that hath a blemish, he shall not approach: a
blind man, or a lame, or he that hath a flat nose, or any
thing superfluous, Or a man that is brokenfooted or
brokenhanded, or crookbackt or a dwarf, or that hath a
blemish in his eye, or be scurvy, or scabbed, or hath his
stones broken; No man that hath a blemish of the seed of
Aaron the priest shall come nigh to offer the offerings of
the Lord made by fire: he hath a blemish; he shall not
come nigh to offer the bread of his God. . . . Only he
shall not go in unto the veil, nor come nigh unto the altar,
because he hath a blemish; that he profane not my sanc-
tuaries: for I the Lord do sanctify them."[14]

There, then, were strong prohibitions against the blemished, the lame, the blind, and the infirm. "Without blemish" took on a moral meaning: to be spotless, blameless.
Here is undoubtedly an obfuscation of the difference between physical and moral stain. It is an instance of transmogrification, a moral "somato-psychism." Society loathes
the blemished and the crippled, frequently causing a deformity of character and mind to fit the physical deformity.
The opening lines of Shakespeare's *Richard III* tell how
the "crookmind" came from the "crookbackt." It should
be remembered that nature formed the latter and societal
prejudice the former:

"But I, that am not shap'd for sportive tricks,
    Nor made to court an amorous looking-glass;

I, that am rudely stamp'd, and want love's majesty,
To strut before a wanton ambling nymph;
I, that am curtail'd of this fair proportion,
Cheated of feature by dissembling Nature,
Deform'd, unfinish'd, sent before my time
Into this breathing world, scarce half made up,
And that so lamely and unfashionable,
That dogs bark at me, as I halt by them;
. . . . . .
And therefore, since I cannot prove a lover,
To entertain these fair well-spoken days,
I am determined to prove a villain,
And hate the idle pleasures of these days."[15]

Richard is matched in literature by the hunch-backed servant girl Maritornes in *Don Quixote*. Deprived of Richard's "assets" of maleness, power, and cunning, she was consoled by the vicarious excitement of tales of adventure and romance. This misshapen woman fares poorly indeed in the mating game. Man seeks for beauty in another as for the holy grail. The "why" of this is anybody's guess. Jean-Paul Sartre sees beauty as a magical protection:

"The beautiful," . . . "seems indestructible, its sacred image protects us. As long as it resides in our midst, no catastrophe can happen."[16]

Nietzsche similarly writes: "What do we desire when we look at beauty? To be beautiful ourselves, we imagine that beauty carries with it great happiness, but this is a mistake."[17]

The quest for perfect beauty was the theme of Hawthorne's tale, "The Birthmark."[18] Here the scientist, Aylmer, deeply in love with his beautiful young wife, nonetheless revealed to her his abhorrence of a birthmark on her cheek, the only evidence of imperfection on her. At first she was unaffected by his revelation, having placed no great significance to it. She said: "To tell the truth, it has been so often called a charm that I was simple enough to imagine it might be so." Not so for Aylmer. He replied: "Oh, upon another face perhaps it might but never on yours. No, dearest Georgiana, you came so nearly perfect from the hand of Nature that this slightest possible defect, which we hesitate whether to term a defect or a beauty, shocks me, as being the visible mark of earthly imperfection." Georgiana's indifference was shortlived after she perceived her husband's obsession. Thereafter the birthmark became a point of fixation for both of them. The blemish threatened to destroy their union. They both agreed that it would have to be removed, as Georgiana said, ". . . whatever be the cost, or we shall both go mad." Aylmer produced a potion against such a blemish but it was untried and dangerous. Georgiana fully ingested it. The "stain" steadily faded from her cheek, as did life from her body.

This tale reaffirms the antinomy of perfection and existence. It also tells of the obsession with beauty and stainlessness that goes back to Leviticus and beyond. It shows the historical misogyny that demands the same virginity and purity in woman as in an unblemished animal to be sacrificed to the Lord. The psychoanalysts could add from familiarity with such phantasmagoria that the tale reveals through "displacement upwards" the fear and loathing of the "castrated" person. The female genitalia, in the irrational part of the male unconscious, are often conceived of as a gaping wound, a defect—an imperfection. The psychoanalyst is at a distinct disadvantage, following an artist like Hawthorne, with a case history. There is some consolation in the adage, "Truth is stranger than fiction." One hastens to add that truth is no stranger to fiction.

Roberta was the elder of two daughters in an upper middle-class American family. As such she had many advantages as well as responsibilities. The crucial trauma of her early life was the death of her father when she was ten. Two years later her mother remarried. The mother was quite aware that with two small children she was at a disadvantage in the marriage and tried to impress on the children that they would have to be well-behaved in the presence of their new father. They would now have to make special efforts to show gratitude toward the man who had taken on this familial responsibility. Although the younger sister was more of a problem in this regard and as a result was subjected to discipline as well as rejection by the parents, Roberta cooperated and capitulated without too much personal attrition. Her adolescence was, however, quite painful. She was very bright, well built, and generally attractive, but she suffered from severe myopia which necessitated the wearing of thick lenses. Self-conscious about this, she showed great timidity about dating and social engagements. She could not participate freely in sports and dancing. Dorothy Parker did not help her morale. Predictably, she became a voracious reader. This made her parents apprehensive because of her poor eyesight. At one time her mother approached their family physician about warning her against reading lest she go blind. This deprivation Roberta passively resisted; she made matters worse by reading in bed with a flash light.

College was some relief from parental nagging. She did well academically and her social relations improved. In her senior year she met Tom, a quiet and serious student in electrical engineering. They were of different ethnic and social backgrounds but shared many intellectual and emotional interests. They fell in love and after their scholastic work was completed they were married. Although Roberta's mother was less than enthusiastic about Tom's background, at least her apprehensions that Roberta would be an old maid were now dispelled. Roberta, herself, was happy, as she put it, "for the first time in my life."

Tom loved her, myopia, thick glasses, and all! She resolved to be a devoted and loving wife. She did not, at this time, make the connection, as with her stepfather, that she would again have to be "grateful." The first years of their marriage were highly successful. One child was born at the end of the first year. Another child followed three years later. It was after the birth of this child that the second trauma of her life occurred. She noticed a disease of her scalp for the first time. This was soon diagnosed as psoriasis. As far as prognosis was concerned, the doctor hoped that it would not spread; it was, however, a most difficult condition to treat. The condition did spread—to elbows and knees—then over the entire trunk. There were ugly red patches which coalesced. They gave great discomfort with much flaking and scaling. There were exacerbations and remissions; and typical of such obscure conditions, there were a large number of treatments, including stringent diets, X-ray therapy, and both internal and external medications. Her life was now transformed into an unexpected nightmare.

Unlike Hawthorne's Aylmer, Tom was most solicitous; he helped with the housework and children and encouraged Roberta to seek the best medical advice. He reassured her that this unfortunate blow made no difference in his love for her. He tried to overcome her newly developed reluctance to undress in front of him and to show her body. Tom was sincere in his devotion and Roberta's apprehensions that he might turn to more attractive women were groundless. They resolved that they would both try to put this disease out of their minds; it simply could not be a relevant issue between them.

Roberta developed a change of character. The evening cocktail multiplied. In addition there were nips of wine during the day. At night there were now the inevitable sleeping pills. Tom was alarmed by this behavior and began to cajole and to scold. She in turn became increasingly argumentative and belligerent. She now accused him of being indifferent and unfeeling. The altercations became frequent and at times they came to blows. One Christmas Eve, Tom arrived to find Roberta in a comatose state, having taken a large dosage of sleeping pills. He rushed her to a hospital where she was resuscitated.

Psychoanalysis followed, lasting four years. In the beginning Roberta spoke exclusively of her disenchantment with her marriage and Tom. She berated his lower-middle class puritanism. Her mother's doubts about him had proved correct: education alone cannot make up for an uncouth background. In listening to her one could hardly detect a trace of the love that had characterized their earlier relationship. She loathed him—did not want ever to touch him. For many months there was no mention of her psoriasis even though its severity went unabated. Now it was as though he had the "blemish." This is how she defended against the humiliation of her own deficiency. She protested that the skin disease was irrelevant to the issues between them. However, in the course of psychoanalytic dialogue, allusions to it emerged. The agony of this seemingly benign disease lay not only in the affliction but in the treatments. Besides the disfigurement and discomfort, the search for treatment was ongoing and generally inconclusive. Each new clinic had to be investigated. Both Roberta and Tom checked the medical journals for new ideas for cures. Fat-free and sulphur-free diets were amongst the least offensive regimens. There were hospitalizations under rigid conditions of isolation and immobility. Concomitant experiments involving the gathering of all bodily excrements had to be performed. X-ray and ultraviolet therapies often produced severe burns to compound the pain. Yet the search went on, as it usually does when medical science has no answers. At times she readily identified with the victims of the inquisition; she recanted a million times with the torture, but she found no redemption.

Roberta's plight was proof that it is more difficult to receive than to give. In her childhood she and her sister were the recipients of her stepfather's generosity; they were no bargain for him. She later felt because of her bespectacled appearance that she was again no bargain. Yet a man whom she loved did overlook her infirmity and she could then hope to show him love and devotion, not merely out of gratitude but of genuine I and Thou concern. The added blow of her biological destiny created a new and irreconcilable imbalance. Uncomplaining and supportive, Tom found himself nonetheless an object of scorn by an embittered wife. He was puzzled; only in his most lucid moments could he understand that Roberta was heaping upon him the shame and humiliation she felt about being unattractive. The more helpful he was, the more ashamed she became of being unable to match his devotion with an equal response. Also, the chronicity as well as the incurability of her affliction caused her to indulge in the magical thinking which turned the blemish of body to that of soul. What had she done to deserve this mark of Cain? She loathed herself as both a physically and morally inferior person. She matched Tom's compassion with loathing until she no longer cared to live. She, in truth, loathed herself for her disease, which she considered a betrayal of her marriage vow. Once again she was to become an object of charity.

Difficult for anyone, disfigurement is a terrible hardship for a woman in a world that still judges feminine worthiness and value on physical appearance. In Tennessee Williams' *The Glass Menagerie,* Laura's lameness is her destiny. Service, generosity, and gentleness as well as intelligence are secondary to appearance. Chekhov's Sonya (*Uncle Vanya*) had all of the above but they went for naught; she laments: "Oh, how awful it is that I am not beautiful! How awful! And I know that I'm not beautiful, I know it, I know. Last Sunday, as people were coming out of church, I heard them talking about me, and one woman said: 'She is so good and generous, what a pity she is not beautiful.' Not beautiful . . ."[19]

NOTES

1. Y. Kuno, *Human Perspiration* (Springfield: Charles C. Thomas Publisher, 1956), Chaps. 10 and 12.

2. M. B. Sulzberger and Herrmann, *The Clinical Significance of Disturbance in the Delivery of Sweat* (Springfield, Ill.: Charles C. Thomas Publisher, 1954), p. 2.

3. F. Alexander and T. French, *Studies in Psychosomatic Medicine* (New York: The Ronald Press Co., 1948), p. 3.

4. W. R. Bion, "Attacks on Linking," *Int. J. Psa.,* XL (1959), p. 40; M. Ostow, "Linkage Fantasies and Representations," *Int. J. Psa.,* XXXVI (1955), p. 387; Robert Seidenberg,

"Household Appliances and the Symbolic Process," *Psychiat. Q.*, XXXII (1958), p. 376.

5. H. Michael Rosow, "The Psychoanalysis of an Adult Nail Biter," *Int. J. Psa.*, XXXV (1954), p. 35; Joseph C. Solomon, "Nail Biting and the Integrative Process," *Int. J. Psa.*, XXXVI (1955), p. 393.

6. Carl P. Adatto, "On Pouting," *J. Amer. Psychoanalyt. Assoc.*, V (1957), p. 245.

7. Clifford M. Scott, "A Note on Blathering," *Int. J. Psa.*, XXXVI (1955), p. 348.

8. Sigmund Freud, *Basic Writings of Sigmund Freud* (New York: Random House, 1938), p. 585.

9. M. Proust, "A Race Accursed," *On Art and Literature 1896-1919* (New York: Meridian Books, 1958), p. 220.

10. Sigmund Freud, "General Remarks on Hysterical Attacks," *Collected Papers,* II (London: The Hogarth Press, 1949), p. 100.

11. Meyer Zeligs, "Acting In," *J. Amer. Psychoanalyt. Assoc.*, V (1957), p. 685.

12. William Shakespeare, "Coriolanus," *The Complete Works of William Shakespeare* (Cleveland: The World Publishing Co., n.d.), p. 706.

13. William Shakespeare, "Macbeth," *The Complete Works of William Shakespeare* (Cleveland: The World Publishing Co., n.d.), p. 926.

14. Leviticus, *The Holy Bible* (Cleveland: The World Syndicate Publishing Co., n.d.), p. 118.

15. William Shakespeare, "King Richard III," *The Complete Works of William Shakespeare* (Cleveland: The World Publishing Co., n.d.), p. 562.

16. Jean-Paul Sartre, *Situations* (New York: George Braziler, 1965), p. 56.

17. Albert Camus, *Notebooks 1935-1942* (New York: Modern Library, 1963), p. 97.

18. Nathaniel Hawthorne, "The Birthmark," *Complete Works and Selected Tales* (New York: Modern Library, 1937), pp. 1021-1033.

19. Anton Chekhov, "Uncle Vanya," *Six Plays of Chekhov.* New English revision and introduction by Robert W. Corrigan. Foreword by Harold Clurman (New York: Holt, Rinehart and Winston, 1962).

20. Albronda, H.F., Dean, R.L., and Starkweather, J.A., *Social Class and Psychotherapy,* in Archives of General Psychiatry, 10:276:1964; also see Hollingshead, A.B., and Redlich, F.C.; *Social Class and Mental Illness,* New York: John Wiley and Sons, Inc., 1958.

CHAPTER VIII

DON'T TOUCH ME!

The water's wide, I cannot cross;
Neither have I the wings to fly.
Give me a boat that will carry two,
And both shall row—my love and I.

Folk Song

Many metaphors exist involving the sea and matrimony.
Together with the achievement of the voyage and the joys
along the way, there are difficulties and dangers. Storms
and shoals, being struck or becalmed, and other external
threats are to be expected. But where is the captain (in
either situation) who fears internal threats? He is not likely
to consciously mistrust his own management. And he certainly does not expect mutiny. If it occurs, he is non-
plussed. The voyage may continue, but it can scarcely be a
happy one. Less dramatic but more familiar, the boat being
rowed by two may go on toward the other side of the lake
if one stops rowing, but the trip is bound to be erratic.
Unfortunately, this happens often in marriage. The owl and
the pussycat were atypical marriage partners, if we assume
that their bliss continued wherever that pea-green boat
went.

A common form of mutiny in marriage is the withdrawal of one partner from the other. He or she "stops
rowing," and in extreme cases will have nothing to do

with the other. "Don't touch me!" the partner says, and is no longer a partner. Eventually there follows emotional chaos—silence, harassment, violence, alcoholism, going home to mother, a triangle or quadrangle, separation or divorce, or other suffering—unless the motivation for withdrawal can be uncovered, understood, and dealt with.

The withdrawal, sudden or gradual, momentary or prolonged, from the male by the female, or the opposite, probably has been an occurrence in every marriage. Freud and other husbands have interpreted the withdrawal of the female as a derivative of the advice of mothers to their daughters: "Don't let *him* touch you." It is understood when the wife recoils from the touch of her husband when she is aggrieved. However, many times this withdrawal occurs apparently unrelated to any known grievance. A husband laments: "I'm completely puzzled. We seemed to be getting along so well and suddenly she won't let me touch her." When asked about her behavior, the wife will appear equally bewildered by her behavior. "He's been all right; I simply can't stand to have him touch me. I don't know why it is, but I cringe at the thought of his arm around me and dread going to bed with him. I don't want any part of him to touch me."

One woman related: "It was after the birth of our second child. Our sexual relations were fairly good up until then; after that I turned cold; he seemed like a stranger or even an enemy to me." Again, in all of these instances the husbands by most standards were fairly attentive, even indulgent, faithful husbands. They were usually powerless to romance or cajole their wives into continuing their former conjugal relations, and arrived at the conclusion that there must be some intrinsic inhibition or sickness. The idea of secondary gain appeared unlikely in the circumstances of these individuals. Their psychological knowledge led them to deduce that there must be a deep sexual block from childhood which had now asserted itself to overwhelm their "happy home." They generally knew about the oedipal complex and all seemed to come to therapy with the preknowledge of an unresolved father attachment which made sex with any man, sooner or later, a cause of deep conflict.

One such woman came to treatment with the "encouragement," if not the command, of her husband. They had been married for six years without incident, but then trouble seemed to begin about three months after the birth of their second daughter. He was a well-educated person of thirty-three, an engineer by profession, who seemed destined to get ahead. He was bright, socially as well as professionally, was continent in his habits, and gave no indication of infidelity or discontent. He was a self-made man, having worked through college, and supported his family in a comfortable style. In his attitude toward his wife, he was generally supportive but never intrusive or demanding. His general behavior made their problem all the more perplexing. If he had been a martinet or a cunning Odysseus, then one could readily point the accusing finger, but this was not the case.

She was unlike him in character makeup. Although also well educated she described herself as a timid person, never at ease in a group, lacking confidence in her ability to manage her own and family affairs. She looked to her husband for advice and instruction in many of the decisions about the household. She admitted, however, that she was generally "good" with the children but worried about doing them psychical harm. Yet she gladly spent her whole day caring for them and never felt either bored or deprived in this activity. She felt less comfortable with her husband in the evenings, for she could contribute little to worldly conversation and was generally in awe of his erudition and poise. In company, she generally deferred to him about opinions or attitudes. She depreciated her own education and skills, describing herself as a "plodder" who did the work. She had gotten good grades but never really learned anything, and should not be expected to be informed on any subject. During therapy, her one positive attitude was her disdain for her mother, whom she blamed for ruining her life. She had been told by a psychologist that her mother was "sick" and it was a miracle that she had grown up as well as she did. She had been an only child and had been the recipient of all her mother's love and the target for all her wrath.

As analysis continued, she began to reveal both facts and phantasies about her parents' marital life. She told of the constant harassment of her father by her mother, wondering how he could take the constant nagging and depreciation that was meted out. In growing up, she experienced continual embarrassment at being a witness to this seemingly "unfair" struggle. Although without any concrete knowledge about it, she phantasied that her parents never had sexual relations after her birth; that her mother withheld sex from her father as part of her punitive regimen. This was imagined, but based on what she thought was good circumstantial evidence.

The mother turned to her daughter for respite from the frustrations she felt so acutely in her marriage. It was then a mother-daughter family, with the father in the role of an outsider. However, the parents never separated; they wanted the girl to "know family life." Later knowledge and insight revealed that this utter coldness between parents, although true to a large degree, was made up by her —motivated by a wish that the parents be divided and that she could be the sole object of her mother. She then operated in the phantasy that there was a cold war between the sexes, and that the male should be excluded from the family constellation as much as possible. It was as if her mother had established a matriarchy to which she was heir and to which she owed her efforts and loyalty. It appeared that after she had secured children of her own, she followed her mother's example and did her one better in shutting out the male for all purposes except financial support, to which he was now morally and legally committed. Rather than having the problem of a "father complex," she proved to be engaged in a role for which she was prepared in the example of her mother's behavior and intentions. Although it would be incorrect to say that sexual fears and taboos were not involved, an overriding motivation appeared to be this deep-rooted antagonism and hostility toward the male. (She did participate and fully enjoy sexual relations in extramarital circumstances.) Her unconscious antagonism was unrelated to any personal grievance toward her husband for what he did or acted toward her, but rested on the basis that he was the enemy as defined by the instructions of her mother. It is akin to the struggles of war engaged in by neighboring countries, such as France and Germany, where the enmity was handed down from father to son.

It was this woman's unconscious desire to establish a new dynasty with her children reared for ascendancy and domination. She was most comfortable in the role as mother, never finding her children's touch or their demands anything but welcome and desirable. She would go one step beyond her mother; she hoped that her husband might be eliminated completely from the family constellation—thereby proving to her daughters the strength, competence, and independence of the female sex.

It was only after the full recognition of this inherited prejudice that this person was able to face the alternatives of living that were open to her, and to put some order into her life. Up to that point she deceived herself by assuming that she had some rare illness or affliction of which she was the helpless victim. She had wanted to see herself as too shy and timid to have a thought or conviction of her own. These defenses of self-effacement appeared to place her on the side of the angels, and thereby promoted a pleasing image, not unlike the Virgin Mary, with whom she privately identified. But they blocked her from an understanding of her covert mission in life, which was to engage in a life-and-death struggle with a male, in the hope of eliminating him as a force in her life and the lives of her children. She therefore had secretly hoped to promote her mother's battle of the sexes.

The withdrawal of the male from the female is seen less

frequently, but probably occurs as often as the reverse. For fairly obvious reasons, a wife is not likely to make the loud complaints that a husband would. She may have been taught that she should have no interest in sexual relations, and she has almost certainly been exposed to the myth of the male's sexual avidity, so that her husband's withdrawal indicates something wrong with her, not him. Also, it is an unwise wife who casts any doubt on her husband's "maleness," so that, by instinct or reason, she remains quiet about the problem.

Current novels, such as Bruce Friedman's *A Mother's Kisses,* portray women who are not at all quiet about sex. The aunt in *Candy* is the all-time high in caricature of this kind of "modern" woman in today's literature. Perhaps the type is increasing in society as well, but the overwhelming majority of women do not wish to announce publicly that their sex lives are inadequate. While a man may call his wife frigid and receive sympathy from all directions, a woman who calls her husband inadequate may very well find herself labeled a nymphomaniac.

A twenty-five-year-old woman who asked an internist for diagnosis of an eye condition was examined and found to be in good health. However, her eyes were greatly swollen each morning. They returned to normal during the day while she was at work, but began swelling again as soon as she returned home. Close questioning revealed that her relationship with her husband was almost exclusively "intellectual." He was a highly educated man and had married much later than his friends and university associates. Before marriage his parents, both university teachers of high caliber and achievement, had impressed on him the importance of intellectual attainments and the necessity for "leaving women alone" until he had finished an extensive education and could marry. He had obeyed his parents.

Of the information obtained, this seemed the most pertinent, and the internist asked to see the husband. Here there was a further problem, for the parents had also impressed on him that if he were "clean" he would also be healthy, that doctors were for "dirty" people. This is an oversimplification, but essentially the husband's attitude was that he was "clean" and therefore did not need to see a doctor. In fact, he became infuriated by the request.

Tranquilizers gave some relief to this woman, but the eye problem did not disappear and she also suffered from insomnia. She had no history of illness and hence no acquaintance with medical attention and, because of her husband's attitude toward doctors, was uneasy about seeing the internist. She felt, however, that he was paying close attention to her and might have some solution, and so continued to see him. The husband was working at a job far below his capacity; in view of this, the internist advised that she "put her foot down," that is, insist that he become a stronger husband if he wished to remain married to her.

When the woman had summoned enough courage to threaten the husband with separation, he explained that he found it nearly impossible to work in a large, "dirty" city. The business world was also "dirty," he said, and he had been thinking for some time of taking a job as a caretaker of an establishment in the mountains. This idea seemed incredible to the wife, but the husband insisted that all that was wrong with their marriage was the dirtiness of the city and his associates, that in the clean air of the mountains they could be happy. They would not have much, but did they need much? After all, they had their intellects, and that was the important thing. Material possessions should be beneath their consideration.

At the same time, the husband pointed out that "animal" behavior was beneath them, and that she would eventually come to realize that her tendency toward this was a mistake. In the mountains they could come to understand each other better. He pointed out that if they drove into the country they could see cows huddled together for warmth. "But we're human beings," he said, "and we have blankets." Her tendency to "huddle" was repulsive to him, but she was an educated woman and could be made to see how ridiculous it was. They could then have a happy marriage. He had expressed himself on the subject before, but now was adamant about it.

Tearful and completely hopeless, the wife returned to the internist. He referred her to a psychiatrist, but this frightened her badly. Her feeling of failure in her marriage, of failure to elicit normal responses from her husband, was complete; now the internist, in recommending psychiatry, seemed to be implying that things were even worse than she had thought, that she was mentally confused. Her husband reacted to the idea of a psychiatrist even more violently than to an internist, and "saw" that he had been right all along, that her attitudes *were* wrong—so wrong that they needed correction by methods unheard of in either of their families.

This case might have had a better outcome if husband and wife could have accepted aid, but the "anti-doctor" orientation prevented this. Eventually the husband disappeared (perhaps to the mountains?) and the wife entered a state mental hospital.

While the situation described is extreme, it points up the suffering caused by inherited prejudices that make satisfactory life adjustments difficult or impossible. Whether it is the male or the female who withdraws from union, there is generally unrecognized deep-seated antagonism or revulsion or fear that must be eliminated if the marriage is to continue.

Noli me tangere—do not touch me—were the words of the newly purified Jesus to a loving Mary Magdalene. They were also the words of the abandoned Philoctetes to a self-seeking, although comparatively compassionate, Neoptolemus. Over the generations this has been the idiom of alienation. Touch we must, if we would live.

CHAPTER IX

SEX: SYMBOL AND MEANING

> Everything points to the conclusion that the child passes
> through an animistic period in the apprehension of
> reality, in which every object appears to him to be en-
> dowed with life, and in which he seeks to find again in
> every object his own organs and their activities.
>
> S. Ferenczi, *Sex in Psychoanalysis*

Sexual impulses are often denied or "extinguished" largely
because they may have been embroiled during their his-
tories in potentially disruptive social situations. They are
capable of causing grave antagonisms, with resultant fears
of loss of love, of bodily parts (castration complex), social
security, and life itself. We recurrently see that sexuality,
although vital to the preservation of race, may go against
self-interest and self-preservation. If one's erotic life can be
so potentially socially discordant, then it would best be
denied. The hysteric truly acts *as if* she or he has successfully freed himself of this scourge. The denial of one's
nature, like the suppression of truths in general, can have
only limited success. The attempts at denial require distortions—of identity, of thought processes, of emotional responses, of object relations—to degrees which frequently
cause clinical syndromes of discontent and unhappiness.

Inextricably linked to the variability of the sexual impulses is the matter of symbolization, the intellection that

more than any other characterizes the human animal. Man soon found that he was able to do many things more economically by the use of symbols—words, numerals, etc., a simple neutral artifact which represents something else, sensory condensations which can be readily understood and communicated. It was infinitely easier to write the numeral 6 and after it a picture of a cow than to take someone all the way to the back pasture and show them that number of animals. This great convenience, working so well in so many instances, was put to use by man to solve the sexual ambivalence to which he found himself heir. Why not—don't we try to apply our newly discovered tools to almost every conceivable task? (Wasn't Dr. Jonas Salk, the discoverer of the polio vaccine, asked to work on mental illness?) But in the application of symbols to his sexual problem, perversion of application and intent occurred. Whereas symbols were meant to be commonly known and easily understood to the communicants, symbols as representing sexual needs and urges were made deliberately obscure and undecipherable by the mind so as to be hidden and misunderstood by others and by one's own conscious self. They might be called negative symbols, for their purpose seemingly was not to communicate the presence of sexuality but indeed the opposite.

Symbol as found in bodily symptoms would, for example, indicate to an observer a severe headache rather than an erotic conflict. The use of symbolization with the purpose of obscuring rather than informing became a chief device in the attempt to deny sexuality. Psychoanalysts and some artists before them were able to "break" the code and discover the reality beyond the representations.

The following case illustrates quite directly this "negative" symbolization. A thirty-two-year-old married woman was referred to a psychiatric hospital by a physician from a nearby town because her malady had exhausted the acumen of many skilled physicians. She had also, one week prior to admission, visited a neurologic center in a metropolitan area. All this was to alleviate unmitigated and unalterable "headaches." The full gamut of therapies was tried. She was gradually becoming addicted to morphine, much to the alarm of her family and physician.

There appeared to be no organic cause for the disorder; none of the therapies proved efficacious. The patient was irritable and openly challenged the hospital's ability to give her any aid in the light of past failures. She had been told in the past that her headache was migraine; but she said it was not the type of "migraine" from which her mother and grandmother had suffered.

The problem was the presenting symptom, the headache. The physician offered to attempt to treat the patient, but his own prerequisite was an exhaustive, detailed description of the presenting symptom. The patient agreed that this request was not unreasonable so long as painful physical procedures were not repeated. The following is the description obtained from the patient:

First of all the headache was not an ache at all, but a pounding—like a heartbeat, but not synchronous with the heart. The pounding was mild at first but became increasingly severe, to a point of intolerance.

The location was then ascertained. The patient pointed to a specific area at the lower end of the head between the insertions of the neck muscles. It was between these "cords" in the midline. The area of activity was round and had the diameter of a silver dollar. The pounding was localized in this area. It penetrated deeply into the head in the midline and did not radiate. It was a rhythmic pounding, relentless and with crescendo.

This, of course, was only the beginning; other questions were asked to determine duration, periodicity, environmental factors, and progress. It was learned that she had been troubled with this pounding sensation for the last eight years, growing progressively worse. The attacks were periodic, on the average of twice a week, and occurred almost always at night when the patient was in bed. The duration was of from one to three hours and on occasions followed sexual intercourse. Her physician was usually called after an hour of the pounding, but as a rule medicines proved ineffective. The pounding would subside, and the patient would lie back exhausted, falling into a sound sleep. She would awaken refreshed and renewed in spirit. In addition, she revealed that this pounding sensation ceased when she left her home and family. These, essentially, were the details given by the patient spontaneously.

Indeed, the syndrome presented by the patient was certainly not typical of "migraine" as the patient herself deduced, nor was it characteristic of anything in the physician's experience of encephalopathy.

The patient had cooperated well and had fulfilled her part of the agreement. However, in the light of previous experiences, it was thought that the patient might be able to make a graphic representation of the head sensation. Pencil and paper were given to the patient and she was asked to draw a picture of her presenting symptom. She smiled at this suggestion, saying she was no artist and anyway could not see how such a thing could be done. After some encouragement, she took pencil in hand, drew the back of the head as an arc—with two lines described as "cords" tangential to the arc. The lines were connected by an arc and circles were drawn between the lines representing the point of contact—the area in which the pounding occurred.

She was then asked what she had drawn. She replied, now a little irritated, with supercilious but somewhat fearful smile: "Nothing at all—nothing—it's so silly—I wouldn't dare say what it is, I don't know." No suggestion was given and the point was carried no further during that session.

During succeeding interviews the drawing came to be an object of derision for the patient—this was indeed a queer hospital! The investigation continued.

The patient became more at ease with each interview. Her attitude toward the personnel and other patients had changed. She became very helpful and participated actively in the hospital activities.

She began to reminisce about her childhood. Her parents

had separated when she was entering puberty, a separation that followed years of marital discord. She and a brother were brought up by the mother. Mother was good but firm. She supported the family without aid from the father. "Daddy had his hands too full with his own wife and her family to support us." Yet the happiest days were the ones spent with the father on weekends and short vacations. Mother was stout, practical, substantial. "Sure," said the patient, "she gave us everything but Daddy always understood me—everyone likes Daddy." She was a popular girl and made friends easily.

When she was sixteen years old, she married a man whom she had known a few months and who had been her first beau. This union was without love, on her part at least; it was a school girl's attempt at getting away from the parental home and a mother whom she should love but apparently couldn't. Her marriage proved disastrous; and she sustained physical injury from a husband whom, she realizes now, she couldn't satisfy sexually. "I was always on the cold side. In talking to other girls, I found that sex was different for them. I'm afraid it doesn't mean much to me." The marriage was annulled after one year.

The patient was remarried four years later to a man from her hometown. "He isn't anything like the first one—he is kind and jolly. Everyone likes him." She spontaneously added, "He's just like Daddy."

Shortly after her second marriage her symptoms appeared. Her menses, always irregular, were not associated with a great deal of pain. Two years later a child was born. Menstrual symptoms—the menses became prolonged to as long as 28 days a month. Now the headaches were associated with irritability, fainting spells and general malaise.

The patient was now known in the offices of every physician in her immediate community and several consultants in nearby larger cities. In addition to strictly medical treatment, in the past ten years she had had eleven pelvic operations. These surgical procedures were allegedly designed to cure the headaches and menstrual disorders. They were in effect piece-meal extirpations of her female organs and the surgical complications thereof. Two years before her hospitalization the last vestiges of her uterus and adnexae were removed; surgical menopause had been effected.

The surgical procedures served to stop the flow of blood; but the complete castration resulted in no alleviation of the patient's symptoms. She became increasingly irritable and was incapacitated by her headaches. She was plagued by a feeling of hopelessness and inhibited to a point where she was neither wife nor mother. She had never understood what appeared to be excessive interest in and assault upon her sexual organs by zealous surgeons. In retrospect she lamented her passivity in allowing the repeated operations to be performed. It was as if the doctor suspected that her headache was rooted in her female organs.

At this point, it is perhaps needless to reiterate that her sexual interests were nil. Her only desire was to satisfy her husband and to conceal from him the fact that sex, in her own words, "Is a household duty—we have to keep our men contented." Indeed, this was a "small" price to pay for the companionship of a husband who was a pillar of strength, one upon whom she could rely, liked by everyone, "just like my Daddy."

Yet the patient began to realize that perhaps the price she was paying was not so small as she had supposed. She made inquiries about her sexual relations with her husband and, for the first time, wondered why the headaches would disappear during periods when they were not having intercourse. Her inquiry was directed back to her with "What do you think?" and "How could that be?" At this point the patient was asked to "draw her headache" again. She was reluctant to do so but finally reproduced with great precision her former representation. There was much visible anxiety—the patient stared at the drawing. She was asked the cause of the sudden change in her behavior and she replied, "Why, that's a man's sex organ—and the round part might be the abdomen that it is placed against."

The genital organ, blocked from functioning by the in-

estuous taboo—disillusionments wrought of past and present traumas—became inert. In the case of this patient, the
head became energized, took over the cathexis and indeed
the actual performance of intercourse. Thus the patient was
able to describe the sex act in terms of a rhythmic pounding in the midline posterior aspect of her head. The pounding, which started when she was in bed, increased to a high
point, a crescendo, and left her exhausted and somnolent.
Deep sleep followed, and she awoke the next morning re-
reshed. No imagination is necessary to recognize the tu-
mescence and detumescence of sexual intercourse, and one
must keep in mind that the headache was not an ache at
all—a point which had eluded every physician who examined and treated her.

It was apparent that the patient had discarded the mother
and had in effect replaced her. The impulse directed toward the father could not be tolerated by the superego;
and the ego, finding the energy of the impulse in its hands,
directed it into another organ, an organ well prepared for
its role because of a family pattern (mother and grandmother having suffered from headaches). With the patient's
first husband, the need for displacement was less because
he did not resemble the parental image. However, the second husband, by his appearance and behavior, became
closely identified with the father, making sexual relations
tantamount to incest. It was not surprising, then, to find
the patient's symptoms arising after her second marriage,
followed by a series of surgical procedures that appeared
to remove genital sexuality.

To leave this woman's dilemma at this point, with the
explication of an oedipal complex alone, does an injustice
to her and to humanity. We know that there is more than
one explanation, more than one truth. Freud, taking from
John Stuart Mill, was quick to learn and apply the con-
ceptual tool of overdeterminism or the plurality of deter-
minations, namely that there can be and usually is more
than one "meaning" to symbols as well as behavior.

The penis juxtaposed to the head picture proved to have

further significance in terms of an identity problem. For, as was discovered later, she was also grappling with the issue of what a woman can be and do. Many women sardonically ask whether brains are supposed to be in the penis since, they reflect, that if you don't possess that organ you are not given credit for any cognitive ability. The male organ supposedly produces what is vital in our civilization, and there is little respect for the opinions and thoughts of those who do not possess this fine organ of "mentation." The woman with the headache in effect drew a caricature of the present state of affairs, pointing out an irony of civilization pertinent to her own hopes and frustrations. She drew a steeple unto the church. She was confronted by a world, inner and outer, where penis and brains were very close, perhaps co-extensive, where you weren't expected to have the one without the other, or where pressing to have the one meant that you had or wanted to have the other. She heard and knew that the woman who attempted to use her brains in areas of social importance would sooner or later be called masculine.

Perhaps this patient had discovered the meaning of the unicorn, that elusive mythological animal that could be captured only by virgin maidens. Assuming that the midline horn is a phallic symbol, does the unicorn tell again that the world equates penis with brains?

As these symbolizations play on the body of an individual, as shown in the above case, where the need is greater and disintegration has been more extensive in an individual, this process is extended to the environment. This will be shown in the following cases of housewives in both their night-and-day-mares.

That cultural patterns and developments affect the psychic apparatus, the symbolic process in particular, is no new knowledge. For instance, the infant is introduced to the benefits and vagaries of household appliances almost as soon as he becomes aware of his parents, his siblings, and his own body. As he starts to crawl and move about, his first warnings and prohibitions, even earlier than those about auto-erotic activities, are against touching such things as the stove and electrical outlets.

In a recent psychiatric case seminar, an instance was revealed of a mother who kept an electric egg beater running outside her child's bedroom supposedly to help him overcome his fear of noises. Later in life this child came to analytic treatment because of extreme passivity. A study of his phantasies revealed a conceptualization of the vagina with internal whirling blades, the modern equivalent or mechanical counterpart of the "vagina dentata."

Household appliances hold many realistic dangers, as well as gratifications, for the child, as well as for the adult, and may thereby become objects onto which affects may be readily displaced. In psychopathological states, as Kubie[1] has brought out, the symbol and its concept no longer are separated, but may overlap to various degrees. In normal development, the use of household appliances provides comfort, as well as a sense of mastery over the environment. For girls, they may be aids in identification with mother in her household work and nurturing duties. Thus, whole toy kitchens in miniature can be purchased so that the daughter may act out in play what the mother performs. The appliances may liberate but for what?

In unconscious phantasies and dream life, these appliances, as noted, readily lend themselves to inappropriate effect. In adult life, in depressive and schizophrenic states, suicides and macabre mutilations are performed in the kitchen; and death by gas oven asphyxiation is a common type of suicide.

Cases are reported where the individuals put their heads into the oven. The obsessive-compulsive neurotic fears sharp instruments and constantly worries about the gas heater being turned off or the toaster being disconnected. In the hysterical individual, the appliances often symbolize objects of both an oral and genital nature, wherever there can be substitute gratification and punishment. The hysterical patient may be fascinated with gadgetry and at the same time be worried about the safety of such automatic

controls as timers, defrosters, and thermostats, as are built
into the appliances.

All modes of energy are transformed, neutralized, and
regulated in the service of making life easier and supposedly
more pleasureful. Very often the hope is that new devices
will be both labor-saving and in the long run "pay for
themselves." Abetting the economic factor is the condensation of many processes and functions in the same unit.
So there are radio-television-phonograph combinations;
clock-radios, coffee-making radios, units that heat and hu-
midify in the winter and do the opposite in the summer.
The multipurpose appliance, par excellence, is the stove.
For instance, it cooks on its surface, broils, bakes, and
grills in the inside and at the same time may heat and give
light to the room. This is aside from such things as timers,
thermostats, clocks, radios, and bells. The stove may be
supplied by one, two, or even three different sources of energy, separately, or in combination. Here is an excellent
object-representation of condensation and overdetermina-
tion. If there is dysfunction, the stove may explode, cause
injury to life and property, become disfigured, discharge
dangerous fumes and odors. Other breakdowns of appliances, often without physical dangers, have nonetheless become major household disturbances. Appropriately enough,
the comic in his skit has captured the disintegrative potential in the household wherein faulty wiring causes music to
come from the refrigerator or the radio freezes over.

In the treatment of certain neurotics, but most often in
borderline cases, one is impressed with the way appliances
are woven into the matrix of phantasy life. Kitchen and
household items very often symbolize conflicts for the
woman about her destiny and identity. Is she to be turned
into an appliance? On a deeper level (that of James
Thurber's now classic cartoon) the house and woman are
fused.

A woman in her early thirties came for analysis because
of difficulties in interpersonal relations. Her marriage of
five years had ended in divorce. Now, male acquaintances

seemed to be frightened away, even though (or because) she frequently fed them and lavished expensive gifts on them. She was fearful of driving her car, having the feeling that oncoming cars would force her off the road. Her history revealed catastrophic circumstances in her early life.

Her mother had died following a goiter operation when the patient was five. Eight months later, her father was killed in an accident on his farm. Thereafter, the patient was brought up in several foster homes, supported by public welfare. She made a submissive, passive adjustment to the women of these homes and managed to get through school and college on scholarships. Thereafter she went into professional life and became fairly successful in her chosen work. Sexually, she "had been" with several men, she had orgasms, and knew of no conscious fears in this regard. However, she revealed persistent fears about the process of childbirth, which she visualized as a gory mess. She had heard weird stories in her foster homes about what a woman went through and about the complications that might occur.

The early hours of treatment were characterized by long periods of silence and the patient's feelings of nausea. Her first dream was as follows: She was at a typewriter. She had a secret which she wrote out. She looked at the paper, then tore it up. No one would know her secret.

There were no associations to the dream, and she had no idea what the secret could be. Treatment was temporarily interrupted at this point by the therapist's vacation. On his return the patient brought the following dream at the first hour of the resumed treatment.

"I was in my apartment. I went to the refrigerator looking for food. I found that it had been turned around, the door facing the back wall and hence unavailable. I was deeply disappointed. I then turned to the stove. I touched a match to the burner. There was an immediate explosion. The stove became charred, gas emanated from it, and a stream of purple liquid seeped out from it. I was terrified and awoke."

The associations were as follows: At one of the foster homes, she had been warned repeatedly that only the foster mother could light the stove, lest it explode in somebody's face, or set the house afire. She is very sensitive to gas fumes; they make her violently ill; she often has to leave the house when there are odors. About the purple fluid, she could make no associations. She recalled that it was purple but did not know what it could have to do with a stove. She was asked if she knew of any chemical or medicine of that color. She then recalled that five years before she had been treated for a vaginal discharge with the use of purple tablets which were dissolved in the vagina.

With this added information, something of her latent thoughts could be pieced together. The stove represented her ano-genital region, not to be touched digitally. This area might become hot, explode, exude gas and colored liquids. Her secret, then, was her infantile masturbatory activity (she had discovered her hidden genitals). During the therapist's absence she was deprived of access to food (the unavailable refrigerator), and her present masturbatory activities increased.

A reconstruction of her problem became possible. Her unconscious fear was that through masturbation she had injured her genital and reproductive organs and had thus impaired her ability to have children. The burner on the stove represented her exterior clitoral region which was touched and heated. This caused an explosion which charred the stove's exterior (anal contamination) and also destroyed the inside of the oven (the womb). She feared that her chronic masturbatory activity had led to her vaginal discharge and to the need for the purple medication. These feelings of self-injury and mutilation were also related to the deaths of her parents, especially that of her mother. The goiter operation was visualized by her as a mutilative procedure, connected with oral impregnation phantasies. Her nausea and silence in the early hours of therapy proved to be on the basis of these oral phantasies.

Another example of this type of primitive symbolization was seen in a thirty-six-year-old married woman with two small sons. She came for treatment because of acute episodes of anxiety which followed the second childbirth. She became overly solicitous of both children and worried about their health, physical and mental. She was likewise very apprehensive about her own health, and often envisaged herself dying without proper medical care. Sexually, she was completely frigid, with neither clitoral nor vaginal sensations during intercourse. There had been orgasms in dreams in which she would watch herself in a mirror. But the frigidity was not her presenting complaint.

She was the only child of doting parents. She described her mother as pushing her out of the kitchen. Her mother had repeatedly told her that it was bad enough that one of them had to be burdened with household chores. Any attempts by the daughter at domesticity were belittled. The mother always pointed out how inept the daughter was at these things. After marriage, in her own home, the patient became uncomfortable in the kitchen. At this time, "knowing" her daughter's ineptness, the mother continued to warn her about household, and especially about kitchen, dangers. She feared that, during a depressive episode, the patient might harm herself with a knife or might "lose control" and open all the gas jets.

During the patient's early treatment hours, there were recurrent dreams about cooking and baking. In one, she was cooking a large turkey in her oven to bring to the therapist. Many sessions were devoted to the automatic garbage disposer which grinds up and liquefies garbage. A screw had fallen into the mechanism and had broken the apparatus. This caused her great anxiety. She became furious at her husband, and at the repair man, as well as at the bill for repairs. She related this affair to the treatment; she felt that she was being treated like garbage, that she was being ground up instead of being put back together. In her neurosis, she attempted to rescue herself from the

conventional expectations of womanhood. Wasn't there
method in her madness?

Recalling Ferenczi's quotation, at the beginning of this
chapter, one can speculate about the effects on the infant's
mental apparatus of perceiving in the inventions around
him the actualization of his own animistic projections. In
the child this may lead to phobic reactions relative to these
moving, sucking, whirling, sound-producing machines. In
the adult, annoyance or the opposite, fascination, with the
"mechanized living," may reflect the persistence of these
fears in latent form.

We have seen in the foregoing examples how the unconscious mechanism of symbolization operates to distort
and hide sexual impulses. It was thought by Freud that this
process is extensively found in the "psychopathology" of
the psychoneuroses. Symbolization here, however, goes contrary to its usual conscious use—that of aiding communication and understanding. For want of a better expression,
we here have labeled this intrapsychic process negative
symbolization.

In popular usage, we have called a mammiferous movie
star the sex symbol of her day. This is, of course, very
different from negative symbolization, for she was consciously built up by movie agents to represent sex, unmis-
takably, and more authentically than any other woman, to
the public. As a result, whenever she was seen on the
screen, or for that matter, whenever her name was mentioned, sex came to mind and perhaps to body as well.
But here as she was a sex symbol, she was also a potential
source of titillation and arousal. The bodily responses may
say a lot about the frustrations or naiveté of the observers
but does nothing to diminish her as a symbol.

A similar degree of passion of another nature can be
elicited by the raising of the flag or the blare of the bugle.
We can readily see how sexual symbolization in the conscious and everyday sense is specifically designed to facilitate and promote passion—whereas unconscious, negative
if you will, seeks to disguise, repress and deny it.

Apart from both the conscious and unconscious process of symbolization as noted above, sexual behavior has taken on meanings throughout history of such significance to the individual and society to a point of its transmogrification. One can see why for apart from its "physiological" and sensational dimensions, it is the sole demiurge of racial survival. A most serious thing indeed. Yet, as Mary McCarthy has said, sex is funny.[2] It is certainly nonsensical, takes no brains, solves no worldwide problems (creating some now). It is coarse, gross, instantaneous, needing no pedantic course of appreciation to enjoy or participate in it. It is available to everyone regardless of wealth and race, color or creed, as they say; this is a God-given right. Even "temporal" law maintains this recognition; there are laws protecting consortium. However, as might be expected, it is held to be a masculine necessity.

For instance in the State of New York, if a woman is injured in an auto accident or on a factory job, the husband may bring suit against the defendant to recover damages for loss of sexual contact due to the wife's physical incapacitation. This right to sue for loss of consortion does not extend to the wife, who according to the philosophy of New York State, does not suffer damage or deprivation if her husband is out of commission.[7] It has been the one institution that the high have shared with the low. In the South during and after slavery, even though the white slave owner would never pray in the same church as his Negro slave, he would have sexual intercourse with her. Sex, then, has been more successful than religion, politics, law, in the struggle to bring people together. James Baldwin,[3] in his novel *Another Country,* seems to arrive at this conclusion although he seems to pre-empt homosexuality. Paradoxically, sex, as democratic as it is, also promotes the fears of miscegenation which in turn delay a true brotherhood of man.

Sex needs no special education, no skill in development that is not readily available to everyone. In fact, its value decreases with acculturation, the greatest premium being placed on primitivism. College degrees are not much help here; bacchanalia asks for no baccalaureate.[4]

Adult sexual relations involve an acceptable hypochondriasis in which intense feelings from all parts of the body can be experienced and reported upon. It furthermore allows a temporary re-experiencing of past infantile sensations dealing with bodily surfaces and orifices which ordinarily would be prohibited. It replaces seriousness and goal-directedness with abandon and aimlessness. It substitutes the concrete for the abstract. Here is something you can touch, something tangible and with results quickly arrived at, a far cry from the agonies and futilities found elsewhere in living. And, it is non-verbal, nothing to be misunderstood or misinterpreted; if there is any tyranny, it is of the flesh itself which, unlike words, can usually be excused. And, it is private, a privacy that is universally respected in a world where intrusion is the rule rather than the exception. It is exclusive, a unique luxury otherwise unknown to most mortals since the infantile nursing experience. As those concerned with the population explosion have aptly observed, for most of the people on earth today "procreation is their only recreation."

The sexual act is a summary of the past, a reminder of one's history, a reaffirmation of one's roots and rootedness in humanity, in the family, and, to a degree, as the French observe, a reminder of the inevitable—memento mori. Sex helps us know our place in the scheme of things, a concatenation of the body and mind, of past and present, of present and future, of our biological and historical dimensions. It is in all a friendly, funny act of communion.

Sexuality, the one "instinct" of man that is capable of an infinite number of distortions, is social as well as physical. You can go just so long without food or water, for substitutes for them are illusory; but you can survive a lifetime without what is conventionally called sexual intercourse. Man has always dallied with his sexual impulses; gratified them, denied them, resisted them, misdirected them, sent them on side trips and excursions, made them tests of loyalty, fidelity, prowess, power, character, weakness, and servility. But the sexual impulses, although capable of vast distortions, denials, and transcendisms, cannot be extinguished. It has long been an ambition of mankind to be free of at least one of his biological givens and necessities. For instance, he has struggled for an antigravity scheme, like flying or a perpetual-motion mechanism that would ignore the laws of energy. (Children engage in breath-holding contests.) There is little doubt that mankind has been trying like mad to accomplish the extinction of sexual impulses. It is in this context that we can understand Freud's debatable and unshakable insistence that sexuality and its distortions underlie psychoneurosis and other mental difficulties. Some of us feel that what he observed as sexual problems are better stated as problems of the sexes. Its unique feature of plasticity gives the illusion of destructibility. In some psychoneuroses, where it appears for all practical purposes that sexuality has been extinguished, it is then discovered in the nooks and crannies and recesses and protuberances of both the body and mind. More importantly, sexuality has taken on a most profound "meaning," that of devotion, justice, and fidelity, as already described in Chapter V. This meaning has led to the importance of kinship and other qualities that have distinguished him from other animals. Since man has given *meaning* to sexuality, it can no longer be thought of as a purely biological function or sensational event.

Of course, love. Love and sex have had a long but restless marriage. Freud did not like to use the term, love; he saw his psychoneuroses as products of faulty sex—not of love. The concept of love is entirely too abstract to handle clinically or "scientifically." Sex and love are often used interchangeably. We say "make" love; it is doubtful whether love can be made; it can only be felt. Sex is what is "made." What is meant by love is usually lust. Fusing love and sex—ideal in the abstract—can be in reality quite burdensome and confusing—doing injury to both. This is not to disparage love as it pertains to marriage, family, brotherhood, country, and work. It may indeed be an important dimension of sexual behavior but not necessarily so extensive or congruent. Most sexual activity in the world today is outside of even the pretense of love—probably without deleterious effects on either pleasure or performance. Yet, we read the following prescriptive passage from a most popular, widely read handbook on marriage, one that undoubtedly has influenced modern thought (and confusion) on the subject: "Voluptuous pleasure *alone,* however refined and varied, cannot bring real happiness, without that solace to the soul which humanity desires, and *must* forever seek. Such pleasure is not only condemned by Moral Theologians and Heidelberger Confessors: Agnostic and Rationalist Ethics are equally severe in their judgment. No person of fine aesthetic insight or emotional nature can think for a moment of winning happiness from sensuality *without* any psychic element. No such person can or will consent to play the loveplay *Ideal Marriage requires, to perform genital stimulation, if Love does not inspire them; Love that unifies flesh and soul. Otherwise they would be impossible, for they would inspire instinctive loathing and repulsion.*"[5]

If these were the normal or average or even the ideal expectations for marriage, love and sex, there would be no survivors. Yet multitudes have read passages such as this with great seriousness and probably worry. Granting the seriousness and importance of sexual behavior to community stability, kinship, and to racial survival itself, one may ask whether altogether too "much" meaning, moral and ethical, has been given to it. Are we really justified in using sexual behavior to discredit and persecute as we now do to homosexuals?[6] Can we in justice withhold welfare payments from mothers who engage in adultery? The above are simple examples of severe and often persecutory judgments that are made on sexual behavior.

Somehow our preoccupation with sexual behavior in general has distorted our moral sense. We have judged the morality and worthiness of people almost solely on their sexual behavior and proclivities. Ergo, a young girl is worthy or valuable because she is a virgin although completely corrupted in values of charity, consideration for others, or ability to love. Similarly a husband is moral if he has observed fidelity but has enslaved his "loved one" and kept her mindless. The preoccupation with sex has kept us from exploring and defining more sensible and authentic calipers for worthiness—better things to measure a man or a woman by. And, there is the grave well-founded suspicion that much of the morality of sex is meant to encourage voluntary servitude as well as *abjuration* of personal freedom. One shudders to think of the number of reputations and lives that have been destroyed throughout our history by our largely irrational attitudes toward sex. It was still another way that we could be cruel to one another. It is not at all difficult to understand sexual fears and abhorrences. There are optimists among us who feel that mankind can make judgments of a person's worth in factors other than sexual. Perhaps de-moralization of sex is a logical contemporary project.[8]

NOTES

1. Lawrence Kubie, "The Distortion of the Symbolic Process," *Psychoanalyt. Q.,* I (1953), p. 59.

2. Mary McCarthy, *The Group* (New York: Harcourt, Brace & World, Inc., 1963).

3. James Baldwin, *Another Country* (New York: Dell Publishing Co., 1960).

4. Mary McCarthy, *On the Contrary* (New York: Farrar, Straus & Cudahy, 1946), pp. 167-73.

5. T.H. Van de Velde, *Ideal Marriage* (New York: Random House, 1965).

6. Lars Ullerstam, *The Erotic Minorities* (New York: Grove Press, 1966), p. 94.

7. Kanowitz, Leo, *Women and The Law, The Unfinished Revolution,* University of New Mexico Press, Albuquerque, 1969, chap. 3.

8. The de-moralization of sex amongst the young is becoming widely apparent. At the annual conference of directors of

B'nai B'rith Hillel Foundation, Jewish chaplains reported a sharp drop in the number of students seeking their advice on sexual matters. One rabbi observed: "The guilt that used to exist no longer does." (*New York Times,* Dec. 18, 1969, p. 41.)

CHAPTER X

INVECTIVE AND INVENTION

Those who love the truth must seek love in marriage, love without illusions.

Albert Camus, *A Writer's Notebook*

Marriage is a union where dreams and nightmares can be shared. These can be phantasies, goals, agonies, and illusions. Individuals may build a milieu on the ground and in the air which will accommodate both partners. They undertake to create a reality which somehow mitigates external actuality.[1] The conjugal pair privately indulge in phantasies which would be generally poorly tolerated by others. These are usually imagined indulgences that they are able to communicate to each other without encountering or bringing down upon themselves shame and contempt. With the burdens of painful disappointments, they help create for themselves a world of make-believe which both of them can carry off in their own home without the stage setting of a mental hospital or sanatorium. The reader will recall the game of playing house with imaginary characters created as needed.[2] Children are able to do this in an unabashed way. They gather to engage in this phantasy play with a natural respect for the imaginative freedom and indulgences of their mates. "Let's pretend that this is a baby" or a "mother or father," one child says to the other.

"All right, all right, and I'll be the doctor," is the reply. This respect for the phantasies of the other is for a few precious childhood years only. After that, with development of conscience and intellectual propriety, children become ashamed of this behavior and will no longer engage in it with one another.

In all marriages, according to varying degrees of need, this phantasy indulgence is present and is a cementing force in the relationship. There is no more disenchanting occasion than that whenever one mate will not tolerate, and indeed ridicules, the secret phantasies which up to that time they had shared. For a private world of make-believe is not alien to human needs. Often these take the form of private religions, theories of health, food fads, ptolemaic systems that one could not want to go beyond the walls of one's home. This is a *folie a deux*[3] that makes for a mutual respect not only for the strengths (this is often easy), but also for the frailties of humanity.

Similarly, married mates allow each other the freedom of aggressive speech and behavior not tolerated elsewhere. The observer might readily interpret this as overwhelming hostility and incompatibility, but in many instances the safety of a firm and secure bond between them allows for behavior of abandon. Often this is very childish and cruel, but nonetheless it should not be cursorily prejudged as malignant. These indulgences can be carried too far, or one or the other may break the rules of their game.[4]

An outsider might meddle and destroy the secret compact. At such a point, one or the other mate might want to play no longer or seek revenge for the unfairness of the other.

A poignant illustration of such an arrangement and its vicissitudes is found in Edward Albee's play, "Who's Afraid of Virginia Woolf?"[5] George is a professor of history at his father-in-law's university. He is in his forties and is reminded by his wife, Martha, that he has not reached the expectations for him on the academic ladder, either in his own specialty or in administration. She, a few years older than he, is childless, the rather aimless but obedient daughter of the college president. Both constantly vilify and tear at one another, especially in Bacchanalian orgies. They drink together and talk together but never spare each other. A young instructor of biology, Nick, and his dull-witted wife, Honey, are invited, not in the evening, but in the early hours of the morning, the time of dreaming and phantasies where spirits have their say. Nick is young, of athletic form, ambitious and practical in his ways of getting ahead; not willing to rely solely on his academic or scientific performance. He married a Dumb Dora with an inheritance from an evangelistic father. She precipitated the marriage with a pseudo-pregnancy, forcing Nick to make a dishonest woman of her through marriage. She is a 19th century maiden right out of Breuer and Freud[6] who not only is prone to pseudocyesis but is pseudo in most other ways. She takes all conversation concretely, has no humor or wit, and gets "sick" when voices are raised in anger. She apparently fears sex and childbirth, associating any private behavior as doing violence to women. George and Martha take the opportunity of this audience to tear at each other with the truths of each other's inadequacies. In the course of all this, the older couple allude to the activities of a son of theirs. This seems to be the foreplay for a seduction of Nick by Martha, egged on by a ruthless, gratuitous explication of the lives of Nick and Honey by George, who remains the historian. All along, George seems to be encouraging the sexual excursion of his wife with the younger man. The sexual experience between them is not successful, Nick proving to be a pipcock. Martha is not kind; she chides Nick and confesses, to the amazement of Nick (but not of the perceptive audience), that her only gratifying sexual experiences have been with her husband. In the last act, seemingly out of pique at his wife's open sexual transgression, but really because she did the unpardonable: she committed the greatest breach of fidelity, she brought out in public their secret about a son—who was in fact illusory. Because she initiated this betrayal to others, he announces that a telegram has come indicating the son's death. Martha responds with, "How could you kill him?" And the shock of understanding comes to Nick that the son was imaginary, a private phantasy that has sustained this disappointed pair. She violated the rules of their game, spoiled it by public exposure. At this point, George, who could give and take almost anything, including flaunted sexual infidelity, reached his limit and spoiled the thing for her too. Her perfidy to their shared indulgence, which could be maintained only when private as well as secret, was for him unforgivable.

What capricious god or whim impelled Martha to destroy their bond is difficult to say. Was unreality between them going so far that it offended sanity? Or did the hostility of the male-female rivalry break through the mutuality that had existed up to that point? We don't know, but it did bring the participants down to earth, and they appeared more hopeful, if not happier.

Perhaps they were better off with their illusion. It may be that married people are entitled to a psychic toilet to share with each other, with the reasonable expectation that it be otherwise private. In this play there are no platitudes. Albee wishes to destroy another illusion, that people can live together for several decades without the intrusion of the worst kind of acrimony. We are generally given a picture of romantic love which knows only tenderness. Albee tells us that the intimacies which characterize a true marriage eventually bring forth all that is vile and contemptible in humanity, as well as all that is good. Those who are unprepared for the worst suffer the greatest disillusionment and do not end up together as did Martha and George. The miracle of marriage is found in the ability of those who can transcend the inevitable cruelties and deformations. Albee's service has been the destruction of the myth of conventional happiness in marriage that is handed down from generation to generation. This unnatural and unrealistic expectation of fulfillment has led to dissolutions of marriages which otherwise might have con-

tinued. These individuals were never prepared for, and
never could tolerate, the agonies which intimacies ultimately bring forth.

In everyday life we generally do not acknowledge the
realities put forth in this play. The shared illusion about
the son of George and Martha is quite exceptional. Usually
it is done in subtler and more socially syntonic ways.
Philip Roth's description of the father in *Letting Go* is an
interesting case in point.[7] There the father, a successful
dentist, is found grief-stricken and in mourning for his dead
wife of a long, seemingly happy marriage. In her last letter to her son she reveals, in the terminal phase of her
chronic and fatal illness, that she had quietly endured much
and had lived out her years in the shadow of her husband's needs. Yet she had been a faithful wife, serving his
needs loyally. Although always healthy and seemingly socially well adjusted, at home he insisted on a regime of
food faddism and obeisance to health cults which went contrary to science and his scientific orientation as a professional man. This usually put a strain on the home routine
and family life, but she seemed to cooperate in his personal
irrationalities, apparently without ridiculing him and above
all never revealing them to others beyond what he would
himself. She is portrayed as only indulging in his make-
believe world and doing nothing to humiliate him. This,
of course, is the long-suffering-wife syndrome. Did he
reciprocate in some way, respecting a secret of hers? Roth
doesn't tell us. She, however, is described as of a scholarly
lineage. She had come from Germany as a refugee with
her family to start a new life in America. Having married
a man she felt to be socially and intellectually inferior to
her, she then apparently turned to her only son for solace
and perhaps hopes of vicarious attainment. But, as loyal as
she is portrayed to be, the betrayal did come in her waning
hours. In the letter, apparently posthumously delivered, she
concretely revealed to her son that all was not as it appeared to be. She had her final revenge in the letter and
laid the groundwork for an estrangement of the son from

his father. Father then spent his remaining time, until a re-marriage, in pridelessly seeking out his son. He became a beggar, helplessly asking for crumbs. The son now might be a substitute as confidant in his secret quest for immortality. The son resisted these attempts and turned instead to finding a meaning and direction to his own life. In the course of this, he experimented with a variety of relationships, vicariously experienced conjugal pleasures and miseries of others, did some helping and meddling, but seemed to have a great reserve about taking the marital step himself. Perhaps he had learned too well that women don't keep secrets even when they appear to. It is not that they are unable to keep secrets but perhaps oppression or feelings of oppression eventually find voice.

At times, the mutually held secret phantasy becomes too burdensome and is revealed to an outsider by both parties. In the Robert Frost poem, "The Witch of Coös,"[8] it is the secret held for years by mother and son about the murder of her husband and the migration of his bones from the cellar grave to the attic. It is the skeleton in the attic that is heard trying to get out the locked and blockaded attic door. They had never revealed their crime and its consequences to anyone, living in the terror of the rattling bones. Was it their guilty consciences that made them "confess" their story of "twilight zone" mayhem, or was it that their shared reality, inhabited now for years with ghost and spirits and the unnatural, was so secure that it could not be damaged or destroyed by an outsider's skepticism or disbelief? The story was told, not as an imaginary problem or a plea for contradiction, but as a confession of unquestionable occurrences. The listener is left with the problem of trying to determine if the story is completely a phantasy or whether the part about the murder might indeed be true. Perhaps it was the cunning of mother and son to add the story of the movable bones, for this brings incredulity to the whole story. It would then be thought that they fabricated the whole thing, whereas the murder of the husband might indeed be true. They then are able to make a confession—one that no one will believe.

Disregarding the cloak-and-dagger aspects of this story, one observes in Frost's poem the obeisance of mother and son to a tale that is part of their shared reality, so firmly coated and supported by their joined authorities that it can be told to the visitor. Now there is no danger that they can be talked out of it, be humiliated or made to feel ashamed. They have been carried beyond such points of communication between themselves and outer actualities. They tell their story with the same confident assurance and total indifference to external authority as the Christs of Ypsilanti or of Islip State Hospital spoke of their divinity. Since their commitment is total and mother and son confirm one another, and since secrecy and isolation have until then insured against intrusions that might cast doubt, the phantasies and illusions become elevated to the level of nonnegotiable truths.

The difference between the characters of the "Witch of Coös" and "Who's Afraid of Virginia Woolf?" is the quantitative aspect of commitment to unreality.[12] George and Martha had too much worldly-oriented conscience to admit the illusions publicly. This would cover them with shame. They apperceptively knew of their own falseness but had too much pride to reveal it. Mother and son of the Frost tale were beyond pride and also beyond apperceptive capabilities. Their primitivism would obviate their ever asking the question, "Who's Afraid of Virginia Woolf?"

Couples are able to maintain their mythologies for years. These often are the "happiest" and indeed the closest marriages. Here there is apt to be a fusion of partners inextricably held in the magnetic field of their fabricated world. Illusion is traffic in illicit stuff, and no one is brought closer than partners in crime. They have transgressed together, strayed together into the Eleusinian fields and must evermore be bound in a secret pact.

Clinically, this was seen in a union between a paranoid

male and a young woman with a strong masculinity complex. Although never married, they lived in a successful conjugal relationship for years. He was an individual of great achievement in his professional field. He had had a disastrous marriage and a daughter therefrom, whom he supported but never saw. He claimed that his misogynic nature was derived from this bitter and disappointing experience early in his life. He was overtaken by periods of black depressive moods which he treated by returning to his mother's home and being attended by her. In the course of a few weeks, he would then recover and be able to resume his work. In his professional life, he traveled a great deal, never being able to remain at one place. This was in part due to the nature of his work and in part to persecutory ideas which would force him to leave the "contaminated" area. His relations with women were poor; he was obsessed with the idea that women were plotting to become pregnant in order to trick him into marriage.

He did befriend the young girl of this story. She was the daughter of a destitute family as a result of the father's preoccupation with an invention for which he gave up his job. Her mother was long-suffering in this and took over all functions of the household as the father had abdicated from them. The daughter, growing up in this depressing environment, was noted to persist in tomboyishness into her adolescence. Instead of trading her dungarees for a dress, and tree-climbing for dancing, she persisted in acting and being drawn to those activities with which boys are generally identified. She showed complete interest in what boys do but showed no interest in being what she called a "receptacle" for them. Her sexual bent was toward her own sex and she had several such affairs. She loathed the sexual aspects of the man-woman relationship; could never see herself as a wife and would not contemplate bearing children.

The two principals met on a ski run and became friends. He confessed his suspiciousness of female motives to her; she readily sympathized and agreed that women were capable of low-down tricks. He then made the demand of sexual intercourse on her, not out of love, or for pleasure, or subjugation of her, but on the basis that he needed sexual release to preserve his health. He would be happy if she would cooperate in this salubrious arrangement. For her, there would be complete equality; they would participate in fishing and hunting trips, mountain-climbing, all those activities generally difficult for her to join alone.

They, then, formed a relationship—not on the husband and wife paradigm, but in another game that children play —that of doctor and patient. She was the doctor, he the patient. In this way it didn't much matter who was the male or female. Sex was then not the fearsome, demeaning, socially disruptive activity, but was instead a curative procedure, a palliation administered out of kindness and benevolence. The bedroom became a recovery room and bodies were not violated but revitalized. The probing, insertions, inspections, palpations were necessary adjuncts of the ministrations of healers rather than lovers. The memories of the childhood doctor games served them well. Because they shared a fear of their sexuality and sexual identities, they were able to establish a relationship on the terms that were still available to them.

They created and faced crises with each other. He accused her of trying to get him to marry her. She would point out that she would never reduce herself to such a role. They would then both deny that theirs was the conventional man-woman union. On the other hand he could escape the image of the powerful and attacking male by subjecting himself to a "cure"—that all but confirming his feminine identification. This allowed her to desert her own dangerous femininity and replace it with a male doctoring role.[9] They helped each other by the illusion they created and shared. They were both helped and were able to maintain a social intimacy which could be maintained only by make-believe that denied those facts of life that both equally dreaded.

These two people were of inestimable comfort to each

other. Both living on the threshold of their sanity, they were unable to fit into the conventional molds in accepting their own biological and social selves and could not therefore relate to others in the social reality of their environment. For him, being a male was too intimately connected with competitive destructiveness which meant ultimate dissolution for him. He would disown his own sex-linked heritage as too cruel to be tolerated by himself or others. She, on the other hand, fearful and disdainful of her femininity, could never enter a relationship where she would be expected to play a role of "subservience and suffering" as she witnessed with her own mother. She was confronted with the specter of what men and women do to each other in their usual relationships. She could have none of this and would deny her own sexual organs and their childbearing functions. As there was an illusory son in Albee's play, there was a phantasied organ in her that could now be life-sustaining rather than life-producing. At the height of their excitement, their organs were mutually owned and they could forget the distinctness of their biological selves; each could feel the relief from the terrors of the differentiation for which each was so ill-prepared.

They fought, had soul-deep crises together, made conventional accusations of infidelity, and displayed petulance and irritability as couples are supposed to do. But they "knew" that each was there principally for the health of the other and their only sin would be one of neglect if one were not there when the other needed him. On the basis of their particular compact, neglect would not be an indication of lack of love but rather a sort of malpractice.

Unlike Quentin and Maggie in *After the Fall* (see Chapter II), the treatment that these two gave each other was always physical. There were never issues of deep convictions or psychological analysis by one of the behavior of the other. There were not efforts of reformation or moral rehabilitation. They never gave any indication that they were out to rescue or to help each other. They never advised nor directed nor condemned attitudes or ways of living. There was not the imposition of intellect on intellect; concern for matters of health meant just that, concrete and physical; there were no esoteric abstractions or normative imperatives here!

That this couple used the doctor game to the exclusion of all others does not mean that this game is not widely used. In the early days of psychoanalysis, Freud[10] told of having advised a reluctant wife that her refusal to have sexual relations with her husband might have an adverse effect on his health! Another early theory of anxiety that Freud promulgated involved the health theme. Here repression of sexual instincts would cause their conversion into noxious substances which produce the symptoms of anxiety and unhealth. In the words of Madison Avenue, there are those who will never relinquish the idea that sexual intercourse is a treatment, rather than a treat.

The possible combinations of mutual illusion-confirming are infinite. Unconscious pacts are made in which one mate may say, "If you put up with my folly, I'll indulge yours." But if there is a betrayal or unwillingness of one to go along with the other, the house may fall in. Thereafter, revenge is sought to make the withdrawing party sorry for his defection.

One wife was very hypochondriacal. She worried about each twitch, ache, or pain that she felt or imagined. Indeed, in her mind these somatic messages represented some dreaded or malignant disease. She had "successfully" converted her emotional and interpersonal problems into bodily symptoms. She preferred having physical diseases, even terrible ones, to mental ones. This was her personal folly, to have make-believe physical illnesses. But she needed confirmation, so she would report her physical complaints to her husband, asking him to look at this bump on her elbow or that discoloration of the skin, wondering if these might indicate cancer. Not being a physician, his opinion offhand would seem unimportant to her, but he would *play* doctor. He would be expected by her to inspect the area, listen to her complaints, and say that it was just a superficial bruise or that perhaps she should see a doctor about it since there was something there. This would satisfy her, and she could thereafter go to bed and sleep. However, on the instigation of friends who witnessed this behavior, the husband was induced to try to change his ways. They told him that he might be doing her great harm by indulging her in these whims. These things, they said, were purely mental and the sooner she realized this the better.

Thereupon, he changed his tactics. When she presented her "lesions," he would make fun of her. "More cancer," he would say reproachfully. At other times he would say seriously to her that she was imagining all of this, that these were figments of her mind, that she ought to face reality or get some professional help. Her tranquility was thereafter replaced by rage and disappointment with her husband and alienation from their dubious friends.

But the friends knew only one side of the picture; they were never aware of the hidden contract that had existed between them. They did not know of his folly; it was not as evident as hers. There had been an exchange of vows of respect which he had violated, and thereafter he became the object of her revenge. These contracts or vows were not openly arrived at, like buying a car or a house, but evolved as an "unconscious" understanding between them. As it was, his folly concerned sexual intercourse. In his personal need to deny sexual passion, he wished to live in a state of celibacy even though married. It was his pride (sickness?) that he could resist his internal desires as well as stimulation from a woman. He would not have sexual relations with her, always found excuses. The wife, preoccupied with physical complaints and worries, looked at his indifference with her own indifference. She said nothing about this most blatant breach of manliness. As long as he sympathetically received her physical lamentations, she ignored his sexual conduct.

However, with his change of behavior, she could not let him get away with his folly. Now she became sexually aggressive; she complained that he neglected her; she taunted him about his manhood and lack of it; she made nightly overtures, now sexual instead of hypochondriacal. With this he became panicky as she was attempting to undermine his passivity. She was getting her revenge for the betrayal that he had initiated. In the exchange it appeared that if he would not allow her to play the role of patient, she would not permit him to be a celibate Christ. He now had to face the facts of conjugal life as he had made her face her use of the body as a sounding medium of the emotions. There were moments of truth that neither of them was prepared to face and their marriage ended. It was a paradox that in this instance the need for "folly confirmation" appeared to eclipse values and commitments of a positive nature.

The doctor-patient game that is so much of childhood phantasies prevails in adulthood more than is generally realized. George in Albee's "Who's Afraid of Virginia Woolf?" chides the young instructor of biology on this point, on learning that he married the girl next door with whom this game must have been his first "intimacy." It was also apparent that this doctor-patient relationship did continue with the younger couple. For Honey expressed herself through bodily symptoms as part of her timidity and perhaps her stupidity. Their marriage had for its basis that most playful occurrence, pseudocyesis, in which her abdomen blew up like a balloon or like a sail in a good wind. This "air" married them notwithstanding the fact that she was also an heiress. Honey continued to have "qualms" in, if not about, the marriage. She quickly became physically ill when confronted by reality and spent most of the time in the bathroom where the doctor-patient game is most often enacted.

Yet we can look upon these games with deep humility and recall the words of the Clown in "As You Like It": "We that are true lovers, run into strange capers; but as all is mortal in nature, so is all nature in love mortal in folly."[11]

No one will be surprised by the statement that the conditions of love itself involve the initiation and perpetuation of an illusion or, perhaps more correctly, illusions. Love distorts judgment, blocks insight, and softens reality. It makes one feel worthy when one is not; it gives a feeling of humility to the great. It tranquilizes the aggressive and propels the passive. And the conjugal two keep the secret of their make-believe world. For love is worthless if it is not secret or private or confidential, just as the games of children in their elaborative machinations fall to the ground when uncovered by intrusive grown-ups. No one, again, will be surprised by the statement that (for reasons too complex for us to understand) illusions are a necessary condition for successful living and perhaps for survival itself. In Freud's idiom, love perhaps gives us an acceptable psychosis, a circumscribed two-person system which takes the onus of suspicion away from it because it is not onanistic, it is shared, and it generally promotes the needs of society. Society always has tolerated shared illusions much better than those held exclusively. If one proclaims that he is a god, he most likely will end up in an asylum; if he is lucky enough to have others believe him, if he gathers a following, he will not be bothered by the authorities. So we might draw from this analogy that one is unsafe with illusions until someone else "believes" them. And lovers are unsafe who can dispute that they seek to lie with each other.

NOTES

1. Erik H. Erikson, "Reality and Actuality," *J. Amer. Psychoanalyt. Assoc.*, X (July 1962), p. 451.

2. Eric Berne, *Games People Play: The Psychology of Human Relationships* (New York: Grove Press, 1964).

3. Richard Michaud, "Folie a deux," *American J. Psychiat.*, CXXI, for. Ross V. Speck (Oct. 1964), p. 1.

4. Thomas S. Szasz, *The Myth of Mental Illness* (New York: Paul Hoeber, Inc., 1961), pp. 223-58.

5. Edward Albee, *Who's Afraid of Virginia Woolf?* (New York: Giant Cardinal Book, Pocket Books, Inc., 1963).

6. Josef Breuer and Sigmund Freud, "Studies on Hysteria," *Works of Sigmund Freud,* Standard Ed., trans. James Strachey (London: Hogarth Press, 1955), pp. 14-32.

7. Philip Roth, *Letting Go* (New York: Random House, 1961).

8. Robert Frost, "The Witch of Coös," *Complete Works of Robert Frost* (New York: Henry Holt & Co., 1949).

9. Robert Seidenberg, "Changes in the Symbolic Process During a Psychoanalytic Treatment," *J. Nervous and Mental Disease,* CXXVII (Aug. 1958).

10. Sigmund Freud, *The Problem of Anxiety,* trans. H. A. Burker (Albany, N. Y.: Psychoanalytic Quarterly Press, 1936).

11. William Shakespeare, "As You Like It," *The Complete Works of William Shakespeare* (Cleveland, Ohio: The World Publishing Co., n.d.), p. 216.

12. Blum, H. P., *The Psychoanalytic View of 'Who's Afraid of Virginia Woolf',* in Journal of the Amer. Psa. Assoc., Vol. 17:888:1969.

CHAPTER XI

DIONYSIAN DILEMMA

Arcanum demens detegit ebrietas
In vino veritas
(*What soberness conceals, drunkenness reveals.*)

I wonder often what the Vintners buy
One half so precious as the stuff they sell.

The Rubaiyat of Omar Khayyam

Many couples live for years like Bacchus and Maenad, spending their hours together in varying degrees of alcoholic intoxication. During these periods they can vent both vituperative and loving feelings in a dreamlike state. They allow each other a full range of uninhibited behavior and expression that could not be tolerated with anyone else or in any other social situation. They allow themselves to be playmates and they play their games completely unabashed. The alcohol causes a mutual ablation of superego so that neither can call the other childish or immature. There is no betrayal, and neither is ever judgmental. The chief danger in this situation is that the inebriation prevents one from being protective of the other. There is no one to set limits, to call a halt, and one or both may end up with delirium tremens.

If it were not for the tragic physical results that often accrue, this union is unique in marriage, for here, unlike most, husband and wife enjoy being together and prefer each other's company to any other. They are oblivious, and want to be, of worldly problems and intrusions which they effectively wall out. It is two against the world, and with alcohol they are able to prolong their honeymoon days for years. They honor each other by a devotion and unity which the real world rarely tolerates or permits. Very often investigation shows that both, in their earlier years, had brother-sister relationships of great closeness where play went on endlessly. It seems that this sibling experience is cherished by both, and in their marriage there is a mutual assent to continue to sanctify and relive these memories. But they could never live in this playfulness with ruthless conscience present. Conscience would never allow these indulgences and therefore it has to be, as Freud put it, dissolved in alcohol.

A picture of serenity in such a relationship is not to be assumed by the somewhat idealized descriptions given above. The state of inebriation can never be continuous; the external world cannot forever be forgotten. One has to buy and pay for the "anaesthesia"; there must be provision made for the "pad" to play on; and, out of the corner of one's eye, social consciousness always comes into view to plague one. One is reminded that he is part of the cosmos and has to recognize, sooner or later, this tie. When the realities of the outside world and internal organs intrude on this phantasy world, the sparks begin to fly and others come into the picture—families, social agencies, psychiatrists, and mental hospitals.

Mary was a lamb. When she appeared in the consultation room, she was dressed in tight white slacks, had her platinum hair cascaded on her head, with pink bows there and on her blouse. This was not the first psychiatrist to whom she had been sent; she generally terminated after two or three sessions. Things had become critical now; the suburban neighborhood was after her scalp, with or without ribbons.

Mary started out the morning and ended each day with

the consumption of at least a few quarts of wine. Her two children were cared for by a nurse, but she was apt to get lonely and call men to her home—often the husbands of neighbors. There were recurrent scenes of violence, suicidal attempts with barbiturates, and slashed wrists. In the evening her husband would return from his inherited business and, after a long assault of invectives between themselves, he would settle down with his bottle of scotch and they would continue to drink together throughout the night. In serious episodes, they were both taken to emergency rooms of hospitals and psychiatric wards.

During their drinking bouts, they followed one another through each room of the house, performing a different play for each new scene. They romped in the cellar, playing tag and hide-and-go-seek in the bins. In the kitchen they made paste of flour and water and threw it at one another; in the bathroom, they would spray one another, and so on. They were re-enacting a slapstick comedy in the tragedy of their existence. Both lived in a state of high anxiety when they were sober; they joined each other to achieve their grand tranquilization.

Mary was raised by her mother and grandmother after her father died of pneumonia when she was five. He had been an alcoholic and died as a result of overexposure; was found one night in a snowbank. The family was poor; the mother supported the family as a waitress. She was now devoted to the young child who had doll-like beauty and was much admired. The mother, however, was obsessed with the fear that the girl would be taken advantage of and placed strong prohibitions on dating, being away from home after dark, etc. The daughter did things behind her back but would have deep feelings of remorse for having deceived her hard-working mother. Mary became pregnant at the age of sixteen and the mother whisked her away for an abortion. The whole illicit episode remained secret, but Mary was impressed that she had struck a horrible blow to her mother's well-being. Thereafter the mother lamented her fate and saw no further reason for living. However, Mary rehabilitated herself somewhat, and a few years later married the errant son of a wealthy family. Mother was appeased: at least her daughter would be saved from the drudgery that she had known. Mary had met Frank at a college fraternity party where several local attractive high school girls had been invited for a "wild" time.

This young man had not been able to become interested in college girls; they seemed too sophisticated for him. He had difficulties in college and was sent from one to another in order to get a degree. He finally did get a diploma but only with the aid of family pressure on the university. He drank heavily and was frequently involved in barroom brawls. His name was always on probation lists, and he was well known to the police, who, because of influence, protected him against punitive measures. Marriage to Mary was frowned upon by his family, but after she agreed to religious conversion, they accepted her as a plaything who might have a settling effect on their scion.

Frank had been an only son of parents who led a divided life. Living between several homes and an apartment in New York City, the father and mother rarely spoke or saw each other from his early childhood on. It appeared that his birth had a divisive effect on them. He was raised by governesses under the direction of his mother. The father became a recluse, manifesting little interest in the household or his son; absorbed in writing unpublishable stories, he preferred to ignore his role of either husband or father. Their family life had no warmth, communication was at a minimum, and loneliness for all was the rule.

Frank grew up in this atmosphere where he knew no congeniality from his parents and few, if any, friends. He too became absorbed in phantasies; a prominent one was that he had a brother with whom he could play and be adventuresome. Later at private schools he had social difficulties because he was dull in thought and action. He couldn't understand the jokes and horseplay of the other boys and was often mercilessly teased and victimized.

This continued at college, but he found some comfort in this generally unkind world in two discoveries. One was the game of lacrosse, at which he became quite proficient, the other was drink. In his game he became quite aggressive with the stick and at times had to be restrained by the coach. In drinking, he would become abusive and assaultive; this was followed by amnesia for the episodes. He was overwhelmed by girls, and was often impotent with them when he tried sexual relations. He was gradually eliminated from his own social class as a desirable marital catch.

Frank and Mary met, and although there was never any passionate love between them, they found a mutual infirmity and affinity which brought them to marriage. She had hopes of money and respectability; he expected sexual freedom and, more than that, the realization of the missed childhood playmate. Both had experienced, in their different modes, extreme loneliness and austerity which blunted their coping abilities.

The above situation brings to mind J. P. Miller's and David Westheimer's *Days of Wine and Roses*.[1] The last lines of the book offer a prayer which might serve all of us well: "God," whispered Joe Clay, "grant me the serenity to accept the things I cannot have."

Alcohol was a tranquilizer long before there were any. The product of the grape marched along with mankind as an integral part of living. Of late it has been much maligned and called the cause of disease. In our Puritanism we tend to frown on self-tranquilization but find it acceptable to be placed under medical auspices. We wonder whether tranquilization through the doctor's pill as opposed to traditional tranquilization of the grape is a mark of progress. If given as a prescription, a medicine which produces flight from awareness seems socially acceptable; drink is not.

Perhaps for some the rigors of existence are indeed too much to be dealt with and accepted without some balm. The grape, like the Church, has been stamped on, but up to now never stamped out. Although our pamphlets and magazine articles will never admit it, many people have successfully achieved greatness in their relationships and work with a daily quart and sometimes more. There are many who would condemn, and be severely judgmental of, Mary and Frank. Their capers were beyond the tolerance of middle-class morality. However, they had a mutuality and mingling of spirit which they were unable to attain in other ways. Mary had to run from the psychiatrists, for she was a child of pain for which reason or intellection or cajoling held no remedy. Frank and Mary would run their course. Who of us is to be their judge?

There is an all too general assumption that alcoholism is an unmitigated evil to be stamped out like cholera.[2, 3, 4, 5] It is a fact that many people, primitives to prime ministers, live active, long, and useful lives on never less than a quart a day. Our middle-class purists of today forget that Dionysus was one of the twelve Olympians ranked with the highest.

Contrary to much of the clinical, condemnatory literature, for many drinking may not only make living with societal hypocrisy tolerable, but may also be the sole medium of protest available. For the forgotten housewife, it may rescue her from total disappearance. The self-absorbed pontifex gets to know of his wife's existence when he finds that, because of her alcohol-induced irascibility, he can no longer count on her for his social and political needs. Now as a problem, she at least no longer is a non-person. Similarly, society becomes aware of its inequities and hypocrisies when good men are driven to anaesthetize themselves in order to keep living.

Alcoholism is often the beginning of a self-rescue mechanism, not invariably the road to ruin which our moralists want us to believe. Every experienced clinician knows that the alternatives to drinking may often be complete disintegration (psychosis) and suicide. It becomes evident that the alcoholic, besides desiring to temporize the pain of living, wishes to communicate a message of despair.

Usually with a history of inordinate timidity and docility, he finds the courage of protest and assertion, usually for the first time in his life.

It is the great paradox of our existence that for ordinary persons we place the highest premiums on complacency and submissiveness. Those people are considered most normal and most desirable who give no trouble or are never heard from. Relatives of alcoholics always long for the time before the "addiction." Yet it takes no genius to detect that in many ways it was only with the start of an individual's alcoholism that he converted himself from protoplasmic nothingness into someone to be reckoned with, perhaps to the chagrin of those around him, but to the benefit of his own self-esteem. Can't he do it another way, one, say, less destructive to his liver? Yes, if originally he were more heroic or had a richer repertory of responses and avenues of expression available to him. For the shy, timid, sensitive, socially deprived and psychologically beaten people, there is, for a particular period in their lives, no other way without becoming completely insensate.

The alcoholic then, at the expense of his liver as well as social penalties, registers a poignant, if not always effective, protest about the condition of his life. In this he is more human than the individual who suffers and is extinguished without a murmur or twitch. As more and more suburban housewives take to drink, as they are doing, and more and more Negroes become "junkies," at least a perceptive few in our society will start wondering if this indeed is the best of all worlds for everyone.

NOTES

1. J. P. Miller and David Westheimer, *Days of Wine and Roses* (New York: Bantam Books, 1963), p. 218.
2. Jo Ann T. Taylor, "New Insights Into Alcoholism," *Medical Opinion and Review*, I (Jan. 1966), p. 14.

3. Keith S. Ditman and George G. Crawford, "The Use of Court Probation in the Management of the Alcohol Addict," *Amer. J. Psychiat.*, CXXII (Jan. 1966), p. 757.

4. Kurt Schlesinger, "Genetic and Biochemical Correlates of Alcohol Preference in Mice," *Amer. J. Psychiat.*, CXXII (Jan. 1966), p. 767.

5. Mary Sarett, Frances Cheek and Humphrey Osmond, "Reports of Wives of Alcoholics on Effects of LSD-25 Treatment of Their Husbands," *Arch. Gen. Psychiat.*, XIV (Feb. 1966), p. 171.

CHAPTER XII

INSTANT SEX

Take off your clothes and lie down; we are not going to last forever—Greek Anthology.

Love takes on the hue of every age.

Balzac

Shakespeare's Cressida learned to her personal dismay that it is ill-advised for a woman to give her heart too quickly.[13] But undercutting the courtship, ending the game with an unfought victory, she apparently makes herself less attractive and leaves the beau feeling gypped. He is deprived of having won his fair maiden; his muscles are left aching from a plethora of unused energy. He is then apt to look at her with disappointment and may quickly lose interest.

Cressida to Troilus:
"My thoughts were like unbridled children grown
Too headstrong for their mother: see we fools,
Why have I blabb'd: who shall be true to us
When we are so unsecret to ourselves?
But though I lov'd you well, I woo'd you not,
And yet good faith I wish'd myself a man;
Or that we women had men's privilege
Of speaking first. Sweet, bid me hold my tongue,"[1]

The "proper" way is represented by Rosalind of *As You*

Like It, who makes very sure of her lover before submitting. Not everyone has Rosalind's opportunity of disguise to learn the mate's true feelings and intentions. Rosalind also gave him a chance to fight and struggle and
suffer before he won his prize.

Rosalind's wisdom decries the animal suddenness and
incontinence of lovers:

> "There was never anything so sudden, but the fight of
> two rams, and Caesar's thrasonical brag of I came, saw,
> and overcame. For your brother, and my sister, no
> sooner met but they look'd; no sooner lov'd but they
> sigh'd: no sooner sigh'd but they asked one another the
> reason: no sooner knew the reason but they sought the
> remedy: And in these degrees have they made a pair of
> stairs to marriage, which they will climb incontinent, or
> else be incontinent before marriage; they are in the very
> wrath of love, and they will together. Clubs cannot
> part them."[2]

Lovers then are the original "sooners."

Rosalind is not blinded by the passion of love and courtship; her apperceptive capability is not impaired. She can
see beyond the moment. We witness this in her dialogue
with the moonstruck Orlando:

Rosalind:
"Now tell me how long you would have her after you
have posses'd her."
Orlando:
"For ever, and a day."
Rosalind:
"Say a day, without the ever: no, no, Orlando, men are
April when they woo, December when they wed: maids
are May when they are maids, but the sky changes when
they are wives: I will be more jealous of thee, than a
Barbary cockpigeon over his hen, more clamorous than
a parrot against rain, more new-fangled than an ape,
more giddy in my desires, than a monkey: I will weep
for nothing, like Diane in the fountain, and I will do

that when thou art dispos'd to be merry: I will laugh like a hyena, and that when thou are inclin'd to sleep."[3]

There is a cult of women today who are taking a view of themselves and of sexuality which departs from the tactlessness of Cressida or the craftiness of Rosalind. They are young women who have placed great value on their intellectual and creative powers. They are bent on excellence, usually in writing, the plastic arts, or science. Yet they acknowledge their need for understanding mates with whom they can build a conjugal life. These women allow for sexual attraction but don't want sex to be more than a minor part of their attractiveness. They generally want exceptional men and want to be held as exceptional people themselves. In order to assure a relationship based on worthiness rather than biology, these women behave in a way the conventional mind finds difficult to understand. First of all, they seek the company of men of high achievement or potential. Once she has found him, this kind of woman either makes direct sexual advances or readily submits to sexual overtures by such a male even though she is fully aware that such eagerness is not conventionally smart strategy. This sexual freedom is not an indication of the high value such women place on sex but, as we would suspect, just the opposite. They look upon sex as an obstacle, so they indulge to eliminate it immediately as an issue. By this behavior they indicate that they do not hold sexuality of utmost importance in their lives. They are saying: "If it is just sex you are after, here it is." If the man thereafter stays, it is for the other parts of her. This woman doesn't want the man to be interested in her for the conquest that he can make or the bodily needs she can gratify. This she sets before him immediately. The sexual concession is made before the game begins; it is then up to him whether he wants to go further. She will not allow sex, or more particularly her biological self, to be all of that game. Her sexual willingness quickly eliminates those men whose role or major interest in women is the chase

and conquest and tabulation. They have been cleverly undone and eliminated as potential objects. The women mercilessly use their own sexual organs as an examination of
the unsuspecting. It is their defense against being defiled.
By sexual submission, they prevent the rape of the intellect.

Conventional morality and its alienists might call these
women sick, whereas in reality they are unique. Because
they hold themselves justifiably in high regard, they have
invented special self-preservative defenses both strange and
unneeded by the *average* person. It is a defense of the
superior woman, needed because she is superior and a
woman. The male does not have to protect his intellect
from a predatory female; he may know full well that his
major asset or attractiveness is not his biology. Not so with
the superior woman. And, because of these peculiar protective defenses she may suffer persecution unknown to the
male. The social pressures may become so great that she
may lose her mind in her attempt to save her intellect.

A twenty-two-year-old woman was granted a fellowship
in the graduate program of a college of fine arts. In under-
graduate years she had shown extraordinary talent as an
artist and had already received wide acclaim for her work.
She was in the unique position of having been sought out
for the valuable fellowship, thus achieving in her young life
that honor of being sought after usually reserved for football players. She, like a football star, had some reservations about accepting the offer, for she wondered if she
would be "on a winning team." She was not at all awed
by her prize, for she was fully confident in her own abilities, but she did not want to jeopardize her talents in a
mediocre milieu. She finally accepted the fellowship and
began her life in the new college community. Her performance and her potential already established, she continued to work with diligence and confidence. Her social
relations appeared limited to her intellectual circle and
then to a few "at the top" among students and faculty.
She, however, was as fearful of mediocrity in her object
relations as she was in her work. She was cautiously dis-

rustful of the people around her lest she be accepted by them for anything but her worth as a uniquely gifted person.

Yet she longed for social relations which, because of her high (or what might be interpreted as queer) expectations, were most difficult to come by. She generally ignored or passed by men and women who appeared hopelessly beneath her standards. This yardstick effectively eliminated most people. She then became devoted to a tiny remnant.

In her work she met a young man of great talent. He had been singled out by his teachers as an extraordinary student and had been befriended by the outstanding artist of the community, who had achieved international fame. This young man she decided to cultivate. She then forthrightly told him of her interest and arranged for a date. They went for a walk and as they returned to her doorstep she asked if he would sleep with her that night. After this less than interminable courtship, they had sexual relations. She thereupon brought out certain sketches that she made that week and asked his criticism of them. The youth apparently was able, like George in "Who's Afraid of Virginia Woolf?" (see Chapter X), to catch on to the rules of this new game very quickly and responded to this strange relationship to her liking. He shifted from instant lover to art critic and spent the remainder of the night in an ardent explication of the art form that she presented.

She gave a history of behaving in this manner on many similar occasions, with some success and many failures. At best she was considered a loose woman, and at worst a nut. Yet as a human being with a most perceptive eye, she eclipsed most other persons; she came by her arrogance legitimately.

Her parents were frightened by stories of her behavior and tried to direct her toward a more conventional mode of life. She was bringing embarrassment to them, and they looked upon her talent as some great obstacle to happiness. Little could they understand that she had transcended their middle-class values and was making a very good adaptation to a different level of intellection which others could neither achieve nor understand. Hers was a morality consistent with her own truths; while most young women spend most of their days either safeguarding their virginity or using their biological selves to attract a man and a future, she held her main virtue in protecting her creative identity. This she would never compromise, and in this she remained sinless. Many said that she was doing nothing but imitating the traditional role of the male in taking the initiative in the mating situation; that her posture and mode were specious, a compensation for an inner fear of being a woman.[4] Although there may have been a component of the latter mechanism, the dangers of being a woman encompassed one of the banalities that psychology usually finds but were in the realm of fear of doing injury to her substance as the person that she was and wanted to be. In this goal, her ideal was to remain pure and undefiled. Yet her interest in people and men remained seminal; she wanted all of the cross-fertilization she could lay her hands on, but only pedigreed.

Her high moral stand, misunderstood and misinterpreted by conventional wisdom, helped her achieve what she wanted. At a relatively young age, her potential became an actuality. And she, because of her persistence and good luck, found a mate with whom she could live and grow.

The novels and plays of today are constructed on this model of instant sex. The agonies and vagaries of courtship that tormented lovers in the fiction of yesteryear are gone. Today, everything is over in the first chapter and the rest of the novel consists of an afterplay in which the characters go on to insanity, suicide, perversion, dope addiction, sadism, and murder. The sexual act itself is no longer a fadeout but is described as in a do-it-yourself manual. No mystery here; as if the author gives the facts of life to his reader, filling in the details that his parents deleted. The author is not the good parent who patiently goes over the whole thing so that there will be no unnecessary detours or errors. Not only the maneuvers but also the accompanying feelings and sensations are described in minute detail.

Is sex so devoid of mystery and desire that it no longer builds tension enough to last two chapters? Or is it the new mode that afterplay has replaced foreplay? It can be an indication that modern man is continuing to handle his sexual urges as contaminated and demeaning—a shameful biological enslavement of his earliest, most premature eras, the first chapter or book of genesis of his existence. Sex is the preoccupation of his inchoate stage and nothing to take pride in or dwell upon. Sex, then, is the most nonsensical aspect of his existence, the very least of accomplishments; it can add absolutely nothing to his worthiness or identity. On the sex mystique, Albert Camus wrote: "Sexual life was given to man, perhaps to turn him aside from his true path. It is his opium. In it everything goes to sleep. Outside it things take on life again. At the same time chastity puts an end to the species which is, perhaps, the truth. Sexuality leads to nothing. It is not immoral, but it is unproductive. One can give oneself to it for a time when one does not wish to produce. But chastity alone is connected with personal progress. There is a time when sexuality is a victory—when it is released from moral imparatives. But it quickly becomes a defeat afterwards—and the only victory is won over it in its turn: that is chastity."[5] The issues that come thereafter are the pertinent ones to be dealt with in a most serious vein, and these have to do mainly with the dangers and vicissitudes of aggressive and destructive drives. Perhaps the thermonuclear cloud has wrought these changes in our literature. No longer is the procreative instinct the chief problem or threat; instead it is man's suddenly developed capacity to destroy civilization. He must now deal with violence and perversion and morbidity. There is an urgency now, a race against the clock, no luxury of time or space to leisurely tame himself of these instincts and built-in immoralities which may bear heavily on that atomic button. The childhood game, button, button who's got the button, comes back like the return of the repressed—but now in most tragic proportions. Perhaps we can no longer afford the luxury of sexual problems, and must view them as the secondary issue of mankind. We can produce manhood willy-nilly, but can we preserve the germ cell?

This attitude toward sex was confirmed by David Boroff in an article called "The College Intellectual, 1965 Model." Mr. Boroff noted that, among the intellectual minority on certain campuses throughout the United States, sex was no longer the hot issue of previous decades. He writes: "Sex is now virtually beyond discussion. A consensus has been achieved, and the attitude seems to be, why bother to discuss it? The prevailing philosophy is a mixutre of sexual celebration and cautious clinicism. Sex is wonderful, but beware of pathology! 'We have a laissez-faire policy about morals,' a Columbia student explained. 'You can do anything so long as you don't turn up the record player too loud.'" [6]

Again, Mr. Boroff writes: "The sexual huffing and puffing of so many of today's novels seems extraneous, the business of an earlier generation. Today's is the post-liberated generation." [7]

This disenchantment with sex has also been noted among Russian youths. [8]

Mr. Boroff indicated that these attitudes were not necessarily held by all on campus but by the five per cent who were the "intellectuals." We can wonder about the genuineness of this liberation. (It could be another masquerade—a defense—a way of being different from their parents.) Yet it is an indication of a swing away from the old saw of biology being destiny. In affluent America, where the securing of food and shelter has become a minor problem for a larger proportion of the population, it is understandable that "biological" preoccupations—those of physical survival—become less prominent. And sex, as a biological entity, would also be lower on the priority scale. The sought-after sensations are then apt to be "mental" rather than physical. This is not to say that the modern intellectual has returned to the life of his monkish antecedents. Without chauvinistic intent, we might give credit to psychoanalysis for lifting the societal repression of sexuality and thereby detoxifying it. Now it can take its unexaggerated place, whereas formerly repression made it unduly prominent in the hierarchy of human functions.

It has been said that Freud fostered a sexual revolution by uncovering the hypocrisy of the Victorian era. It may have been the important beginning of many things that are now happening and are about to happen. These new changes in both sexual attitude and behavior may be secondary to new discoveries, "the pill," and new conditions, population explosion, but more than these new perspectives. The new turn of the revolution against hypocrisy, now that sex has been "uncovered," is to put it in its proper place. Contraception, which was rarely if ever mentioned by Freud, with its effects of separating the sexual act from inevitable procreation (also from venereal disease) has on the whole made it a less serious and consequential event. Other things being equal, it can be taken as a fun thing which need not necessarily be major and inordinate determinant of one's destiny. And, because contraceptives today can be in the control of either sex, an equitable distribution of power is attained. No longer need one fear, or be at the mercy of, the intrigue or machinations of the other. Many have expressed concern about the liberating effects of contraceptives, especially "the pill," on morality.[9, 10, 11] Will the lessening or elimination of dangers and penalties lead to looseness and a cheapening of sex, and in its course, people? This is largely a spurious and maliciously diversionary issue. The cheapening of mankind will come, has come, not from his sexual behavior but from the inauthenticity of other facets of his life. He will be cheapened by being reduced to a speck in mass society, by having his privacy ignored, and by having inequities perpetuated as in the case of women and other minority groups. For too long has morality been cleverly tied to sexual behavior allowing the significant sinfulness of people and society to go unseen and unchecked. Exploitation, persecution, and war march together as normal expectations whereas the chief determinant of a person's morality has been his or her sexual behavior. Humanity must look elsewhere and on other qualities to judge a person's worth or character. And typically, sex-based moral judgments have been more ruthless on the woman than the man. In the past, as well as in the present, her reputation is largely a sexual one.[14]

The alienation which this spurious issue has produced has been documented by a leading sociologist, Edgar Z. Friedenberg, who writes: "The stress, as they see it, comes not from sex but from living in a society which prevents people from having human contact with their sexual partner, especially if they are young. Even sexual relationships become shallow and sporadic in a society that affords the young no privacy and not enough jobs, in which they must accept an interim, sub-adult status that delays marriage for 10 or 15 years after puberty; in which competition and status-seeking induce young men and women to make use of each other while denying them the opportunity to get to know one another."[12]

It is no wonder that the perceptive college youths of today do not preoccupy themselves with sexual issues, though the jobs of many college administrators would be simplified if they only would. How happy many deans and presidents would be if the principal demand of students was sexual freedom! Students will no longer be diverted from the authentic issues of their existence. We never promised them a bed of roses; they, in turn, will not settle for a bed.

For man, sex has an urge and a meaning. At times the two are indistinguishable, but the importance of "meaning" has transcended the biological aspect. This statement may be disputed. However, the evidence points to man's getting hung up not on biological frustrations but by the vicissitudes of object relationships. Thus the principal meaning of sex in our civilization is that of love. Love in turn encompasses matters of loyalty, fidelity, trust, as well as possessiveness, jealousies, and enslavement. These effects and drives have already been alluded to in Chapters I, V, and X. It appears that our playwrights, and some of the young intellectuals referred to above, would like to strip sexuality of its meaning and transfer this meaning to the intellect and its products. Thus one might be faithful to work or loyal to a community or a country. Thus Albert Camus writes: "I have had an illicit love affair with this country, that is to say, I have reasons to love it and reasons to hate it. For Algeria, on the contrary, it is unbridled passion and abandonment to the pleasure of love. Question: Can one love a country like a woman?"

Whether this new posture is salutary to man's existence cannot be answered. Of course, if carried to extremes, it must eventually become misanthropic. However, it may be that there has been an inordinate amount of passion attached to sexuality because of man's chronic disingenuous confrontation of the realities of his sexual nature. This lack of candor has undoubtedly led to the overt and covert sexual obsessions which have characterized the human condition for so long.

NOTES

1. William Shakespeare, *Troilus and Cressida,* ed. G. B. Harrison (New York: Shakespeare Recording Society, 1963), p. 58.

2. William Shakespeare, "As You Like It," *The Complete Works of William Shakespeare* (Cleveland, Ohio: The World Publishing Co., n.d.), p. 230.

3. *Ibid.,* p. 226.

4. Joseph C. Rheingold, *Fear of Being a Woman* (New York: Grune & Stratton, 1964).

5. Albert Camus, "A Writer's Notebook," *Encounter,* XXIV (March 1965), p. 28.

6. David Boroff, "The College Intellectual, 1965 Model," *New York Times Book Review Section* (Dec. 6, 1964), p. 134.

7. *Ibid.,* p. 135.

8. Gregory Frost, "What Russian Girls Are Like," *New York Times Magazine* (Jan. 24, 1965), pp. 16-17.

9. "Impact of 'The Pill' Under Debate," *Medical World News*, ed. Morris Fishbein (Jan. 21, 1966), p. 62.

10. Lee E. Dirks, "Will the 'Pill' Affect Moral Standards," *The National Observer* (Nov. 22, 1965), p. 1.

11. Andrew Hacker, "The Pill and Morality," *New York Times Magazine* (Nov. 21, 1965), p. 32.

12. Edgar Z. Friedenberg, *A Polite Encounter Between the Generations,* New York Times Magazine, Jan. 16, 1966, p. 10.

13. See Hays, H.R., *The Dangerous Sex, The Myth of Feminine Evil,* New York, G.P. Putnam's Sons, 1964, chap. 12, *As False As Cressid . . . .,* p. 123.

14. The rights of women concerning their own reproductive functions, long overdue, are beginning to be honored in the matter of abortions. A recent decision of Justice Gesell of Washington, D. C. declaring the abortion laws there invalid (Nov. 1969) awaits an appeal to the United States Supreme Court. In California (Nov. 1969), the Supreme Court ruled the 117 year old statute limiting therapeutic abortions as unconstitutional. (see report in *Medical Tribune and Medical News,* Nov. 17, 1969) A report formulated by the Committee on Psychiatry and the Law of the Group for the Advancement of Psychiatry entitled: "The Right to Abortion: a Psychiatric View," reads: "A woman should have the right to abort or not, just as she has a right to marry or not," and that anything short of this "stands foursquare against the right of the woman to control her own reproductive life." (same periodical, p. 39.)

CHAPTER XIII

LOVE AND MONEY

Ergo sollicitae tu causa, pecunia, vitae es,
Per te immaturum mortis ademus iter.
(*Money, thou art the cause of the anxieties of life,
and through thee we go down to the graves
before our time.*)

                                                    Propertius

The all-time expert on this matter was, of course, Honoré
de Balzac. He more than anyone lifted the societal repression about the money of love and the love of money.[1, 2, 3]
He talked and talked and talked about it, as Freud later
was to talk about sex. Balzac must be credited in fully
acknowledging the commercial aspect of the marriage contract and other "love" relationships. By lifting the veil of
repression surrounding these matters, he hoped that contracts could be made wherein nothing was obscured by
double talk and fine print. Perhaps then, catastrophic
shocks of recognition, which would ultimately come, might
be cushioned by both preparation and by fuller knowledge
of the rules of the money-power-love game. Ironically,
France learned, or knew, Balzac's lesson all too well.
Knowing the power and significance of money as related
to love, despite its avowed devotion to liberty, fraternity,
and equality, she, until 1966, along with suffrage denied
the wife the right of property. The male-dominant society
made sure that there were few or no alternatives to the

woman to staying happily married and in love with her husband.[9]

Psychoanalysis' contribution, although sizable in that it always promoted frank and candid discussions of money matters, suffers in this regard because of its reductionistic tendency relegating money matters to the anal stage of development. With this reductionism, it has often failed to understand many of the existential meanings of earning, of giving, and of spending money. By promoting a genetic, orificial formulation, psychoanalysis tended to undo Balzac's explications, which have proved to be more consequential in understanding human struggles. Money is filthy lucre and cannot buy happiness and is certainly an inauthentic goal in itself, but it does bring power and esteem, does often determine whether a person can act autonomously or remain enslaved. It brings esteem, for instance, to the one who makes it and degrades those who have to beg for it. And, earning power, whether it should be or not, is a most prominent measure of one's worthiness. The housewife gets little personal prestige from being the great spender. Her lament usually is: "The significant person is the earner, not the shopper." "Madison Avenue" is trying to convince her otherwise; not many women are permanently seduced.

Much of the anxiety and concern in married life for the male involves his "providing instinct"; this in turn, in the modern mode, has to do with money and paying the monthly bills.[4] Money has more meaning than excrement, as any responsible husband and parent knows. It is well to conceptualize it as an end product if you have never been confronted with the onerous task of making ends meet.

Yet the monthly, very necessary, and often critical ritual of being confronted with and paying the bills has an effect which is almost organic and biological in its consequences. If the woman has her monthly menses, the male also has his regular overflow of substance. It too may be accompanied by all sorts of tensions which euphemistically may be called fiscal and may begin several days before and have effects which last longer than the event itself. That the male feels bled to death on these occasions may be carrying the metaphor too far, but the gut reaction that he has cannot be discounted. It is also not his period of fecundity, more of depletion and, possibly, of grave discouragement. It can also rekindle any misanthropic instincts that he may be latently harboring. The monthly fiscal period serves to mobilize all of those hostilities forgotten or deferred during the distractions of everyday living. Then the day of literal reckoning serves, and becomes the acceptable occasion for, the great outpouring (*sic*) of pent-up resentments and grievances. The mate may be brought to account for her wanton budgetal recklessness, her unabashed fiscal emasculation of him.

One recalls the cynical words of Thornton Wilder in *Our Town* quoted recently in an article on the financial pages of the *New York Times*. "A man looks pretty small at a wedding, George. All those good women standing shoulder to shoulder, making sure that the knot's tied in a mighty public way."[5]

Judges and lawyers of divorce courts relate that the most frequent causes of marital disharmony are sex and money.[6] At least, they say, these are the subjects around which most of the arguments and discord seem to arise. There may be deeper and more complex reasons, but these are the manifest and presented ones. We therefore cannot ignore the problem of money and financial responsibilities. And we cannot deem it beneath discussion because it is too superficial an approach or because it is specious (*sic*).

If not the root of all evil, money is an acceptable object of controversy in marriage. In certain instances, it saves one from facing more sensitive issues such as object withdrawal and emotional bankruptcy. When a person may be ashamed of complaining of other things, or is puzzled at what is bothering him, money complaints serve well.

Pecuniary goals appear to be more communicable and image-saving than any others. Some prefer to say they have married for money rather than for love. And society often feels better when they conclude that is the case. When a young attractive girl of eighteen marries a middle-aged man, they are happy to explain this anomalous situation by assuming that she married him for his money. People might shudder about the possibility of any love between Spring and Fall—or that daughter is marrying father. That she married for "security" is satisfying and eases suspicion. This is similar to the ceaseless quest for concrete motivation in criminal investigations. When an entry or act of personal violence has been committed, there is great reassurance to the police and public when money or jewels have been stolen; otherwise the act appears nonsensical and is apt to be the work of a maniac. Society does not like grave acts of passion and is relieved if there seems to be a profit motive. Similarly, in marriage there is great suspicion when there are motives of passion and/or love.

When a crime is committed without apparent motivation, hopefully of theft or self-aggrandizement, the culprit is apt to be sent for psychiatric examination as if he had violated the rules of a capitalistic society. Similarly, in courtship and marriage, money motives and preoccupations are acceptable coin of the realm. Relationships and acts out of pure passion are poorly tolerated, for they are not usually amenable to punitive and corrective procedures that may be applied by outsiders. There is also probably an understandable envy of those people who may be able to indulge in emotional unions which appear to transcend banal values. It is indeed the principal paradox of our times that greed and avarice are understandable but love is not. Those who profess doing things for love are accused, at the least, of folly, and usually of insanity. So in marriage, irrational motives are replaced by understandable ones, the chief of these being money.[7] Just as one can be reassured by marrying for money, he can feel on safe ground if he fights about it. He is thereby not a "sucker" in allowing himself to be taken in. Nor is he a petulant child; he would not fight over anything but very basic and worldly matters.

Nevertheless, there are practical realities of adaptation and real needs of personal and family survival. With an irresponsible spouse, what else can one do but confront, or restrict, or apply sanctions, or blockade him or her for behavior in financial matters which could wreak havoc for all. This is seen when there are great drains of resources due to excessive drinking or gambling or "manic" behavior in which there is no concern about tomorrow. As economists tell us, most people are honest about money matters, but tend to spend when they have it. We are told, for instance, that a voluntary social security program would not work because too many people would never, without compulsion, feel it necessary to participate in such an insurance fund. They need parental restrictions and compulsions to provide for their own future needs. Similarly, in family living, one could predict that the power of the pleasure principle under which, unfortunately, all too many operate would overwhelm prudence and lead to financial insolvencies.

As our society becomes more affluent, will there be a concomitant diminution of money arguments? It would seem that if there were money enough for necessities in the present, and government-sponsored social security and welfarism for the future as well as state-provided education and health benefits for the whole family, the agonies of money altercations would be eliminated or diminished. There are already a good many upper and middle income families where the saving or spending of money does not have to be an issue. It is there in abundance, and since depletion or bankruptcy is practically impossible, do mates in such circumstances fight over money? They do, but with more subtlety. The bank accounts and stocks and bonds belie any threats of possible insolvency so that the husband could not reasonably use this as a weapon. He cannot say: "You are ruining me financially," but is more apt to say, "You are ruining me!" He would then bemoan his fate in terms of Quentin's father in Arthur Miller's *After the Fall* (see Chapter II), that he had to buy his love and that everyone else loved at his expense. Here the money is hated as an attraction for others in lieu of being attractive and loved for oneself. So it appears that money cannot win. Its absence brings threats of alienation and disenchantment, its presence brings grave fears that its glitter eclipses the virtues of its possessor. King Lear is another example of the obsession that can overtake an individual in regard to the love he can muster from others. The ultimate humiliation, then, is to have one's identity confused with one's possessions. The eternal search for knowledge of one's worth is frustrated by one's worth. Lear gave away his wealth so that he could learn his value to his daughters. He took a risk beyond the heroicism of most men and he was considered mad for such extremism. Who but a madman would expose himself to such knowledge? He did become poor and "mad" but, like Oedipus, became one with the gods.

We see the paradox: the desire for money to increase status and power, and the agony of having accumulated money and being loved solely for it and not for oneself. For Lear the world became distorted, populated solely by those awaiting his death. "Pelican daughters" Lear called them, all mouths and no hearts. The money once so highly coveted became the chief disturbance of social relationships. The myth of Midas gave civilization its early warning of the personal tragedy incumbent on accumulation. The magic touch of the financial wizard may indeed convert those he would love, and be loved by, into hard metal, thereby defeating the alleged motive for accumulation. To have a heart of gold is a paradoxical euphemism generally connoting generosity. In the Midas sense, however, it is the least desirable of conditions.

If there is agony in love, that seems to have been bought, there is considerably less dismay about the control of the other person that monetary power gives. Husbands who provide their wives and children with the goods of life often take to themselves a feeling of extreme generosity.

In feeling generous, they are apt to obfuscate the reality that they are only doing what they themselves demand to do: produce the purse, control the strings, and give what they privately feel are handouts. They may even be unaware that these are regarded and resented as handouts by their families.

It has been a fact of life (although it is becoming less so) that in most middle-class homes the husband, in bringing support to his family, feels like a benefactor and expects some reward of unflinching fealty and more for his sacrifice of going to work. He also becomes completely perplexed when his "generosity" is met by ingratitude worse than a serpent's tooth. It is difficult for him (as for those in charge of American foreign aid) to comprehend that the position of benefactor in relation to recipient often sets up an inequality which, carried to its logical end, can lead to a master-slave relationship. The husband as breadwinner cannot escape this accusation because he is witness against himself in his most common and natural expressions on the subject. What middle-class male has not said: "I have given her everything," or "I have tried to give my family what they need," or "I have given you the proper education," or "I gave my wife a new car," etc.? These are all words and expressions of generosity, clearly indicating that the male is benefactor in spite of any talk of sharing, mutuality, different but equal roles, and loving partners. Can there be love in situations of inequality, of master-slave, of donor and recipient?

There has been recent confirmation of observations to indicate that the male's bread-winning capacity has in reality made him an accessory rather than an integral part of the family unit. The resentments and humiliation which are engendered in the woman due to her enforced financial dependence frequently cause her to extrude him from meaningful and deep relationships with herself and the children. He is frequently depreciated and his judgment and opinions are, secretly and not so secretly, undercut.

Domination of the household is her revenge.[8] Sensing his own diminution in his family, like Willy Loman, he seeks consolation elsewhere.

NOTES

1. Honoré de Balzac, *A Marriage Settlement* (New York: Jefferson Press, 1836).

2. Honoré de Balzac, *Father Goriot,* trans. E. Marriage (Philadelphia: Gebbie Publishing Co., 1898).

3. Honoré de Balzac, *Eugénie Grandet* (St. Louis and Philadelphia: Thompson Publishing Co., 1901).

4. Robert O. Blood, Jr. and Donald M. Wolfe, *Husbands and Wives, The Dynamics of Married Living* (New York: The Free Press, 1960), pp. 79-114.

5. *New York Times,* April 5, 1965, p. 48.

6. Louis Nizer, *My Life in Court* (Garden City, N. Y.: Doubleday & Co., 1961).

7. Albert Lauterbach, *Man, Motives, and Money* (Ithaca, N. Y.: Cornell University Press, 1959), p. 134.

8. Marya Mannes, "I, Mary, Take Thee John, As . . . What?", *New York Times Magazine* (Nov. 14, 1965), p. 52.

9. Are we to believe Orwell: "In the last resort, what holds a woman to a man, except money?" (Orwell, G., in "Keep the Aspidistra Flying", Harmondsworth, Middlesex, Penguin Books, Ltd., 1962, p. 111.)

CHAPTER XIV

MARRIAGE, MEANING, AND "MITTLER"

> People set out to remedy evils at the point where they
> appear; nobody pays any attention to their actual source
> and origin. This is why it is so difficult to give advice
> and have it heeded, especially by the general run of men,
> who are quite reasonable in everyday matters but seldom
> see beyond tomorrow.
>
> Goethe

The psychoanalytic tradition has been that one doesn't
treat a marriage, or marital partners, but persons. A psychoanalyst may treat one person and not see the mate in
treatment or even in consultation. This has led to a great
deal of criticism of the analytic situation as being detrimental to marriage and family life. This type of criticism
is consonant with the modern social welfare concept which
looks beyond individuation to what is good for the family,
the group, and the community. Perhaps sanctifying the
individual, as psychoanalysis does, *is* an anachronistic ideal
with a diminishing position in an era of mass action and
communal enterprise. Psychoanalysis was quickly liqui-
dated behind the Iron Curtain, where the nation's "truths"
and goals pre-empt the individual's.

Psychoanalysis, in its classic form, fiercely defends matters of privacy and confidentiality. This has engendered
criticism of it as being some type of secret cult that de-

mands of its practitioners and analysands a fealty, exclusiveness, and devotion, at the sacrifice of mate, children, and job.[3] This is patent nonsense, for in respecting the rights of the individual, psychoanalysis acts consonantly with the enlightenment that freed man from the tyranny both of the horde and of Heaven. The basic proposition of psychoanalysis is that man is not owned by the external world and hopefully that he should not be enslaved by internalized irrationalities. Intimately involved in this liberation is the new imperative that he make choices. The capability to make a choice, encompassing as it does freedom from internal and external shibboleths, is the goal of psychoanalytic treatment. It is in the pursuit of this goal that psychoanalysis seeks the exclusion from the therapeutic relationship of all forces, good or bad, which might possibly interfere with the progress of choice-making.[16]

All the seemingly "crazy" rules of psychoanalysis are in the service of creating this atmosphere. This is often done, paradoxically, even against the wishes of the analysand himself, who, in his own perplexity, may have relinquished to varying degrees the human rights of privacy, autonomy, and chance for choice. However, if these rights are meaningless, or if even the wish for them has been effectively extinguished, then psychoanalysis is not for him any more than a democratic form of government is for Saudi Arabia at this time. When psychoanalysis is undertaken subject to external pressures and intrusions, it ceases to be psychoanalysis. By its very definition, it deals with the needs and/or anxieties of an individual, not of a marriage, or a family, or a community; although these are not necessarily antithetic, they may be. A woman may have important responsibilities to her husband, her children, and her household, but none of these can be well served if she is not self-fulfilled. Psychoanalysis does not aim at divisiveness, nor does it promote a secretive mode. But it does sanctify privacy; without a secure modicum of privacy, there can be no identity. An individual is of many minds: he minds his wife, his children, his business. But without a mind of his own, there can be none of these other minds and mindings.

Psychoanalysis of one or both mates may be indicated and yet not be feasible. Its impracticality, however, does not mean that other methods are suitable substitutes, any more than French is a suitable substitute for German for someone living in Berlin. Too often people are lured into the folly of using what is available rather than what is right. Usually what appear as problems of marriage are problems of individuals or problems of living, so that marriage counseling, like advice to the lovelorn, may be specious in theory and operation. Both the giving and receiving of advice, as well as the application of gratuitous homilies, are weak balms. More than that, they are insulting to any but the simple-minded. These words may seem harsh and untrue, especially to many who have felt helped by professional marital advice. They may also sound extremely chauvinistic coming from a psychoanalyst who could easily be accused of promoting his own show. And the efficacy of psychoanalysis, even when formally applied, holds no guarantees. It too has many disappointed participants who may bitterly recall no help derived therefrom. But psychoanalysis as intervention can only do the best it can, limited in its results by the participation of the analysand, the skills of the analyst, and the intensity of the problem at hand. As treatment, it is not meant for all men or all seasons. It is, in fact, for reasons of economics and factors of intellection, in reach of a very few, just as a college education was in the past century of this country.

The "social awareness" of the therapist is of utmost importance in helping a client toward understanding and possible remedial action. By social awareness is meant the sophistication of the therapist in matters of forces in the culture and society which can be more consequential, helpful, or eroding than some legendary and perhaps mythical relationship at the age of five. The therapist must be at least relatively free from the prejudice that the middle-class marital contract and family life are the best and only way of living. He must be aware that a woman, for instance, may be the victim of persecution even with the most loving and "generous" husband. In such situations it really matters little that she happens to be married to a benign master. The marital situation itself may realistically cause her enslavement. To treat such a woman as a sick, paranoid person because she complains or is belligerent, or seemingly inappropriate to her husband's benign behavior toward her, is to miss the point. The therapist may be unaware, or may not want to be aware (he himself may be a slaveholder in his personal life) of the persecution because society has generally defined these inequities as "natural." Why is it that women more often institute divorce action?[5, 9]

It was the rare white Southerner who could ever feel that the Negro was persecuted. The roles of white and Negro were "natural" since it was always that way. It is entirely possible that the client may be ahead of the therapist in understanding the importance of human rights and dignity. In many instances the despair and disillusionment of clients are entirely justified. The lament that "the therapist just didn't understand me" can be all too true and not a case of stubborn resistance which we too often hear about from self-righteous therapists in clinical conferences.

Another instance of the need for awareness is the frustrating and corrosive effect of conformity in mass society for the male. The compulsion to compete, to win out, to get top dollar has become a virtual hallmark of maleness. The therapist himself in his own life has generally proceeded in this fashion and might really feel this is the best and even the only way of life. To achieve, to get ahead, to dominate at home and at the office are prime virtues of middle-class morality. Is it good for everyone? In psychoanalysis, when confronted by a man who did not seem to want to get ahead, the therapist all too often invoked the Oedipus complex as the main reason for this man's otherwise unexplainable passivity in worldly affairs; he was either fearful of competing with or overtaking his father.

Even if such elements may be present, they may be less consequential than a latter-day honest appraisal and renunciation of conventional values in the service of the pursuit of personal idealistic goals. The therapist must be aware of at least the possibility of such "honestly" derived goals which may not be consonant with the usual expectations of a marital partner. To hack away here at poor old Oedipus makes a mockery of true understanding. Therapists too often make the error of defining the client's condition as "sick and regressed" rather than seeing it as a valid attempt to free himself from the prejudices of parents, tradition, and society. It may prove to be the gravest error of psychoanalysis that it has called "neurosis" and "sickness" those attempts of young people to purge themselves of the demonolatry of their parents. It is unfortunately too often the case that the therapist attempts to cure the patient instead of healing himself.

In lieu of the understanding of the spectrum of operative forces both of the past and present, there are in our professions the disease of reductionism and the cult of simplistic derivations. For instance, it is not unusual to find in psychoanalytic writings that the "character" of the male and the female is largely determined by the shape and direction of their bodies and sexual organs. To wit, the woman must forevermore be passive because her organ "receives" the penis. Is anatomy destiny? It unfortunately is, and may continue to be, unless we abandon our self serving euphemisms and cant in favor of existential appraisals.

It may sound condescending and arrogant to ask for awareness in one's colleagues. But there are all too many amongst us who not only are "unaware" but take pride in their aloofness. They take the position of medieval monks, fearing that contact or knowledge of the temporal scene is contaminating. Some (analysts) indicate in their protocols of cases that the talk of patients of "here and now" events is "resistance" and non-consequential to the work of the analysis. They would prefer to work with the "internal disease" derived from eternal and static maladies of the soul without integrating these with the tensions of the age in which we live.

Yet the reader will rightly say that people have been helped throughout the ages by priests, wise men, good friends, and, in the present era, by social agencies. This observation is valid, but we are talking here of another dimension. People who seek and respond to this order of help would neither seek nor qualify for psychoanalysis. They generally want to be told how to behave or what are the expectations of them as mates. They also may want to justify their behavior and, at the same time, seek a moral judgment of that behavior or that of the mate.

There are innumerable people who need managers in marriage. Lacking responsibility and judgment even about the simplest matters, they seek out someone to tell them how much to spend on rent, whether beatings should be allowed, and how many times a week sexual intercourse is necessary. And for the fights and arguments, an arbiter is needed to pass judgment on who is right, who is the aggressor, and who is the victim.

Another intervention frequently sought is a scolding for an errant mate so that, with the authority of a psychiatrist or a social worker, she may be induced to take better care of the house. Or a wife wails, "Tell him he mustn't drink so much." This is like a child asking the adult supervisor to warn an adversary to be cooperative and play nicely. Camus is quite cynical about the appearance of the married couple in front of the third force. ". . . the man tries to shine before a third person. Immediately his wife says: 'But you're just the same. . . .' and tries to bring him down, to make him share her mediocrity."[2] This has always been the role of the clergy and often the judge and sometimes the attorney. They give the moral or legal warnings, and they may chastise and punish. It is the legitimate use of authority to bring about submission where internal control or judgment is inadequate.

Individuals with no adequate internalized tools of opera-

tion and bereft of powers of persuasion must look to others
to make their mates and themselves behave. Is this managerial role a proper one for a psychiatrist, psychologist,
or social worker? It is not psychotherapy in the sense of
producing great insights or profound character changes,
but nonetheless there can be some help in it. It is psychotherapy in the broad sense of the modern-day tendency
to call nearly everything people do by themselves or together "therapy." Some people indeed do look upon life
itself as a basic disease, and everything we do as part of
the treatment. Everyone today seems to be philosophically
therapy-minded. Hobbies, relationships, and careers are
identified as therapies. Almost no one does things now
because he likes to; he does them because they are "good
therapy." Perhaps the world *is* one big mental hospital,
as some of our cynics would have it. Certainly our diseases
are mulitplying faster than are doctors to care for them.
Idiosyncrasies, quirks, and extremisms are now diseases
whose bearers are to be placed in isolation wards.

Since marriage traditionally has been connected with
religion, it is quite natural for the clergy to play a major
role in marital problems. Religions have imposed the
principal regulations and moralities governing conduct in
marriage; the religionists thereby become the arbiters of an
overwhelming number of issues. The clergyman may be
able to counsel and advise whether certain behavior does
or does not violate the moral code to which the marital
partners have already committed themselves. For people
who live by edicts of external authority, the force of approval or condemnation by such an authority has a regu-
lating effect and may curb errant behavior. The dread of
alienation from one's church or, even worse, the threat of
losing the chance of a benevolent hereafter, may serve
to keep many in line. This helps and it may change conduct; so it is psychotherapy?

The other institution with which marriage is inextricably
involved is the law. Marriage must be performed in either
a religious or a civil manner, usually in both. Along with

religious edicts, the state governs the conjugal state with
an iron fist. It insists on a minimal age for participants,
requires blood examinations, and in some areas regulates
the union of the "races" of man. It is therefore no surprise
that judges and lawyers are frequently called upon for
advice. Here civil authority is depended upon to settle
conflicts of interest or misunderstandings about prohibitions, liberties, rights, and responsibilities. Has one been
victimized or has one stepped beyond the pale of the law
in one's behavior? Of his attorney the mate may ask, "Am
I within my legal rights?" Or, "What are my responsibilities in this matter and what are my mate's?" And the
punitive arm of the law can be invoked when personal
power or influence fails. Let the judge or lawyer threaten
with the possible consequences. And finally, perhaps six
months in jail is the lesson that is needed. So the law is
another vital intrusion into the marital state—present at the
onset and called upon thereafter as an aid. Can this be
psychotherapy too?

Marriage counseling was once solely the prerogative of
the clergy. With the intrusion of the state into marital
matters, the situation became more complex, necessitating
both spiritual and temporal information. With the advent
of psychological knowledge, a new dimension was added;
thus the modern marriage counselor combines, with varying degrees of success, all three roles—spiritual, legal, and
psychological. This worldly knowledge, plus his personal
skills in "handling" people, may enable him to act as a
mediator of current issues involving rights, duties, and responsibilities, both moral and legal. Goethe beautifully described both the evolutionary history and role of such an
individual in the character appropriately named "Mittler"
in *Elective Affinities:*

"Mittler told them what he had done that morning and
what he still planned to do. This strange man had once
been a clergyman and, apart from his untiring activity
in his ministry, had distinguished himself by his skill in

pacifying and settling quarrels in his own parish as well as in the neighborhood—at first between individuals and then between communities and between landowners. . . . Early in his life he realized the necessity of a thorough acquaintance with the law; and he devoted himself zealously to that science, soon finding himself a match for the shrewdest lawyer. The sphere of his activity widened remarkably, and some people tried to persuade him to move to the city where he could carry on in more influential circles the ministrations he had begun at a lower level. . . . He firmly determined—or rather followed an old habit and his inclination—never to stay in a house where there was no quarrel to settle or no assistance of any sort needed. People who were superstitious about the significance of names insisted that the name *Mittler* ('mediator') had compelled him to choose his strangest of all vocations."[4]

Today there is a buyer's market in the choice of therapies. Excluding the physical therapies, from psychosurgery to tranquilizers which make no pretense of intellection, marital partners who seek help through understanding can visit the clergy, attorneys, social workers, psychologists, psychiatrists, psychoanalysts, and others who set themselves up exclusively as marriage counselors. This is a listing of professionals apart from friends, relatives, the police, and even neighbors who are often called upon to intervene. Not to be discounted, of growing importance in our mass society, are the columnists of our newspapers and other media who also diagnose, prescribe, and refer. And, apparently the buyer needs no *caveat* because most reports and "scientific" communications regarding results indicate successes from *all* interventions. As Thomas Szász has wryly observed: "In this field everything works."[17]

Symptomatic of the advent of mass man and social engineering is the appearance of a myriad of group enterprises and team efforts. It seems now that no possible combination of therapists and clients has been overlooked; but the nature of "progress" being what it is, there will be more. Without engaging in an exhaustive explication and critique of each, some of these will be presented.

That everything "works" in psychiatry finds confirmation in the approach of Markowitz. His is "Analytic Group Psychotherapy of Married Couples by a Therapist Couple." Male and female therapists together either act as substitute parents or act as the good example for their misguided clients. Markowitz feels "most encouraged by our therapeutic approach" proving the "efficacy of heterosexual therapists working as a pair."*

The idea of providing a "mother" and a "father" as a therapeutic experience lacks a subtlety of approach that must be offensive to self-respecting adults.

Undoubtedly with the diversity of needs that exist in this world such an arrangement might be acceptable to some persons. Nonetheless, do the purported benefits outweigh what must be a humiliation in the procedure? Or, are we to accept this degradation as therapeutic? Perhaps one can become mature by being treated (sic) as a child.

There is "married couples group psychotherapy" directed toward couples whose main problem is their marital relationship, especially when the partners are relatively effective in other sectors of life and personality. The group herein described consisted of four couples, two cotherapists and a silent recorder. The sessions continued for twenty months. Most of the objections and obstacles predicted for it by non-orthodox therapists were readily overcome it was reported. Furthermore, "the group process seems particularly effective for clarifying distorted communications, for helping couples to clarify ambiguous marital roles, and to resolve neurotic behavior primarily involving the marital relationship. Most significant is the fact that the symbiosis is dissipated and the partners become

* *The Marriage Relationship, Psychoanalytic Perspectives,* Edited by Salo Rosenbaum and Ian Alger, Basic Books, New York, 1968.

Max Markowitz, "Analytic Group Psychotherapy of Married Couples by a Therapist Couple," pp. 267-82. Chapter 19.

individuals who live real, rather than defensive, roles in their marriage."[6]

Another approach to airing marital disharmony is "collaborative therapy." Here each partner was treated by different therapists who communicated with each other at intervals, according to some, to "maintain the marriage" and to others, "for the purpose of facilitating therapeutic changes in their patients." This is also known as "stereoscopic technique," showing at once that psychiatry too is up-to-date.[10] The psychiatrists met individually with the partners and thereafter consulted with one another, "of necessity" comparing notes on the therapeutic problems of their couples. The conferences of the therapists, it was pointed out, were held not only with the full knowledge and consent of the marital partners, but frequently at the *insistence* of particular partners who wanted all possible help. Emergencies such as possible suicide, homicide, and desertion arose requiring "management."

What is accomplished? We learn that the regular review of the situation helps the partners recognize reality distortions. It also helped the therapists recognize the complementary neuroses that existed between the partners, that "both drew them together and pushed them apart." Another advantage, one of the greatest it is claimed, is that the stereoscopic technique affords the psychiatrists the opportunity of ending "transference-counter-transference duels" by having different psychiatrists work with members of the same family. In other words, it is a supervisory check on the therapeutic situation.

Stereoscopic technique, basically psychoanalytically conventional in that in substance it reconstructs even the earliest infant-mother relationships, is deemed by its inventors as an effective instrument and a "welcome addition to our therapeutic armamentarium." One advocate of this method relates that many techniques can achieve the same thing; there are "many ways to skin a cat."[11]

For others, there is "concurrent psychoanalytic therapy." Here both partners are treated separately but concurrently by the same therapist. The purported advantages here are four. This combined technique extends hope for the restoration of the marital relationship. Also emotional support for both members becomes immediately operative. Thirdly, the therapist gains a multidimensional view of the marriage transaction; a "triadic communication system" is established so that knowledge of both past events and current conflicts can be gained in minimal time. And, since each partner knows that the other is also reporting, possibly on the same marital problem, there may be more "accurate" reporting by each. The fourth advantage, it is stated, is the "triangular transference." Feelings are directed toward the therapist and also toward the other patient, the mate. This allegedly might be an aid in the full explication of the oedipal constellation.

Patients are "directed" to report their dreams and as part of the therapeutic effect they agree not to discuss the contents of their respective interviews. These are the only stated demands of the therapist. This treatment, although using *some* conventional psychoanalytic techniques, is alien to most analysts because, the authors tell us, "a great majority are biased by their one-to-one patient orientations."[15]

It may be pure coincidence that a chief advocate and promoter of this triadic, judicially structured therapy is named Dr. *Solomon*.

Another opportunity for the distressed couple is "conjoint marital therapy." Both partners are seen together by the same therapist or by cotherapists, one male and one female. This arrangement is for married couples without children. With children, all are brought in, then the "family therapeutic approach" is instituted.[12] Emphasis is placed on the opportunity to communicate which this setup allegedly provides. We are told that "this experience can serve as an ego-enhancing corrective and eventually reflects in clearer, more specific, and more direct communication between husband and wife."[13]

Alger is amongst a growing number of therapists who have confused "disease" and "treatment."

"Psychoanalysis, which was born at the turn of the century, and therefore originally reflected the more mechanistic thinking of that era, conceived of the individual as a closed type of system, and understood neurotic symptoms as resultants from the disturbed equilibrium of an inner economy of instinctual forces. Interpersonal, sociocultural, and communicational theories have all emphasized the point that an individual cannot be understood apart from his relationships with other human beings." (page 251)

For these reasons, Alger contends, ". . . psychoanalysts in increasing numbers are openly using the techniques of conjoint therapy of marital partners, as well as other methods which include the marital partner in the therapy plan. Conjoint therapy: concurrent therapy in which each spouse is seen by the same or by a different analyst, but not together; and combined therapy, in which conjoint and individual concurrent sessions are both arranged, are all variations which take into account in a direct way the fact that the primary patient is a member of a family and that his behavior, whether or not to be labeled neurotic, cannot be understood in isolation from other people."[11a]

The logical fault in Alger's statement is that his sound observation, about the patient not living in a vacuum and the interpersonal relations, sociocultural considerations, etc., does not lead inevitably to the conclusion the only or best way to be of help to a person is in a "social" or family type therapy—any more than a violinist should be given group or "conjoint" lessons because he is destined to play in a symphony orchestra. No one to my knowledge condemns individual and private instructions in that area. The shortcomings of this analogy notwithstanding, the private, confidential, one-to-one therapy which psychoanalysis provides does in no way exclude an understanding of either interpersonal relations or socio-cultural considerations. It may actually increase understanding of these crucial factors by the *distancing* that the private contract facilitates, distancing that we generally recognize of prime importance in the learning process. Distancing allows for a modicum of reflection needed for insight and decision making. I don't know of any great novels or music that have been written on battlefields! Furthermore, although we have been told that families who pray together stay together, there is no surety that this is also true of "therapizing" together. Sometimes therapy of this "social" nature may compound the crime in that the principal problem is likely to be too much togetherness, too much community, too little privacy with a resultant too much intrusion into each other's lives.

Lastly, treating both partners together or alternately burdens the treatment with an implicit value judgment about *the* marriage and marriage. It is like learning about the choice of religion versus atheism in the Vatican![11a]

The above is but a partial list of the available therapies. And, apparently to leave no hole in the net or, if metaphors may temporally be mixed, to leave no stone unturned, there is the serious use of "individual, concurrent and conjoint sessions as a 'combined approach'." This treatment, a combination of the best of all those mentioned above, "is based on a plan of active support, including environmental manipulation; complementary goals; clarification of role expectations and enactments; redirection of intrapsychic and interpersonal energies; and evocation of 'healthier communication'."[7]

Psychiatry obviously can never be accused of lack of zeal and inventiveness. And, as already indicated and confirmed by each "scientific" study, "everything works." Who can resist the doctor's prescription? Who cares if the doctor's prescription makes no mention of individual aspirations, the rights of privacy and confidentiality, the hypocrisy inherent in the role of judge-therapist, or the total blockage of meaningful communication which an "adversary-structured" situation, such as conjoint therapy, really is? Courts of law for centuries have clearly recognized the principle that the accused should not be asked to testify against himself. In marital problems each is the accused. In all these "social therapies" the inherent judiciary nature of their operations is never mentioned. Without the protection of basic rules of evidence, can one then expect more than a modicum of disingenuousness on the part of the accused? We shudder at the image of a kangaroo court in modern society and yet they may be operating at full steam in the most unsuspected and most respectable places. We must not forget the kangaroo courts "work"; the accused is found innocent or guilty and is sentenced. What is missing, of course, are the rules of procedure and evidence that guarantee basic human rights *even if the accused himself may not be aware of them.*

Relatives, enemies, and friends play a variety of roles in a marriage. They may be helpful or destructive. The destructive role makes the best dramas, so it is better known. Everyone knows about sinister Iago and his instigation; what hateful families did to Romeo and Juliet; what a malcontent tried to do to Hero; what a malicious adventurer attempted with Cymbeline and Posthumus; what a lustful Tarquin did to Lucrece. All were waiting in the wings ready to destroy happiness. Shakespeare, for one, seemed out to warn humanity that there was always some force, some Lucifer ex machina, ready to put asunder what God had joined.

"All the world loves a lover" is a lovely but inaccurate popular quotation. The sight or knowledge of people deeply in love and trustful of each other seems to stimulate the desire of some to split them apart. Perhaps it is some inherent human capriciousness. It may be the work of misanthropes who, unable to find suitable mates themselves, cannot tolerate the happiness of others. Or it is a lingering hostility from the oedipal stage of development, where the impotent youngster is overwhelmed with frustration at the closeness of his parents; divisiveness is his hobbyhorse thereafter in life.

The third force seems to be a vital part of most human

progress as well as tragedy.* The third party is most often portrayed as the intruder, the disruptive force, that within humanity which casts doubt, encourages deceit, promotes suspicion. On the other hand, the third party in *Troilus and Cressida* who brings the lovers together is the coarse, disreputable Pandar, whose voyeuristic tendencies are not even thinly disguised. His role as a love broker is an inglorious one, never reaching the stature of the spoilers such as Iago, Tarquin, and even the bastard John in *Much Ado About Nothing*. Shakespeare wanted the word Pandar forevermore to connote pimpishness. The marriage broker has always been a derided character, an interloper who is generally contemptible, yet respected for sensitivity and tragic involvement even in villainy. Perhaps Shakespeare wanted to alert humanity to the strength and cunning of the third force, to warn against ignoring or underestimating the power of the enemy which love likes to hide. Or was it part of Shakespeare's tragic vision or existential cynicism which caused him to portray the mind as easily poisoned, trust quickly overturned, and conviction routinely cuckolded?

Perhaps Shakespeare understood that the third force is necessary in most human relations and vital to marriage. This is why there are so many intrusions, both solicited and gratuitous. Posthumus was under no moral obligation to test his wife; yet he could not resist the gamble offered him. He thus reveals the perversity of mankind that seems to have to introduce controversy where none exists, to risk doubt when there is certainty, to feel pain rather than pleasure. But it is only a seeming perversity, because it is too extensive and ubiquitous to be considered the erratic behavior of a few. Lederer and Jackson† in their book,

---

* We may recall the cynicism of Alexandre Dumas: "The chain of wedlock is so heavy that it takes two to carry it—sometimes three."

† Lederer, W. J., and Jackson, D., *The Mirages of Marriage*, W. W. Norton, New York, 1968, Chap. 48 (The Use of a Third Party in a Marital Dialogue).

The Mirages of Marriage, recognize the importance of this inevitable third force in marital situations.

The third force may be the needed, often self-created, frustration and stimulus to carry one to the next stage of development; to counteract that tranquility which encourages stagnation and involution. In the modern idiom, it is needed for one's creative identity, in the sense of testing oneself in the cauldron of doubt, destruction, and dismay. Only in such a position can one concretely learn one's true mettle. It was Shakespeare who also wrote, "Sweet are the uses of adversity." Love is, then, never enough of a test for the developing human being any more than the caliber of a race horse can be fully known on a dry track. A basic characteristic of man's mentality is that he is problem-seeking: if he does not have any problems, he will manufacture them. It seems that his mental growth and general maturation depend on finding and attempting to solve them. If he cannot manufacture them in reality, he will do so in phantasy.

Othello is the tragic figure who succumbed to the third force, Iago. When tested, he knew of no accommodation other than to destroy his fancied oppressor, Desdemona; yet his actions are understandable in the light of his problem-solving mode. His life was devoted to the sword; this was his principal, and perhaps only, means of solving problems. If you are taunted or threatened, go to war; wipe out the enemy and the anguish the enemy appears to bring. With one blow you eliminate both. For Othello, having few or no social skills, knowing little patience and forbearance, never cast in the role of mediator or conciliator, it was natural enough to kill that strange and complex being, his wife. His entrapment by Iago is no surprise, for warriors are regularly goaded into uncritical fury in order to destroy the enemy. Some rationalization is needed for the organized murder that war permits, and this entails the total degradation of the adversary. For Iago the female was the enemy and it was his job to indoctrinate the warrior. Othello remained true to his calling, the dutiful soldier to the last. He acted like Jephthah, who, coming home from successful combat, killed his only daughter because he had promised to kill the first person who appeared. The third force of Othello was "brotherly" intrigue in the form of Iago, spurring him on to destructive goals. But like the golem, he killed and killed, a repetition compulsion devoid of discrimination. Like Coriolanus, he was the sword that could be directed toward either foe or friend. Like the psychoanalyst who analyzes his family when he comes home at night, the soldier can be expected to ply his trade in off-duty hours, with similar results.

The third force brought to bear on the problem, whether analyst, friend, clergyman, social worker, or attorney, must be at best a temporary expedient. The ideal to be achieved by outside help is not a third leg for a stool (although often this is the most that can be achieved) but ultimately inner strength, the growth of the inner person. Familiarity with the inner self is the chief source of what is left to man in matters of troubled relationships. Hopefully man can transcend some of his miseries through understanding.

The passion of love always carries with it expectations that for the most part are destined for disillusioning frustration. When the other person does not fill all the vacancies of one's soul, abject bitterness and hatred may result. The solution in most instances can only be the accretion of inner tissues to call upon when the outside fails, as it generally does. In the jargon of the trade, we can say that the fruits of affinity can never be known unless there is identity. It is wonderful to love and be loved, to protect and be protected, but none of these is possible until or unless one is able to be alone. And it is impossible to be alone unless there is a firm, ongoing communication with an inner self. Stripped of its mystical trappings, Soul can be called the chief sustaining force of life. Soul is a reservoir of ideals, convictions, memories of pleasure and pain, of sustaining objects of the past and present, of associations with the world of people and things, and of proofs of achievement and worthiness. Hopefully, one has access to such an internal entity—and, most importantly, open communication with it rather than having something inside encased in a leaden pipe. This leaden pipe is the repression that effectively cuts off from our chief sustenance. Psychoanalysis has as a chief goal the establishment of full communication between the outer and inner self. It is only here that ultimate reassurance and consolation will be found.

When people with marital problems come for help, they are rarely interested in the "inner man." The wife is more involved with that outer man who is reducing her to a state of impotent rage. After a battle, the urgent need is to get the wounds dressed and to justify the war. "Treatment" in these instances consists of a series of "white papers" issued by the aggrieved party attempting to justify the behavior which is "defensively" derived. Kubie's words can be readily confirmed by every psychoanalyst. "Psychoanalysis in marriages which are already on the rocks almost always encounters one particular complication. In marriage individuals usually come not to get well, but to prove to a spouse that they *are* well; not to find out where they are wrong, but to prove they are right."[8]

The husband comes to treatment because it is the thing to do, but it is hard to see how treating him is going to change "her obnoxious behavior," which is the cause of all the trouble. Then the inventory of oppressions begins, with the only area of self-doubt being, "I wonder in what state of irrationality I was to have married her." All of his grievances are reasonable; he is right. Yet he would have put up with all of them if only she had brought the fulfillment that no outsider can provide. And he could not do it for her and must face the humiliation that the promises of love alone are no substitutes for inner strength. If he is lucky enough to be able to see beyond his wife, he will gradually get down to the work of self-accretion, instead of self-justification, for preparation for a world which never lacks injustice, corruption, and chaos. The ultimate reunion with the self, which understanding brings, helps both to defend against these three and to rail against them more effectively.

Central to marital problems, after the pettiness is stripped away, is the awkward issue of human rights, rights such as self-fulfillment, autonomy, privacy, as well as expectation of compassion, sharing, and mutuality. Marriages frequently land "on the rocks" because there is an assumption of one or both partners that the marital union somehow abrogates these rights, as if the holy writs give license to strip the other of what is generally held dear and sacred. Loving someone then appears to some as giving themselves liberties to overwhelm, to entrap, and to enslave. Love then becomes a strange and puzzling experience indeed if, in its name, almost any indignity and intrusion of rights can be perpetuated.[1] Bruno Bettelheim told us that love is not enough. It is nothing and less than nothing, if it is not inextricably bound to a sense of justice. Love without justice is a yoke, which more often than not, not only enslaves but strangulates the human spirit. The sense of justice in human relationships is the consequential contribution of Martin Buber in his "I and thou" concept. Before him, love seemed the solitary requirement.

Because the issue of human rights in its variegated, subtle expressions is of paramount importance, the structure of therapy and its sensitivity to this issue takes on great meaning. Therapy, it would seem, should be a corrective paradigm in that it should respect with utmost care matters of goals, privacy, confidentiality, and highly individualistic, even if disturbingly eccentric, aspirations. In this it seems appropriate and reasonable that the therapist be the client's exclusive agent, apart from the mate, children, relatives, other therapists, etc. It is in this situation, one which psychoanalysis alone most closely approximates, that human rights can gain validity. It is difficult to see how therapies which by their structure downgrade and even denigrate, either by design or accident, the importance of *individual* worth and aspirations can enhance either self-esteem or personal hope. A person must, in T. S. Eliot's idiom, seek his own salvation with diligence before he can save another, a family, or his marriage. Does this type of individual "attention" promote megalomania and selfishness? Isn't it the traditional job of therapy to shrink heads rather than expand them? No danger. The erosions of the human spirit are usually so immense that the restoration of human dignity and feelings of heightened self-worth can only be salutary. No marriage should ever be held of more importance than one of its participants. Persons, not marriages, are worth saving. It is the grand hypocrisy of our morality that we have attempted to sanctify and glorify a compact often irrespective of the plight of the human beings involved. Every lawyer knows that no compact or contract is ever worth more than the signatories. We will someday learn that this verity applies to vital human relations also.

Andrew S. Watson,* a psychiatrist and attorney, urges psychoanalysts to involve themselves in the problems found in the law of the family—domestic relations law—and to assist the legal profession in understanding human behavior. That this would be most rewarding for all concerned, we can wholeheartedly concur. However, I would suggest that psychoanalysis has already profited and can enhance itself further by the example of the law tradition especially in regard to the client-advocate relationship. Psychoanalysis has imitated the legal model, and in my judgment, psychiatry in general would do well to study it. As the attorney is the advocate of the client he therein acknowledges an adversary situation. That inevitably develops in the marital state —those either "on the rocks" or otherwise.

It follows then quite logically (and ethically) that an attorney does *not* speak privately to the mate of his client. It follows that the attorney does *not* reveal to the mate personal data gathered in confidence. It follows then that the

---

* The Marriage Relationship, Psychoanalytic Perspectives, Edited by Salo Rosenbaum and Ian Alger, Basic Books, New York, 1968.

Andrew S. Watson, Psychoanalysis and Divorce, Chapter 23, pp. 231-339.

attorney does not sit in judgment of the pair as to who is right and who is wrong or who is mature and who childish. His role is that of agent or advocate of his client and he behaves as such under penalty of malpractice. Who would advocate changing this set of rules? Psychoanalysis, to its credit, felt that these rules should be applied to its own work. This basic structure of the psychoanalytic situation is not derived from the "mechanistic thinking of a past era" as some like to claim, but from the advocacy tradition which our colleagues in the law taught us. Knowledge of worldly socio-cultural forces as well as the interpersonal ones have not impelled lawyers to stray from their basic rules for dealing with a client. Nor should it. Learn we must and should from one another. At this point, the psychiatrist or analyst has more to learn from the attorney than the converse.

The problem of therapy involves ties and bonds to the past. These ties often remain to influence, often detrimentally, the new affinities the mature life demands. This is a lesson each generation must learn; it is contained in the mythologies of every culture. Hymen was worshipped as god of marriage by both the Greeks and the Romans. We generally think of him as the promoter of ties and bonds; his role of instigator of revolt and escape is often overlooked. He in fact gained his prominence in helping young maidens flee their captors.

This tale, of course, can be interpreted in a variety of ways. As the protector of womanhood, Hymen gave his name to the well known female structure.[14] However, we may derive from this myth the universally acknowledged necessity of young people to free themselves from bonds and bondage which characterize childhood. It would not be a product of wild analysis to assume that the pirates from whom Hymen rescued the maidens are symbols of enslaving parents.

The adult who has not freed himself may find, through psychoanalysis, that he is in the paradoxical position of Byron's Prisoner of Chillon:

> "My very chains and I grew friends,
> So much a long communion tends
> To make us what we are."

Freeing oneself does not mean the ability to forget family traditions, as some existentialists would have us believe possible. Both the forces of the sequence of generations and the reality rooted in love and work make us what we are. In our forging of an identity, we may modify this reality a little. This "little" may be more than enough. As Horace said to Sestius: "All of life is only a little, no long-term plans are allowed."

In summary, everything works in the "helping" professions and therefore all types of interventions are tried, rationalized, and established as "therapies." Since all claim good results and none can be placed under "scientific" scrutiny, the observer, as well as the client, must use moral criteria to make critical judgments as to their value. It is herein suggested that the structure of the therapy and the rules governing the behavior of therapist and client are of central importance. For the manner in which therapist and client conduct themselves can be the crucial and significant educative experience for other relationships. In terms of modern idiom, the medium is also the message. A therapeutic relationship, in which human rights are scrupulously honored as well as disciplined inhibition of exploitative and coercive instincts, is a salutary model that will be remembered for other relationships including marriage. Unfortunately this model for human interaction is too often ignored by the new, really old, breed of interventionists.

In terms of humanistic tradition the structure of psychoanalytic therapy scores high. The innovators with their disregard for privacy, confidentiality, and the autonomous strivings of the individual appear to run counter to this tradition. There may be a legitimate role for the "mittler" in modern society, but is he a therapist?

NOTES

1. Blood, Robert O. and Donald M. Wolfe, *Husbands and Wives, The Dynamics of Married Living* (New York: The Free Press, 1960), pp. 221-35.

2. Camus, Albert, *Notebooks 1935–1942*. (New York: Modern Library, 1965), p. 42.

3. Giovacchini, Peter L., "The Clinical Approach," *The Psychotherapies of Marital Discord*, ed. Bernard L. Greene (New York: The Free Press, 1965), pp. 39-81.

4. Goethe, J. W., *Elective Affinities*, trans. Elizabeth Mayer and Louise Bogan (Chicago: Henry Regnery Co., 1963), p. 18.

5. Goode, William J., *Women in Divorce* (New York: The Free Press, 1956), pp. 133-54.

6. Gottlieb, Anthony and E. Mansell Pattison, "Married Couples, Group Psychotherapy," *Arch. of Gen. Psychiat.*, XIV, Feb. 1966, p. 143.

7. Greene, Bernard L., Betty P. Broadhurst, and Noel Lustig, "Treatment of Marital Disharmony: The Use of Individual, Concurrent, and Conjoint Sessions in a 'Combined Approach'," *The Psychotherapies of Marital Discord*, ed. Bernard L. Greene (New York: The Free Press, 1965), pp. 135-51.

8. Kubie, Lawrence S., "Psychoanalysis and Marriage," *Neurotic Interaction in Marriage*, ed. Victor W. Eisenstein (New York: Basic Books, 1956), p. 38.

9. Lasch, Christopher, "Divorce American Style," *New York Review of Books*, VI, Feb. 17, 1966, p. 3.

10. Martin, Peter A. and H. Waldo Bird, "An Approach to the Psychotherapy of Marriage Partners, The Stereoscopic Technique," *Psychiat.*, XVI (1953), pp. 123-27.

11. Martin, Peter A., "Treatment of Marital Disharmony by Collaborative Therapy," *The Psychotherapies of Marital Discord*, ed. Bernard L. Greene (New York: The Free Press, 1965), pp. 83-101.

11a. *The Marriage Relationship, Psychoanalytic Perspectives*, Edited by Salo Rosenbaum and Ian Alger (New York: Basic Books, 1968).

Ian Alger, Joint Sessions: Psychoanalytic Variations, Applications and Indications. Chapter 18, pp. 251-65.

12. Satir, Virginia M., *Conjoint Family Therapy* (Palo Alto: Science and Behavior Books), 1964.

13. Satir, Virginia M., "Conjoint Marital Therapy," *The Psy-*

chotherapies of Marital Discord, ed. Bernard L. Greene (New York: The Free Press, 1965), pp. 121-33.

14. Seidenberg, Robert, "Psychosexual Aspects of Hymen," *Psychiat. Q.,* XXV, July, 1951, pp. 472-74.

15. Solomon, Alfred P. and Bernard L. Greene, "Concurrent Psychoanalytic Therapy in Marital Disharmony," *The Psychotherapies of Marital Discord,* ed. Bernard L. Greene (New York: The Free Press, 1965), pp. 103-17.

16. Szász, Thomas S., *The Ethics of Psychoanalysis, The Theory and Method of Autonomous Psychotherapy* (New York: Basic Books, Inc., 1965), pp. 11-28.

17. Szász, Thomas S., "Recent Letters to the Editor," *New York Times Book Review,* June 11, 1961.

CHAPTER XV

FOR THE FUTURE—EQUITY?

After the so-called expert presents his cases and clinical data on the vagaries and vicissitudes of marriage as he has seen them in his consultation room and in life, the legitimate question is asked of him, "What of the future for marriage?" The nihilist can of course indulge in all sorts of hyperbolic pronouncements, such as "It is altogether rotten to the core and will destroy all those who enter into it"; or, in the same tone but opposite vein, "There is nothing wrong with marriage. It is the participation of 'sick' people who ruin it."

Marriage as the predominant way of living will be with us long after 1984. Socialist countries in our time have not eliminated it nor do they anticipate doing so. Capitalistic countries find that the marital state is consonant, perhaps all too consonant, with the ideology of personal possession.

It is the author's hope that the marriage of the future be perceived in a way quite different from that of the present. Firstly, it will become dissociated from divine sanctity and be placed in the hands of the participants. It will become a wordly compact, an open covenant openly arrived at. (Monarchs no longer rule by divine right, but all too often today husbands (occasionally wives) appear to be doing just that in their marital provinces.) The religious ceremony will be retained just as the coronation of the kings and queens of England is retained in that democracy. Pomp and ceremony are delights in an all too rationalistic world, but henceforth few women will take seriously the idea that they are to become either God's or their mate's servant or "handmaiden." The enlightened young people may demand that the words of submission in the wedding ceremony be eliminated in favor of "I" and "Thou" expressions which are really much more beautiful as well as right. Marriage will be placed in the hands of the people, taken away from a Deity who has never had the time or the will to partake of it Himself. By His own celibacy, He has indeed forfeited His claim to expertise in these matters.

In the matter of the conjugal union the major religions have not kept up with egalitarianism. Drastic changes are needed in church dogma, relevant to the concept of the equality of men and women. Up to the present time, religions have envisaged by prescription and example relationships based on the dominance-submission model. Invoking the authority of a male godhead, parents, ministers and rabbis have never failed during marriage ceremonies and during subsequent pastoral counselling to corrupt men by causing them to believe in their own dominance and superiority while at the same time encouraging women to suffer the demeaning effects of passive submission. While it is true that many marriages are held together by the threat of external damnation for the errant partner, again it is often true that the means eventually undo the ends. Religion, hopefully the instrument for morality, has now lagged painfully behind the times. How long it can creditably remain the arbiter in interpersonal relations is debatable. The church establishment is a laggard in the questions of both civil and human rights: since it has excluded women from its inner circles of decision making, its administration, and its clergy, its credibility as the authentic agent of both partners in a marriage contract is under great doubt. Although one can legitimately debate the issue of whether God is dead, it is unlikely that human beings will continue to suffer injustices in His name.

If the above statements appear to address themselves to the inequities toward women in the religious imperatives of the marriage contract, it is not because the inequities do not have a deleterious effect on men also. But for the moment the urgency of the oppressed must pre-empt the plight of the oppressor. Men ultimately suffer the corruption of unearned victories and ascendancy. Their personalities become warped by the myth of their own dominance and superiority. It places them in a position of having to be the literal oppressors of those they profess to love. They decorticate their own sisters, wives and daughters, fulfilling a vow no less ruthless than that against Jephthah's daughter.[1] This "heroic" Judge of Israel immolated his own daughter in exchange for winning a battle. Agamemnon did the same with Iphigenia to get his ships moving. Unfortunately these inglorious deeds of our heritage continue to the present day in more sophisticated and malignant forms. Wives and daughters are sacrificed today for men's ambitions. These go largely unreported. There are no modern-day chroniclers. There are an articulate few who can communicate their feelings in words rather than symptoms. One is Caroline Meline of Philadelphia, Pennsylvania, who wrote to the *New York Times* (Magazine Section) as follows under the rubric "Alienation: Housewife Dept."

"To the Editor:

"Steven Kelman makes the point in 'These are Three of the Alienated,' Oct. 22, that alienation today takes many forms. This corps of the alienated may be larger than he or many people suspect, because I have the feeling that many of America's most stable group, the housewives, are included.

"I am the wife of a promising young businessman, the mother of two small boys and I work at home as a free-lance copy editor. I have been out of college almost five years. The college is Smith. At 25, I am faced with the crisis of finding some meaning in life or, if that proves impossible, finding a satisfactory way of living and functioning despite it.

"No, my family is not enough. Yes, I want to make their lives as happy and problem-free as possible, and I will, no matter what, go through all the necessary motions. But I really do want to be more than a smiling zombie. The more I think the less real enthusiasm I can muster, and unfortunately I can't stop thinking.

"The question is, how do you find something to look forward to? And how do you achieve that sense of purpose in what you are doing that will end this questioning? Like Bill in Mr. Kelman's article, I wonder how you go about feeling committed. What difference does it make whether I go back to school and get more educated or just read or go to painting classes or try to make a career out of something? Basically, what good are goals of any kind in the face of death? Yet how is it possible to be happy in the present, forgetting goals, if there is no sense of accomplishing anything?

"The trouble is that I, probably like many of the other alienated, can't get out of myself. I think deeply mainly of me, and I am isolated in my thoughts. To be able to communicate in this impersonal way, that is, write a letter to The Times, is a pleasant relief, but still very self-oriented and of course very temporary.

"What is the answer? Keep busier? See lots of people and communicate like mad? See a psychiatrist? Drugs?"[2]

These sentiments can no longer go ignored or discredited as the products of a "sick" mind or a spoiled, maladjusted adolescent. They are in fact the laments of one who takes neither her life nor her "voluntary" servitude lightly or cavalierly as the "alienists" (sic) have up to now been prone to do.[11]

Something is terribly wrong with a social contract that results in such real deprivation. It is ludicrous to say, as some do, "Well, she didn't have to get married. If she wanted to pursue a career, why didn't she stay single?" The reasonable rejoinders should be apparent. No man is ever asked to make such a choice. He is expected to have both. Furthermore, in life today, marriage is a woman's only *acceptable* destiny. She really has no choice but to get married. Yet the understanding "humanist" who is appalled when the man-in-the-street says, "If the Negro doesn't like the Ghetto, let him come out," is as likely to ask his own wife, "Why didn't you stay single if you wanted a career?"

The inherent inequities of the customary contract blind and corrupt the male. His often accurate vision of broad social issues and problems stops at his own doorstep, invariably skips the one he "loves." The corruption of the male usually shows its effects on both sides of his own doorstep. John Stuart Mill in 1869 was able to write:

"All the selfish propensities, the self-worship, the unjust self-preference, which exist among mankind, have their source and root in, and derive their principal nourishment from, the present constitution of the relation between men and women. Think what it is to be a boy, to grow up to manhood in the belief that without any merit or any exertion of his own, though he may be the most frivolous and empty or the most ignorant and stolid of mankind, by the mere fact of being born a male he is by right the superior of all and every one of an entire half of the human race: including probably some whose real superiority to himself he has daily or hourly occasion to feel; but even if in his whole conduct he habitually follows a woman's guidance, still, if he is a fool, she thinks that of course she is not, and cannot be, equal in ability and judgment to himself; and if he is not a fool, he does worse—he sees that she is superior to him, and believes that, notwithstanding her superiority, he is entitled to command and she is bound to obey. What must be the effect on his character, of this lesson?"[3]

It would be pleasant to report progress in the hundred years since then, but that is unfortunately not possible. There is little or no progress to report either on the domestic scene or in man's general ability to inhibit his "aggressive drives" in dealing with diverse political and social problems. In the latter he is constantly driven by his insatiable need to be superior to his neighbor, to save face, and to be a winner in war.

Does this corruption start in his relationship with women as John Stuart Mill and R. V. Sampson seem to think?

Perhaps there is a need now for a massive reappraisal. In the idiom of the day, might not we now leave "love" aside for a while and wonder about redistribution of power in the marital contract? This will be no simple task, for, as minority groups have painfully learned, power is not readily relinquished by those who comfortably and traditionally possess it. The problem becomes even more complex because maleness itself has become identified with the possession of power and the innate superiority that it brings. Any step in the direction of equity between the sexes must then be unfairly called emasculation. The woman then is placed in the hapless position of "emasculating" her brother, husband, and son. It is probably this particular mythology which has deterred her from either effectively resisting or rebelling against her voluntary servitude which is part and parcel of most marriage contracts. The tragic aspect is that the servitude indeed is voluntary—she has internalized her role of inferiority; the chastity belt is now unneeded. "The Story of O"[4] tells of a woman who has to be beaten into submission, then submits without being beaten; having lost her identity, all she wants is death.

The magic word in psychiatry today is "identity." It can be defined in many ways. It encompasses having some uniqueness and distinguishing features in a world of three billion people. It means standing for something. It also means being what you are supposed to be and, more than that, *doing* what you're supposed to do. It's being an engineer and as Ralph Nader might say, "Being allowed to build a well-engineered car." It is being a lawyer and being able to defend clients instead of routinely pleading indigents guilty. In the idiom of Arthur Miller's *The Crucible*, it is having and defending one's name.

We soon realize that these are fine-sounding ideals which apply almost exclusively to the male. Perhaps it is picayune to discuss, but in the marriage contract in the United States the woman is automatically deprived of her very name, and she is glad to lose it, without a whimper. As though it were not enough to relinquish her good family name, rules of etiquette require that even her given name of Jane is replaced by John. Whatever became of that Marjorie Morningstar we used to know? Where in Westchester is she now? What name does she go by? Her conversion is complete. Stripped of her name, she now knows on whom her destiny rides. And, unlike the male, whose marital status need never be identified by his signature, hers invariably is. He begins and remains forevermore "Mr." She must forfeit this privilege.

The reader may say this is quibbling and ask with Shakespeare, "What's in a name?" Some say "nothing"; others have died defending their names. A Negro woman took her case to the U. S. Supreme Court because a "friendly" prosecutor insisted on calling her "Mary."

A man works hard for a name. Names often work magic, as politicians will readily tell you. It would seem elementary that woman should not have to submerge her own heritage in this way. In many cultures in the world today, the woman's name is not so cavalierly obfuscated; both lineages are represented in the resultant family name. But one suspects that the "repression" of the woman's name is the message of how things are and what they are to be. That she had better forget her own search for identity in the meaningful world. Can this "custom" be modified? Simple and as innocuous as such a move is? Probably not, because this is but one of the many ways that our cultural misogyny has been institutionalized. Who wants to pull one fiber in the fabric?

It may be that there has been too much emphasis placed here on the oppression of women in the marital situation. Ironically, it is quite probable that men become victims of their own advantages. An unearned superiority is thrust upon them. This places a constant burden of proof upon them which causes distortions of character and personality which are tragic to behold. The man is placed, often through no personal need or desire of his own, in a position of proving why he, of two people, should automatically be the standard-bearer for the family. Often to prove his doubtful superiority, he must resort to pseudo-self-enhancement such as uncalled-for bravery, bravado, cunning, tricks, and outmoded feats of courage. On the other hand he must assume an often unneeded executive role with his wife. This entails both a dictatorial attitude and at the same time a subtle campaign of depreciation of her talents, ability, and intelligence. Authority must often be exerted, as upon children, to prove and maintain dominance.

In other words, the male is expected to wear the "emperor's clothes" even though he risks pneumonia. Even though psychoanalysis has labeled the female as the narcissist, it is in fact the male who is forced consistently to show and prove himself, leading to the "hang-ups" of eternal competition and inevitable oneupsmanship. Albert Camus recognized and hated this distorting compulsion in men: "Every time a man (or I myself) gives way to vanity, every time he thinks and lives in order to show off, this is a betrayal. Every time, it has always been the great misfortune of wanting to show off which has lessened me in the presence of truth. We do not need to reveal ourselves to others, but only to those we love."[5]

He must be superior whether he is or not. Whether this man-woman supremacy myth has led to or encouraged concepts such as racial supremacy, chosen people, and master race is an interesting speculation, but one which must be seriously considered, given the serious social and political problems that such concepts have created. In entertaining such speculations one does risk the sin of global extrapolations; we must concede it has been the male sex that has controlled governments, and has brought the world to the very edge of disaster. Women have had little say in the inner councils of high-level decision making. R. V. Sampson asks about the price we pay, politically and morally, when we allow urges to dominate and to submit to control our lives.

As the inequities of marriage were enforced by "Divine Will" the marital status quo has been reified by modern sociology and psychology in their theories of roles, role-playing and role-taking. Marital partners then are not dominant or submissive in marriage but play proper dominant or submissive *roles*. Problems of equity need not arise. Then the unction of "instinctual" drives are applied to prove that it is natural enough for the male to dominate and the female to submit. To complete the male self-serving mythopoeism, evidence is gathered from lower animals to show predetermined patterns. Ergo, if a man dominates and a woman follows, they are correctly following their biological givens. Therefore, accusations of exploitation as well as hopes for correction of inequities become irrelevant. These types of justifications have successfully kept people enslaved for centuries. The problem of autonomy inherent in "assigning" roles to the male or female, to black people or white people, is that the roles *are* assigned. Perhaps justified in a play on Broadway, the reader in his self-preservative wisdom would like to have a say about the role in life he is to play—even if that say turns out to be pitifully small. At least there is the hope that everything about one's destiny is not preordained by mythologies of the past and present. If the concept of role foredooms, the addition of the word "natural" condemns. Nature is by and large neutral in social and political matters. The history of the word *natural* is not a happy one. It has too often been applied as a self-serving demiurge amongst individuals, nations, and races. Even though everyone glibly speaks of them, inherent sex-linked character traits are products of pseudo-science and more often than not are used to create differences for purposes of prejudice or self-justification. But character is indeed formed through both training and role-imposition. With the assigned role of dominance and superiority inevitably come arrogance, feelings of self-love, favored access to opportunities, a right to decision making, and expectations of leadership. Pejoratively, the role of dominance too often means the right to exploit, to prevail, and to show off. The role of submission has little to commend itself for in the context of the "good life." It is a condition that a man might endure as the price of failure or ineptness. Yet society generally recommends submission on the part of women as both virtuous and beautiful. Above all it allows fully for the quality of humility. It leads to character traits which, although often allowing for good adjustment to the dominant counterpart, stymie genuine expressiveness, discourage noetic functioning, and promotes abdication of personal responsibility. Secondary consequences are malaise, retreat to biological preoccupations including hypochondriasis and self-hate. The clinical ramifications of this self-hate is involutional melancholia—the woman's menopausal syndrome—the outcome of twenty years of submission.

As everyone knows, nothing succeeds like failure. Lederer and Jackson* speak of "the stable—unsuccessful marriage." Historically, marriage worked best when it was the "sickest." Dreikurs correctly observes:

> "It was much easier to maintain marriage and to find peace in one's home as long as the man was dominant. (There was no conflict about sex; women considered their sexual role merely as one of satisfying the needs of their husband). . . . As soon as one wants more than the other, the relationship is disturbed. The one who wants less feels imposed upon. . . ." "These difficulties, which discourage and demoralize husbands and wives alike, are partly due to this new relationship of equality, which developed as part of the democratic evolution. There is no tradition that teaches us how to live with each other as equals, in mutual respect and trust."†

Is there an alternative to the dominance-submission model for marriage? A majority of people will not admit

* Lederer, W. J. and Jackson, D., *The Mirages of Marriage,* W. W. Norton, N. Y., 1968. Chap. 18, pp. 153-60.

† The Marriage Relationship, Psychoanalytic Perspectives, Edited by Salo Rosenbaum and Ian Alger, Basic Books, New York, 1968.

Rudolph Dreikurs, "Determinants of Changing Attitudes," Chapter 7, pp. 83-103.

that marriage today is based on this model; this reality offends the egalitarian image. They admit to a difference of roles but with equally important functions. Their argument does not hold up under close scrutiny. They ultimately must fall back on the argument of what is "natural." Other people admit the dominance-submission model and praise it. They talk of the dominant role as a heavy responsibility, almost as a yoke, and submission as a manifestation, or as an intrinsic necessity of love and devotion. They ultimately invoke Divine evidence as the authority for ordering the man-woman relationship in this manner. In answer to them, the cynic might reply with Camus, "Do not confuse sanctity with idiocy."

In suggesting alternatives for personal conduct in marital relations, one need not fear now the accusation of utopianism, simply because time may be running out for the human community. It may be the changes at the "precinct level" that will give impetus to the re-ordering of social and normal values of our foundering society. And the alternatives carry with them no guarantees of happiness, elimination of mental illness, or the elimination of war. They are proposed in the simplistic and naive framework of doing what is right. This may betray a personal arrogance on the part of the writer but here again the alternatives that are to be proposed are not original but have been a neglected moral theme of the liberal humanistic tradition of Spinoza, John Stuart Mill, and Martin Buber. It was Spinoza who exposed the hoax of humility—the keystone on which most bias leans. John Stuart Mill, a hundred years ago, wrote of "The Subjection of Women" in which he carefully explained the corrupting effects of the dominance-submission model. Martin Buber more recently doubted whether there could be love at all if it were not on a basis of equality. This writer, lacking originality, compensates for this deficiency by placing himself in good company and taking a job that will be, in Irving Howe's idiom, "steady work."

It is probably impossible to change the marital contract

without demythologizing the traditional images of maleness and femininity. This will probably have to start in primary education in the content and illustrations depicting the roles of the sexes. Children might see a woman doctor treating patients and women in the church pulpits. They might at least see them in textbook illustrations if not in real life. Small boys might be allowed to play with dolls, as so many long to do, instead of being directed toward toy tanks and gun sets complete with Russian cosmonauts as targets. These are but a few examples of the type of patterning that the educational establishment actively promotes in "forming character." It is an ironic joke to say that the school system omits "sex" education.

It is indeed preoccupied with sex education, actively creating artificial differences to fit the male and female children for the dominance-submission yoke which is to come. There is rarely an attempt to educate the young girl to think that she is just as good as anyone else, but just the opposite. She is too often discouraged from serious subjects such as science and mathematics "because girls really don't need that." Boys are quickly directed toward athletic games which exclude females to impart to them the message that this physical superiority is meaningful, indicative of a "natural" superiority which can be spread to everything else. For in terms of the scholarly curricular pursuits, no such superiority for boys is evident; often the evidence is to the contrary. Neither sex would suffer if superiority or inferiority were earned by mental achievement, eliminating the artifices of the football hero or the beauty queen. Both of these symbolize "unearned" victories and represent specious standards of worthiness. These activities are innocent in themselves; the trouble begins when these "stars" are used in toothpaste ads as the best we have in society.

There are many who say that a drive for equality breeds a new form of bitterness and frustration. A new competition is nurtured which augments and unleashes aggression. Thus "love" and "peace" along with harmony are destroyed. Here the world continues to be a vast hunting ground—now with everyone fully armed. Mr. John Wilson, the British philosopher, writes as follows: "A belief in equality is no real improvement over a belief in privilege or meritocracy: people still continue to compete, to measure themselves—only this time they measure to see that they are equal, rather than to see that they are getting what they deserve or what they are privileged to get. *We need to get away from the notion of achievement and competition altogether.*" (Italics mine.)[6]

Mr. Wilson's point must be taken seriously because it is utopian. Yet it may be discouraging to those affected to find that fair play is no longer relevant when they finally get a turn at bat. It is like the chagrin of the black person in America who, after finally being allowed in the white man's church, is told from the pulpit that God is dead! Similarly, the woman is to be told that the fight for equality is now spurious and that achievement as well as competition are to be immoral. Perhaps in some millennium this may prove to be so, but it seems to this writer that achievement in its authentic sense is something that can be preserved. The issue of competitiveness as it is too often practiced in our society is a legitimate one for reappraisal. Here there has been an over-emphasis; it has become a way of life rather than a necessity for achievement or even survival. One can agree with Mr. Wilson that achievement has often been obscured by the inordinate need of the male to show off. There is no need to discredit achievement; instead there is a need to sharpen our discriminatory abilities. We must desist from calling everything that gets attention as an achievement. But if not achievement, what? Is man destined to spend his years in "Peyton Place" preoccupations? But then in all fairness, Mr. Wilson, in wishing to eliminate what he considers a scourge, is under no obligation to supply an alternative. On the other hand, he can leave us naked but not skinned. Even though much can be said for the life of pure contemplation, this has proved inadequate for modern man. Camus' modification of Socrates reflects this: "To know yourself you must act."

Can one then at this point prescribe action for women? One would think that they can lay claim to our heritage too. But tradition, as well as text books in psychology, tell us that to be feminine is to be *passive*. Thereby women are all too effectively eliminated from seeking those values in living that philosophers espouse and recommend.

The passivity of women, like the purported laziness of the Negro, is another instance of male self-serving mythopoeism. Even Freud, no patron saint of women, had to recant on this score. Yet the discrediting continues unabated. The male has sold this idea and the female has, outwardly at least, accepted it, or at best her rebellion against it has largely been indirect and circuitous—to be understood only by the casuist.

Both male and female might be re-educated about alternatives to the dominance-submission model—in lieu of indoctrination, which now prevails. In this re-education, there might be included the "sinfulness" of powerlessness. Matters of power especially in the romance of relationships are never brought to conscious awareness. How can one mention power to people in love—a state of being wherein for a short time intrusive worldly matters are denied. Power is a dirty word—abhorred especially by those who possess it.

The wholesale repression of the subject of power (and its distribution) as it affects human relations is scandalous. Freud, who unlocked the subject matter of sex, never mentioned power as a determining factor in marital relations. Here again the interest was centered on *impotence* of a physical (sexual) nature, as if sexual power was the principal demiurge of relations. The term *power* is herein used, not in the sense of the physicist as a neutral force or energy, but as Lord Acton saw it. Differing from influence, it functions through coercion rather than reason; it operates to prevail and dominate rather than to cooperate. It worries little about equality, justice, or fair play. Mr. R. V. Sampson defines it as follows: "By power is meant the production of desired consequences in the behavior or belief of another, where the intent to exercise personal ascendancy is present in the one producing the effects. Motive is all important, although the motive may be unconscious. Usually the victim of another's power will be aware of at least some sense of psychic constraint. But this is not necessarily the case. The victim may have long since come to accept his position and regard it as natural."[7]

The elimination of "power" in this sense in international relations or in marriages should have highest priority. However, before it is reached, there must be some defensive stances to discourage the use of power and to protect against its effects. One might for purposes of expediency talk in terms of corrective action to create a "balance of power" or a system of "checks and balances" in the idiom of the political scientist. We do not live in a pristine world in which we can fully rely on the "power-ful" to relinquish their easy advantage. A profession of love has been used as a justification for many unfair tactics. Yet love is the answer but only when the heart becomes informed.

The black man in the ghetto cannot lift himself one inch out of his destiny with all his purported or fancied sexual strength.[8] He has now offended the sensibilities of the classes of people who have the significant power of living, economic and social, by bringing forth power as a subject of discussion. Black power, practically non-existent as it is, has become a major threat to the white community. The black power leader has offended because he has attempted to undo a repression; he has called attention to the reality that power, and principally economic power, gives people control, allows them to dominate, to exclude, and to exploit. This same power may control relationships between father and son and husband and wife. It may even determine one's state of sanity. A sociologist[12] is convinced that it is the principal determinant in the admission rate to mental hospitals. He shows convincingly that the admission rate of these hospitals is inversely proportionate to the prosperity of the country. He theorizes that mental breakdowns occur in those who had economic power and have suffered great losses.

Love hates to discuss money. Yet in most marriages the woman is expected to give up her economic independence, to relinquish her own earning capacity. While it may be true that most husbands are generous and considerate as providers, control remains with them and more often than not they see themselves as both responsible and generous. Furthermore, amongst the sophisticated at least, the withholding of money punitively is rare. Generally it is the male's great pride that he can "give" his wife and children more than the next fellow does. Yet there is always an overhanging "terror in reserve"—the potential for the male's self-righteous nastiness about being ruined or being run into bankruptcy. And the wife, with her children, all euphemisms aside, is placed in the role of recipient and dependent. Using Kierkegaard's formula, the woman loses doubly. He writes: ". . . it is better to give than to receive. . . . it is far more difficult to receive than to give."[9]

A sort of economic independence is being reached by many wives. In 1969 thirty-four per cent of them were in the labor market. They work allegedly to supplement the "family" income, to finance houses, cars, boats, educations, and other needs which characterize an affluent society. They have jobs—not careers. Rarely are they able to reach high incomes or decision-making levels. Their purported flightiness has been of no help in penetrating outer space. Wives who are trained professionals do badly. They are less in evidence in the world today than twenty-five years ago. They are hopelessly incapacitated by their lack of acceptance in the world and by their inner panic about competing with (thereby castrating, they are told) their husbands.

Coming into marriage with economic reserves of her own (inheritance, etc.) gives a woman more leverage, and is to be highly recommended. This unfortunately is still a rarity. To obtain an economic balance of influence it would seem mandatory that the woman never relinquish her earning capacity—even when it is not "needed." The main obstacles here are the shibboleths of society rather than rational considerations. With minimal ingenuity arrangements can be made to run an office and a home, providing the spirit is willing. Husbands will have to help in the menial work—no biological factor precludes him from such tasks. Only inequality will be castrated. Day-care centers for children may become as highly recommended for the middle class as they now are for the poor. Why must only low-income or welfare mothers be "liberated"?

It is this writer's contention that behind the facade of love, devotion, and compassion, the spectre of power looms to take its toll in marriage. The toll that is taken is really not measurable in terms of divorces or separations, for power can create inescapable traps in which all that are left are resignation and apathy. These, ironically enough, because there is no movement or resistance in them, are often called happiness and contentment. Here there may operate a relentless spirit-destroying machine that leaves the body intact but spineless without an apparent wound.

The power that each of the mates can use on the other might be described simply in terms of positive and negative —each can be destructive. The male has the power that has been institutionalized and supported by tradition. These come from earning power, religious authority, and social approval of the male's dominant role. He has advantages of education and access to worldly opportunities. The woman generally lacks these or gets them through union with her husband. With this power, the male can keep the woman from fulfillment of goals and can effectively bind her to his needs and directions. The woman's power is negative in that she can act as an impediment, slow up progress, cause embarrassment, and great expense. She may overspend and bankrupt her husband. She may cuckold him, discrediting him before all. She may turn to alcoholism or drugs to frustrate his ambition, and there are hysteria, psychosis, and suicide. This is not to suggest that these latter are purely linear to the husband's behavior, but often enough they are. This is negative power which damages the husband but is also self-defeating. It is Medea, Salome, and Turandot; it is also Samson, who suffers self-destruction as he pulls down the temple. The woman's negative power has the shortcoming of lacking much disguise or subtlety. The positive power of the male, derived from generations of experience and practice, has become incorporated into what is "natural"—ironically consciously accepted even by the victim. And, it is often the case that a man is despised and ridiculed if he does not use power.

It then becomes unmanly not to oppress. It makes one almost agree with Sartre that most marriages are exercises in sadomasochism.[13] This represents the malignancy of positive and negative power. If the use of power in interpersonal relations is inevitable, the confrontation of power with counter-power would seem preferable. Hopefully, this confrontation too may eventually become vestigial for human affairs.

Can we afford to become optimistic in this direction? We may if people become educated to human rights as they pertain to themselves and others. There must be the recognition that the days of ownership and possession of human beings are over. That the time of adults asking "permission" should be at an end as well as the postures of the generous donor and grateful recipient. People must make social contracts such as marriage both out of passion and strength, the passion derived from a wish to cooperate and build, and strength that comes from equality. People in marriage need not be either authoritarian or dependent; both may be autonomous.[14] Autonomy and passion are not antithetic. One would hate to think that the price of love is the sacrifice of dignity and identity.

All of our humanistic words have become so overused as to vitiate their meaning. One such is "cooperation." Marriage might be based on the basis of cooperation rather than the dominance-subjection paradigm. This would obviate the need for or use of power. It would, however, mean that our culture would have to become accustomed to the manliness of cooperation and give credit to women for independence. In a union of self—as well as other—loving, autonomous persons, there would be the expectation that the destiny of one is congruent but not fused with the other. Personal as well as family goals will co-exist.

Autonomous persons cannot be chattels; the conjugal contract cannot include ownership of bodies or "free access." Similarly, a person's worthiness must be loosened from his sexual behavior. Sex must undergo demoralization. To consider a person moral solely on the basis of one's sexual impeccability cheapens virtue.

Under the guise of the expectation of sexual fidelity is the covert demand for possession of the body and soul of the other. To insure this "fidelity," liberties and human rights which normally would prevail in society are abrogated. Demands for sexual fidelity, a generally expected accompaniment of love and devotion, have too often taken on the force of total ownership of the mate.

The British philosopher, John Wilson, made sense when he wrote: "'Fidelity' means keping a sexual contract, analogous to as economic contract, whereby both partners agree not to spend money except on each other: this, for us, is the basis of 'marriage.' 'Love', in a sexual sense, is supposed to imply a similar situation: the concept is so used that if one is 'in love' with someone, or even if one 'loves' him or her it is supposed to follow that one can have no proper sexual interest in anyone else. Even more obsessive is the concept of specifically 'romantic' love; this too implies sexual fidelity, and 'romantic' is thereby contrasted with 'promiscuous', 'animal', and other unfashionable concepts. Without discussing these and cognate concepts at length, we need only contrast our attitude to sexual relationships with our attitude to the ordinary relationship of friendship; although friendship too can be possessive, it is generally recognized that this is abnormal and undesirable, whereas in sexual relationships we accept it as the norm."[10]

We must respect a high degree of sexual fidelity in marriage if it can be separated from exclusivity and possessiveness with the attendant jealousy which they promote. Few of us now have "nervous systems" strong enough to withstand the total sexual freedom of our mates. However, we should strive to worry more about fidelity in other areas in our living. We might more profitably be concerned with *fidelity* in our work, and with our ideals in the conduct of our public as well as personal affairs. This, in short, means being faithful to one's own identity—that is, being what you are supposed to be and doing what you are supposed to do. This writer suspects that the morbid and obsessive preoccupation with the faithfulness of the other represents a compensatory projection of the corrosion of one's own integrity—the doubts that exist about one's own real worthiness in areas other than sexual.

Sexual fidelity must be kept in perspective; it is not the ultimate virtue, nor does it make a person moral. Fidelity to a mate, a friend, or a client encompasses a sincere concern for his fate and a respect for his human rights. One can be sexually faithful to a mate and deceive him or her in a myriad of ways both subtler and more vital.

Another issue that is most significant to marriage is the respectability of the alternatives to it. Society might make it a great deal easier for the single person to exist. This acceptance may come sooner than expected because of the population explosion and the imminence of "standing room only" for the human race. Tax advantages for the married person will disappear. Staying single may become an act of patriotism; necessity is frequently the mother of morality.

Today the opposite exists. The male who prefers bachelorhood is charitably considered "a mother's boy" and more frequently someone with homosexual tendencies. Our psychologists are happy to confirm these views. The girl who finds herself a spinster is in far worse shape; she is accused of being unwanted, deemed not valuable to the least of males. Whatever she does or attains in life is looked upon as a poor substitute for the real success that passed her by —namely marriage. She is an object of pity to all except some housewives who have found themselves marooned and forgotten in a plush suburb. Today for the young woman the only real success or proof of one's worth is via marriage. One-half of all women who enter college leave before graduation for marriage, and, for a short time at least, feel wonderful about it! They are never considered to be drop-outs; they rarely, if ever, are sent to psychiatrists to uncover psychological reasons for their intellectual failures. No papers are written about this "drop-out" problem, for in this situation nothing succeeds like failure. Here the woman who completes her college work, and is not married, is apt to be an object of concern by now nervous parents and relatives.

The stampede to marriage can be viewed as a rigidity of our times. Society, with an unhealthy assist from psychiatry, has been the cause of this. The frantic attitude does a tragic disservice both to the young people and the institution of marriage.[15] It prevents adequate experimentation and deadens adventuresomeness. Only a few are able to declare a moratorium and properly examine themselves and the world around them; the hippies are the exceptions which prove the rule. Conformity is still the role for young people—long hair and street demonstrations notwithstanding.

If, hopefully, the single state does gain respectability, marriage will cease to be the unalterable imperative that it now is. With that pressure relieved, better and more equitable social contracts may evolve. The frenzy may disappear and there would be more time to read the fine print or change the wording. One need not dwell here on the old phrases such as "free love"—"trial marriages"—and other brave pronouncements of the 20's. These were more air than substance and are irrelevant to our times.[16] No movement or crusade for liberation is necessary. The hope for our times and the future is a climate of understanding that may allow young people to work out their destinies *with passion* but also with autonomy which demands the elimination of power as an interpersonal demiurge, and with love which has an authentic concern for the identity of the other and self.

NOTES

1. Robert Seidenberg, "Sacrificing The First You See," *The Psychoanalytic Review*, Vol. 1 (Spring, 1966).

2. *New York Times Magazine*, Nov. 12, 1967, p. 40.

3. John Stuart Mill, "The Subjection of Women," *Three Essays* (London: Oxford University Press, 1966), pp. 522-23.

4. Pauline Réage, *Story of O.* (New York: Grove Press, 1965).

5. Albert Camus, *Notebooks 1935-1942* (New York: The Modern Library, 1963), p. 58.

6. John Wilson, *Logic and Sexual Morality* (Baltimore, Maryland: Penguin Books, 1965), p. 144.

7. R. V. Sampson, *The Psychology of Power* (New York: Pantheon, 1966), p. 233.

8. Robert Seidenberg, "The Sexual Basis of Social Prejudice," *The Psychoanalytic Review*, Vol. 39, No. 1 (Jan. 1952), pp. 90-95.

9. Sören Kierkegaard, *Fear and Trembling* (Garden City, New York: Doubleday & Co., Inc., 1954), p. 113.

10. John Wilson, *Logic and Sexual Morality* (Baltimore, Maryland: Penguin Books, 1965), p. 67.

11. For a contrary view, see Ginzberg, E. et al., *Life Styles of Educated Women*, New York, Columbia Univ. Press, 1966. Ginzberg contends that the American educated woman has the opportunity to do just about what she pleases!

12. Brenner, Harvey M., *Economic Change and Mental Hospitalization: New York State, 1910-1960*, in *Social Psychiatry*, vol. 2: 180-188: 1967.

13. Some investigators have found an association between the occurrence of psychoneurosis in husbands and wives who have been married many years. They attribute this to "contagion." Are we being told of the dangers of prolonged marriages? See Buck, C. W., and Ladd, K. L., *Psychoneurosis in Marital Partners*, in *British Journal of Psychiatry*, vol. 111: 587: July 1965.

14. For the woman to adjust to marriage and in the process to acquire those attributes which endear her to the world, that is, to be the good or beloved wife, she most often accepts, or has to appear to accept, the role of an inferior person. Of one of his female characters, the British novelist, William Golding writes: "She was beginning to look up, to belong, to depend, to cling, *to be an inferior in fact* (Italics mine), however the mar-

riage service may gloss it." (Golding, W., *Free Fall*, Harmondsworth, Middlesex, Penguin Books Ltd., 1966, p. 91.)

15. Margaret Mead, drawing on her knowledge of how other peoples live, has recommended a dual marriage system. She writes: "I have recommended that we have different kinds of marriages. An *individual* marriage in which young people who are not ready to have children can legally live together. I don't think they should be ready for children until they have tried marriage for a couple of years first. Thereafter a couple knows they can get on together. There could be a second kind of marriage involving parental *responsibility*. I propose it because the only alternative today seems to be getting married and getting divorced and getting remarried and getting divorced. But this idea doesn't find favor with the young. Young people want society's permission for every kind of premarital behavior. They would like their parents to support them while they live together in the playroom. And so, on the one hand, they say, 'Why get married?'. And on the other hand, they still want marriage presented as irrevocable. The ideal of young people in this country is still totally monogamous marriage for life. They want the ideal to be what it has always been, so that when they finally decide to get married they can believe it will be forever. It's a hopeless position, a ridiculous position, and utterly untenable. We live in this unreal world where people still assume in spite of the divorce rate that marriage is going to be different." (Mead, M., from *Life* magazine, Aug. 23, 1968, p. 34.)

16. Yet, we must view with compassion and deep interest those social experiments, such as communes and similar types of group living, that some of our young people are now attempting. Probably no replacement for the traditional diadal arrangement will emerge, but instead, alternatives for the adventuresome few. This alone would be advantageous. They are handicapped in their search by naiveté of approach and by external harassment. It may be too much to ask that our *proper* people desist from persecuting them. Hopefully, our "mental experts" may resist their well-known propensity to find "deviants" amongst those who move away from the "missionary" position and other conventional modes. Is this too much to ask of our literate element?

Undoubtedly traditionalists will feel smug with the news (*New York Times*, Dec. 7, 1969, p. 20) that the much publicized commune of West Berlin known as *K. Eins* (Commune No. I.) has "fallen apart." Reasons given for the failure are: ". . . the group got tired of political activity and began to concentrate on pot and other drugs, so that the members lost themselves in a form of passivity in which even group sex no longer served as a stimulant." The news report indicated, however, that "dozens of other communal experiments still flourish in Berlin, some based on left-wing political activity, others formed by narcotics addicts and still others more conventional groups that offer students and other young people the experience of common living quarters." In a city which was to be the world capital of an authoritarian empire, it is difficult for literate people to be other than sympathetic with young Berliners who seek to abandon a patriarchal family system which, many claim, provided the fertility for Nazism. And, for women, it was the Germans who invented the aphorism, "Kirche, Kuche, und Kinder." (Church, kitchen, and children.)

INDEX